IMAGES
of America

PITTSBURG

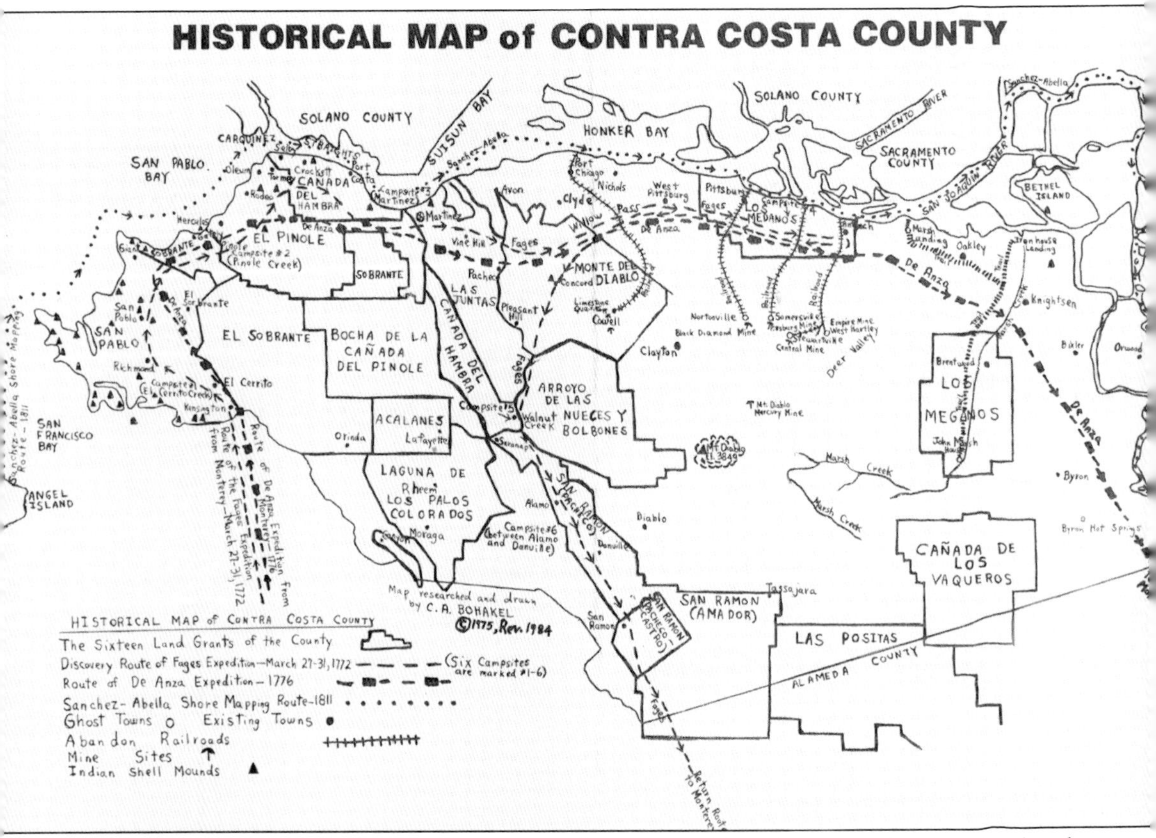

This hand-drawn map of Contra Costa shows the county's 16 land grants and various landmarks, including ghost towns, mine sites, and Indian shell mounds.

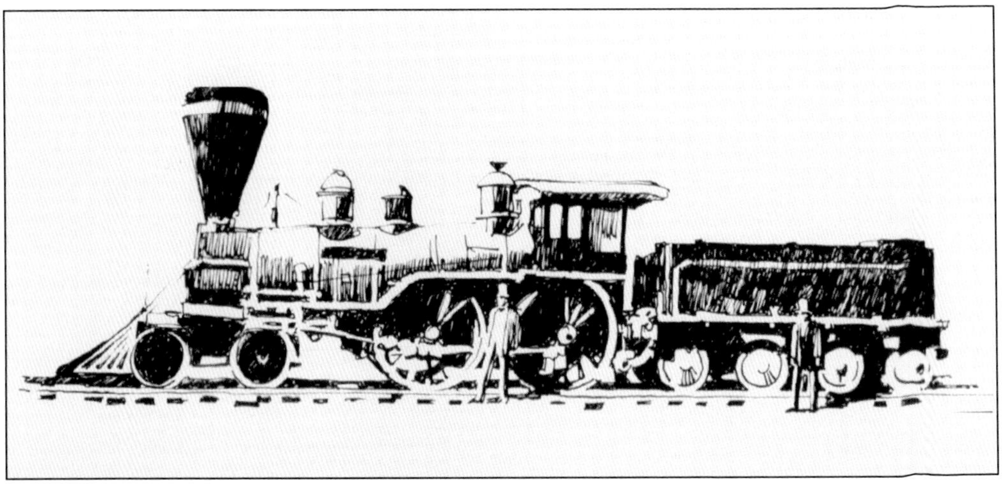

The *L.L. Robinson*, the first locomotive in California, was shipped around the Horn for use on the Sacramento Valley Railroad between Los Medanos Ranch and Sacramento.

IMAGES
of America

PITTSBURG

Marti Aiello

ARCADIA
PUBLISHING

ISBN 978-0-7385-2904-2

Published by Arcadia Publishing
Charleston, South Carolina

Printed in the United States of America

Library of Congress Catalog Card Number: 2004105266

For all general information contact Arcadia Publishing at:
Telephone 843-853-2070
Fax 843-853-0044
E-mail sales@arcadiapublishing.com
For customer service and orders:
Toll-Free 1-888-313-2665

Visit us on the Internet at www.arcadiapublishing.com

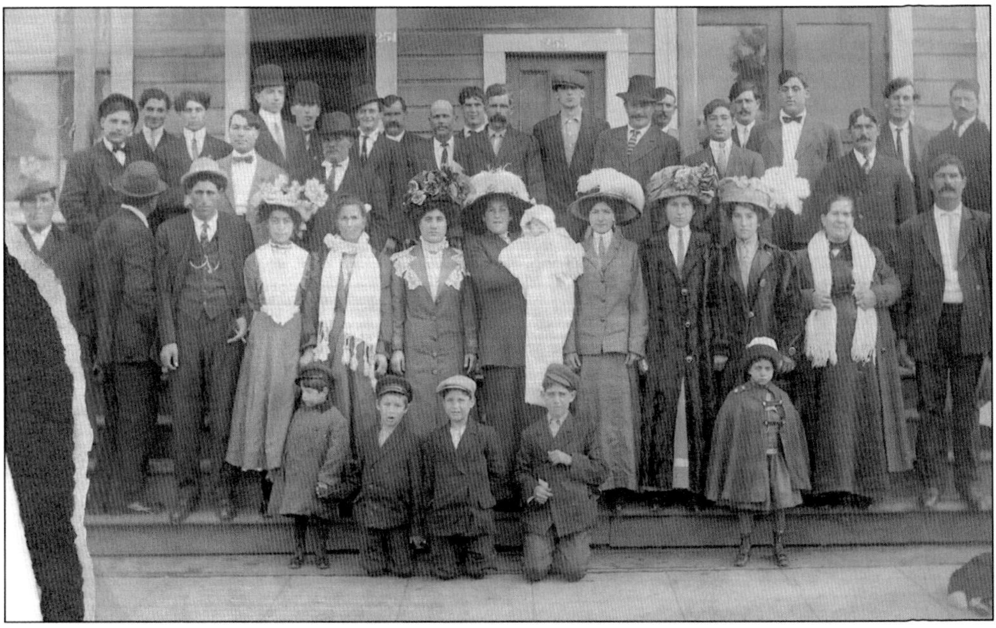

The immigrants who arrived in Pittsburg in the 1880s were an impoverished but hard-working lot. By sheer will and determination, they created a new life here. Italians, Chinese, Anglos, and Filipinos lived together in harmony and created a healthy economy within a short span of time. Coal mining, fishing, canning, heavy industry, and commercial enterprises employed a burgeoning population.

Contents

ACKNOWLEDGMENTS

In commemoration for his work, I would like to dedicate this book to Jack Aiello, historian and curator from 1973 to 1978. In his long career as curator, Aiello became a virtual history book on local lore. His interest in photography resulted in a collection of images that were reproduced for slide presentations and, subsequently, became part of our film library. Aiello also produced a number of pen-and-ink drawings of items of historical interest when no photos could be found. He was able to secure old 8mm film of early fishing in local waters and of fishermen working at the wharf, Columbus Day Parades, and other aspects of our history.

I also wish to thank the Pittsburg Historical Society for its generous provision of photographs and other materials. This chronicle of the life and times of a unique community is a tribute to the people of Pittsburg and their descendants.

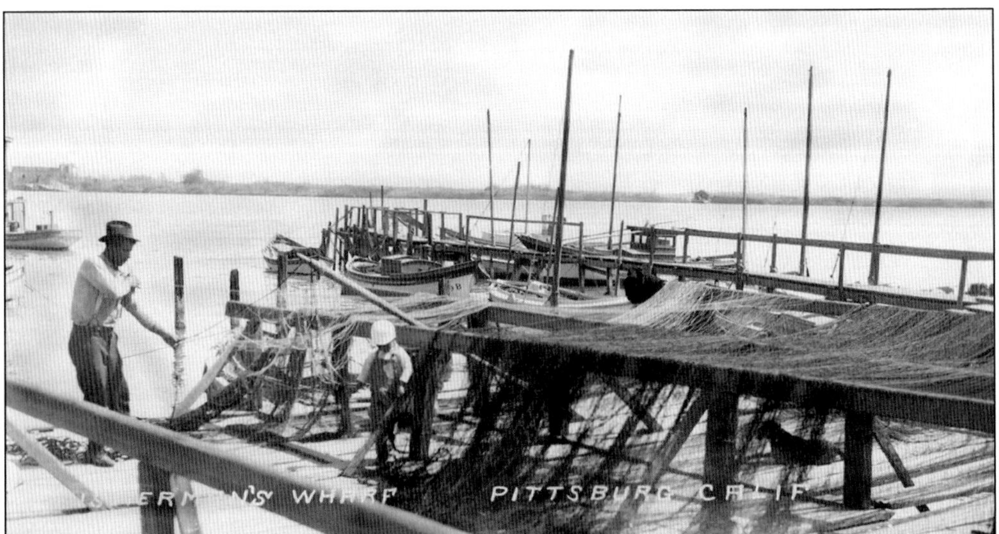

The rivers played a large part in the development of Pittsburg. The area's commercial fishing industry lasted 80 years.

PROLOGUE

Consider this book a pageant, a procession of photographic portrayals of an ever-changing city of promise. Attempts to define Pittsburg change with each new discovery.

The earliest recorded history of this area was in 1772, when Spanish explorers, led by Juan Bautista de Anza, ventured into the territory occupied by the Ompin Indians. In 1839, the Mexican government granted approximately 10,000 acres of land to two brothers, Jose Antone Mesa and Jose Miguel Garcia. Called Rancho Los Medanos (the dunes), the land extended south to the foothills of Mount Diablo and north to the San Joaquin and Sacramento Rivers. It was dotted with oak trees, and tules lined the river banks and marshes along the seven-mile-long property where the Ompin Indians lived.

By the 1840s, nearly all of Contra Costa was owned by a few military officers, retired from the Mexican Army. To encourage rapid settlement in the state, territories were allotted to them. They built adobes, several of which survive to this day—in Martinez, Moraga, Alhambra Valley, and Pacheco. Some have been restored, and some altered.

In a matter of 10 years, the Los Medanos grant changed hands. In 1849, Col. Jonathan Drake Stevenson, commander of the New York Regiment, who had earlier passed through the area, sought the blessings of President James Polk to "conquer and occupy the land" in California. In addition, President Polk gave Stevenson permission to raise a regiment of New York volunteers to accomplish his purpose.

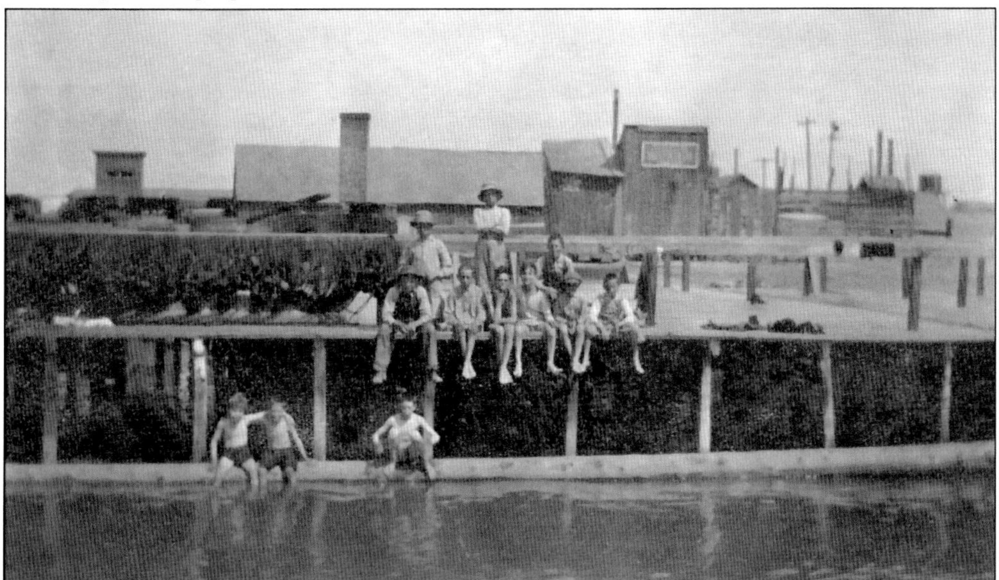

Today, the rivers are used for recreational sports.

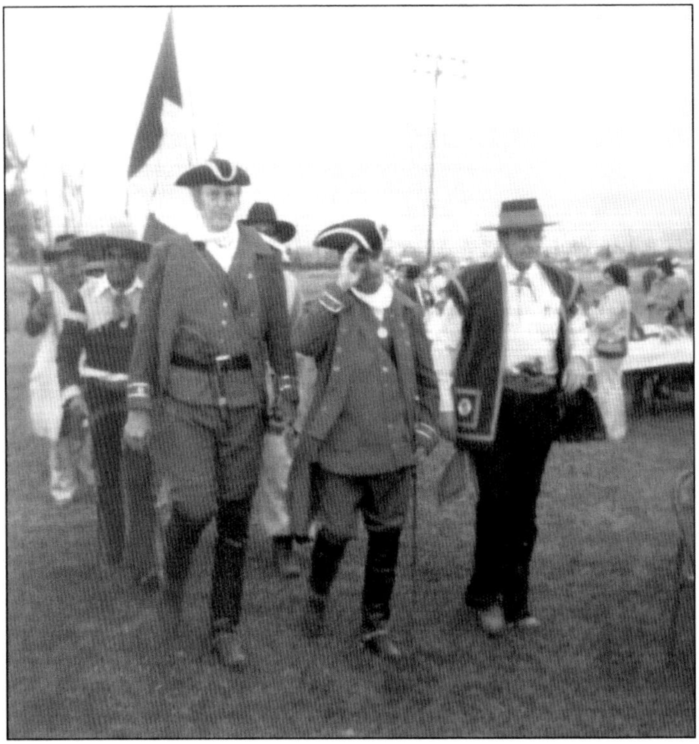

The first expedition was led by Don Pedro Fages, the acting governor of Alta California, in 1772. The Spanish hoped to locate sites for missions to be built in the area. In 1774, a second expedition was led by Juan Bautista de Anza, who was sent by the Mexican government to explore the region

The coming of the Americans changed the West forever. Gone was the slow-paced life of early Californians, replaced by the frantic activity of prospectors, farmers, coal miners, and businessmen who saw gold and hard cash coming their way. Eventually large populations were sustained on smaller and smaller lots. Visionaries purposely sought to engage in commerce that might bring success and wealth, and industrialists wanted to enlarge their empire. Farmers reaped the benefits of the rich virgin soil. It seemed the newly acquired golden state of California was ripe for just about anything.

Colonel Stevenson bought the property from the Mesa brothers as the first step in a grandiose scheme to develop the land and entice investors to settle here. The name, however, may have seemed pretentious to its new inhabitants, for it began to be called instead by its geographic location near the water—New York Landing and Junction. Near the train depot was Cornwall, home to a settlement of farmers. When the city was incorporated in 1903, it was called Black Diamond for the coal found in the hills. The city finally assumed the name of Pittsburg in 1911.

In its 150-year history, Pittsburg had passed through many phases, beginning with the coal miners who worked the mines until a better source of energy was found. During this time, investors poured out their money into the mining industry. Black Diamond Coal Company and the Empire, Cumberland, Eureka, Union, and Pittsburg Mines operated for nearly 50 years in both the Pittsburg and Antioch side of the hills.

Around 1904, during the great Industrial Revolution that took place during the 18th and early 19th century, Pittsburg began to develop an industrial base. It grew rapidly and flourished until the 1970s, then went into decline after a recognition of the damage being done to the rivers by factories pouring contaminants into the waters.

Beginning in the 1940s, the war with Japan and Germany and the building of a large army camp in the south of town generated a booming economy for a 14-year period. Camp Stoneman became the largest debarkation center in the West, where soldiers received final training before going overseas, including amphibian exercises at the waterfront of Pittsburg.

Col. Jonathan Drake Stevenson, commander of the 7th New York Regiment, was sent to California at his bequest, and by presidential approval, to conquer and claim the land for the United States.

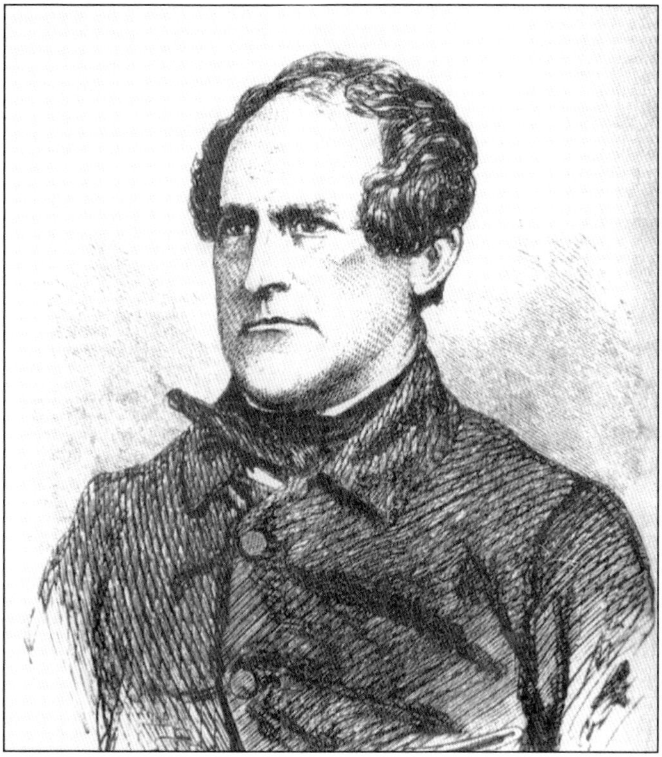

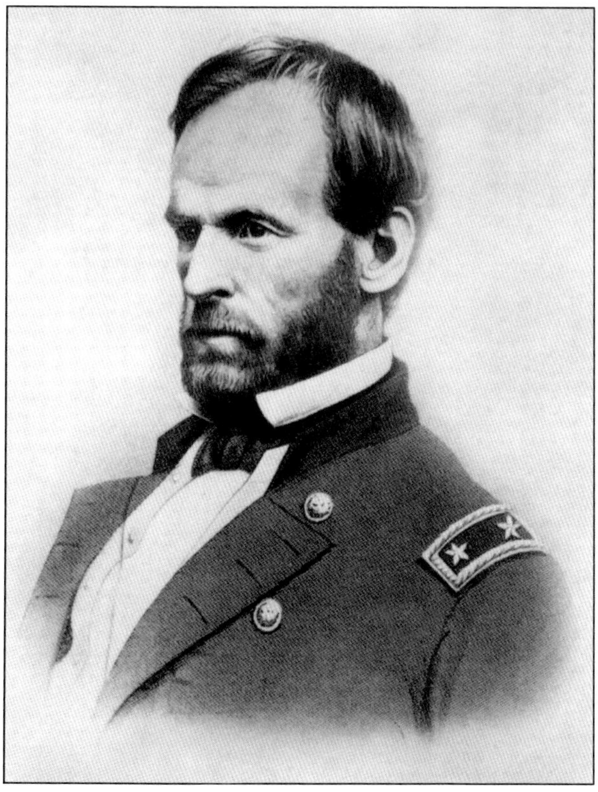

Famed Civil War hero William Tecumseh Sherman was hired by Stevenson to survey the townsite of New York of the Pacific and to make a plat of the area.

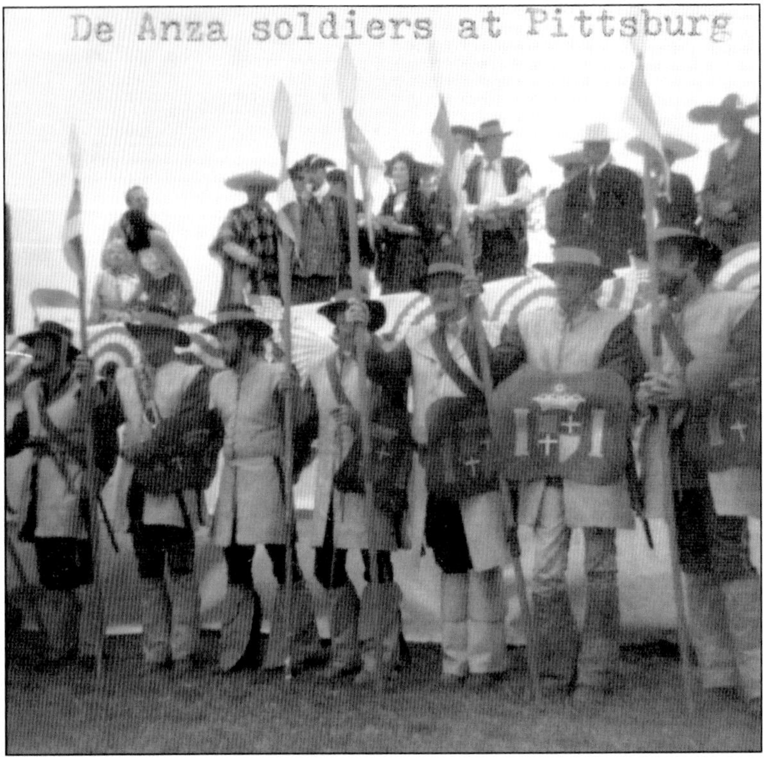

In 1976, a parade of men representing the 1776 exploration came into Pittsburg on horseback and dressed in period costume.

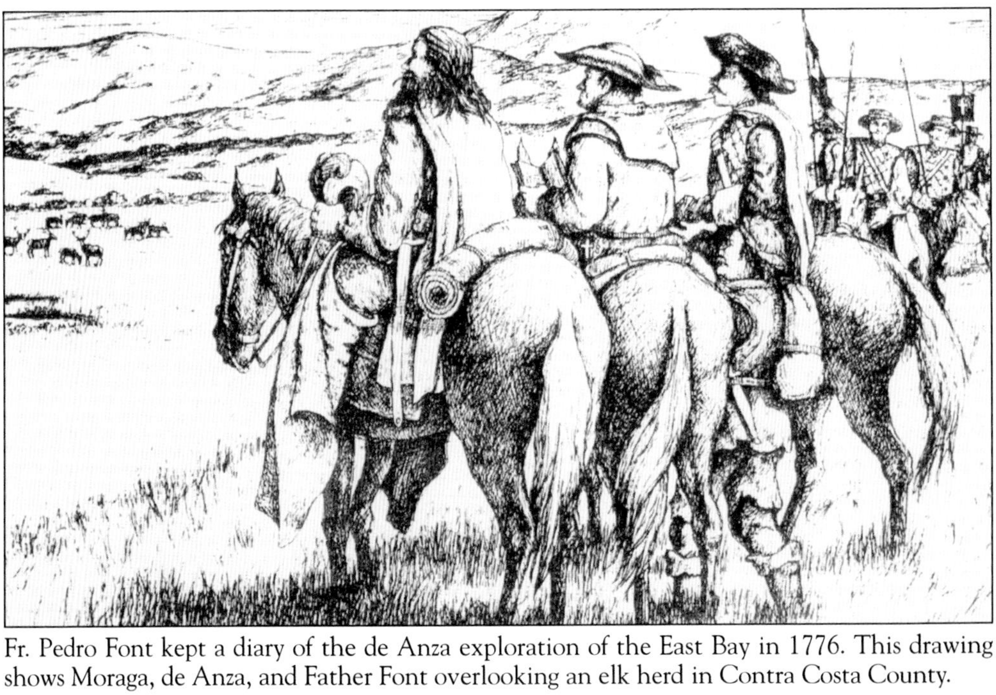

Fr. Pedro Font kept a diary of the de Anza exploration of the East Bay in 1776. This drawing shows Moraga, de Anza, and Father Font overlooking an elk herd in Contra Costa County.

One

The Beginning

The founding of the town in 1849 was the dream of Col. Jonathan Drake Stevenson, who saw the possibilities of establishing a great city along the river route to gold country. Stevenson, leader of the celebrated New York Volunteers, came west to guard the province of Alta California from the Mexican Army.

Exploration into the area led Stevenson and his aide, Dr. William C. Parker, to see the merits and advantages of locating a city near the deep-water channel of the Bay of Suisun. The Sacramento and San Joaquin Rivers were a gateway to gold country. San Francisco was already a great seaport and commercial center. Sacramento was established as a portal to the gold mines of the north. Everything in between was fair game to an opportunist like Stevenson.

Antonio and Jose Miguel Mesa had received the Los Medanos land grant from the Mexican government and sold it to Stevenson. A land sales announcement appeared in the *Alta California* on May 17, 1849, touting the advantages of procuring choice property with abundant water, a healthy climate, and other enticements of business opportunities. The new town of New York of the Pacific was duly plotted, streets were laid out, and carpenters were sought out to build a large structure that would accommodate families. (Later this first building was to be used as a hotel for those en route to the gold country.) William and Joseph Smith were hired to build the hotel, called New York House.

P.B. Cornwall came to the town in 1862, and with D.O. Mills and Alvinza Hayward as partners, he established (and was president of) the Southport Land and Improvement Company for the mining and shipping of coal. A small settlement that grew up around the Southern Pacific Railroad station, located south of New York Landing, became known as Cornwall. It extended to land beyond Tenth Street, to the plot now occupied by the Pittsburg Unified School District administration building, and beyond to the foothills, south of the city. The central path of a horse-and-buggy trail coming from Nortonville crossed the area. A village blacksmith shop was then located at the corner of what is now Railroad Avenue and North Parkside Drive, and the Southern Pacific train station housed a telegraphy office. Chinese farmers had chicken coops and truck gardens in the area that would become a city park. There was also a post office, a hotel, a row of modest homes, and several saloons. The Santa Fe Railroad station was just two blocks away.

Daly's Saloon was built in 1906, next to the Southern Pacific station, by Andrew Daly and was used as a gathering place for the community. Water troughs for the horses were located in the front of the saloon, which sold steam beer for 5¢ a glass and good whisky at 10¢ and 15¢ a shot. An old iron stove provided customers with heat in the winter, and the front porch with a latticed veranda presented weary travelers with a place to rest and refresh themselves.

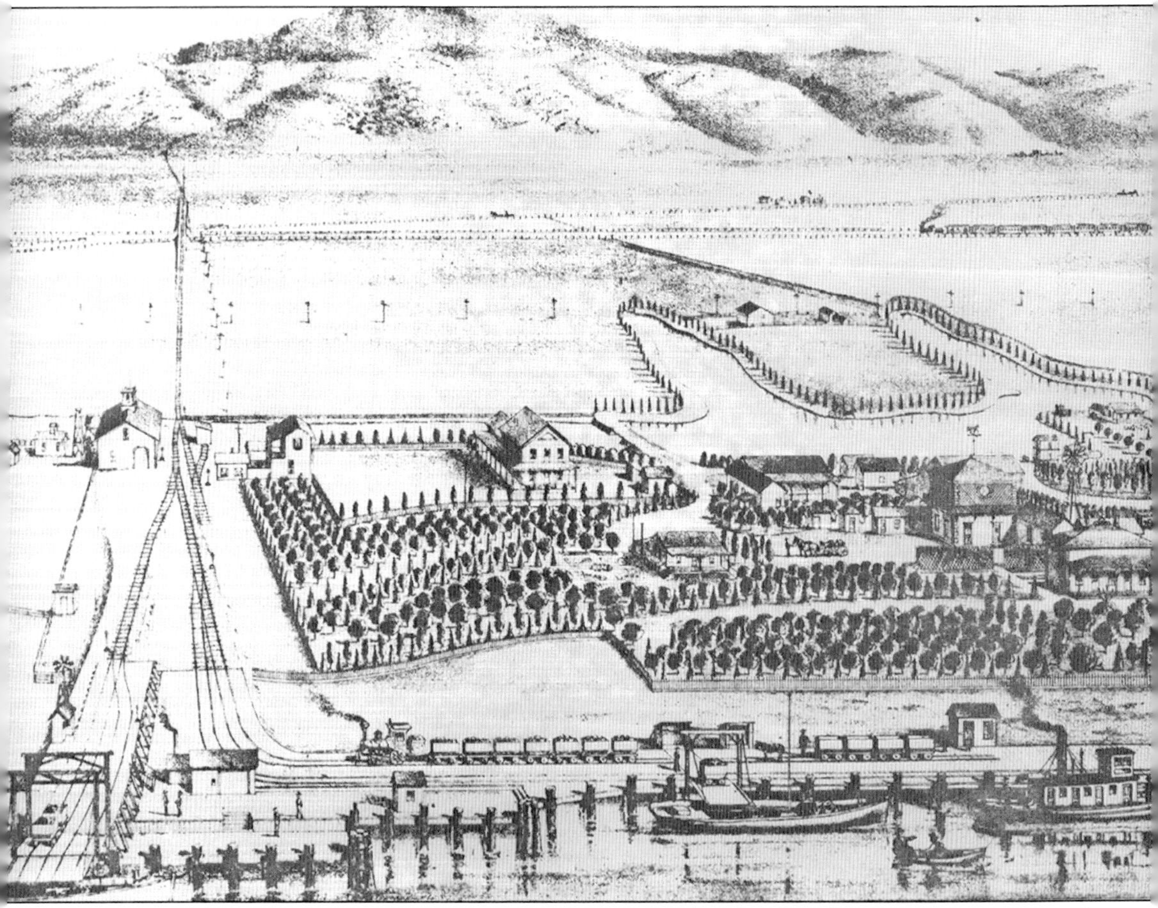

Pictured here in the late 1800s, Los Medanos Rancho developed over a 50-year period,

The town grew, but not to the great expectations of its founder. The community's name was changed to New York Landing, and Colonel Stevenson eventually sold his interests to a banking firm in San Francisco. The property was later sold to L.L. Robinson, famed for his building of a train, the *L.L. Robinson*. He also established the Sacramento Valley Railroad Company. Robinson's property, located along the twin rivers of the San Joaquin and Sacramento, had rail lines leading to the Central Pacific Railroad station called Cornwall, the first of the tracks in the area linking Sacramento and San Francisco. Santa Fe Railroad would later follow Robinson's lead. In 1855, the Black Diamond Railroad coal cars heading

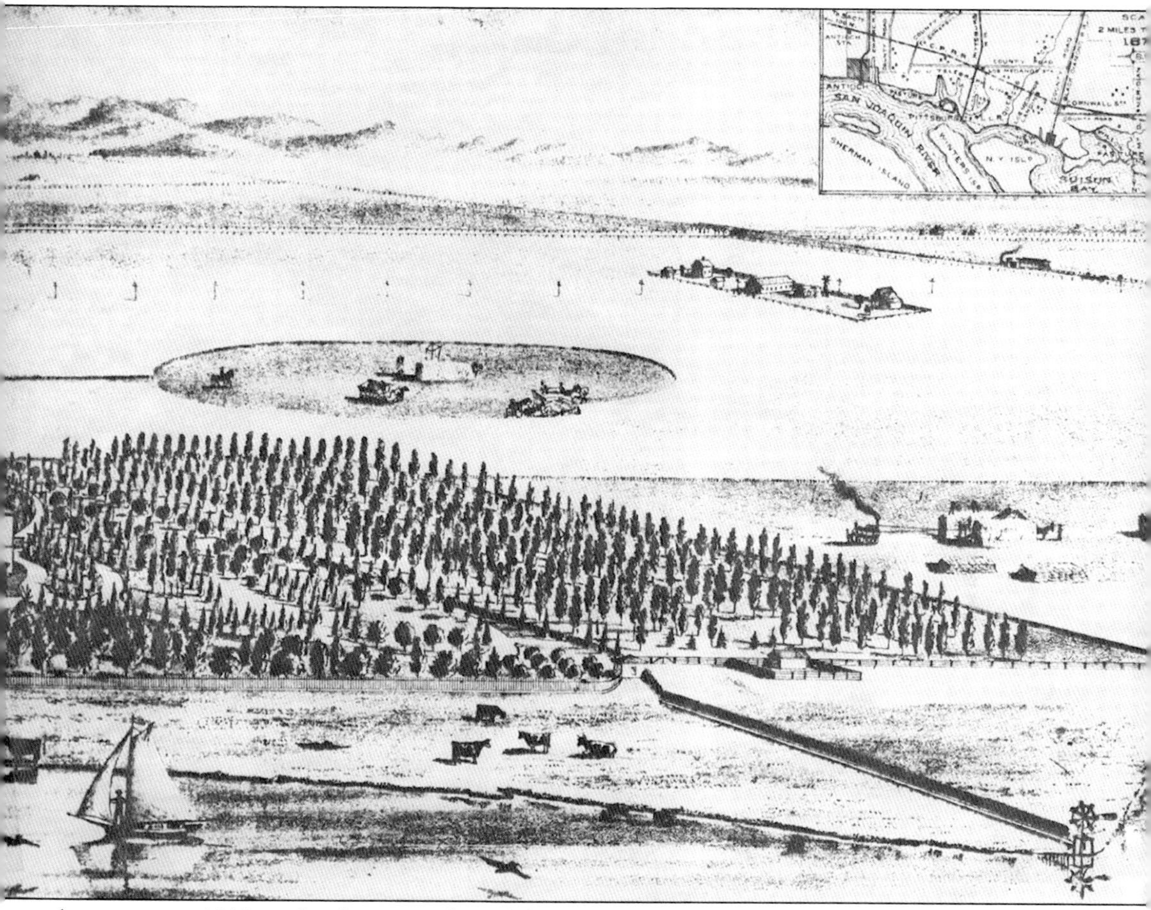

beginning in 1849, under the ownership of three men: Stevenson, Robinson, and Hooper.

south to north would cross these tracks to deliver coal to the waterfront for shipping to various points.

Even though Stevenson's grand scheme to establish a metropolis did not materialize, immigrants from Europe carved out a life for themselves by ranching, working the coal mines that opened in the south of town, and fishing the rivers. The fledgling city also became a canning center for fish and produce. As foreseen by Stevenson, such natural resources as the flat land and rivers, coupled with water and rail transportation, became a catalyst for industrial development.

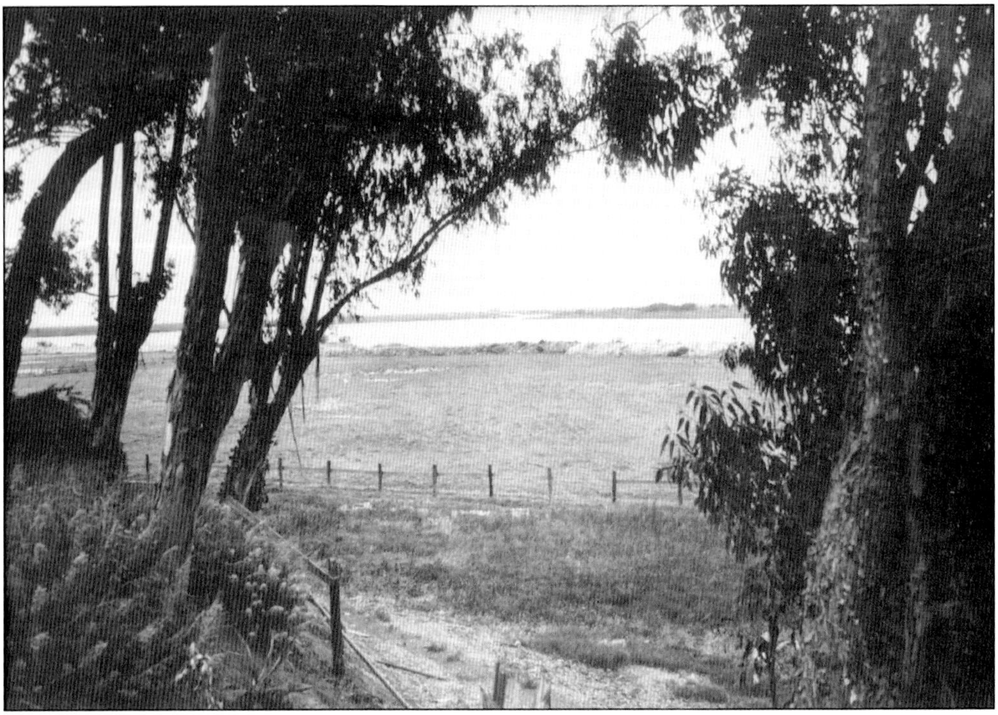

The grounds were beautiful. Trees and shrubs lined the pathways down to the river, which provided the irrigation that kept the landscape lush and green.

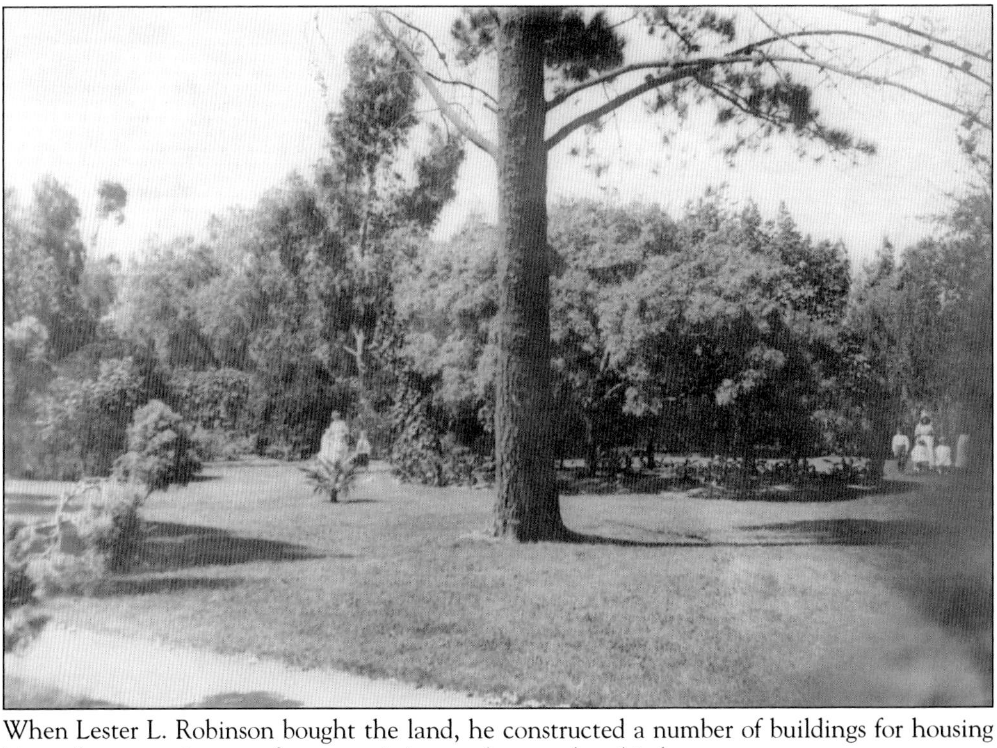

When Lester L. Robinson bought the land, he constructed a number of buildings for housing his workers, a main room for entertaining, and an outdoor kitchen.

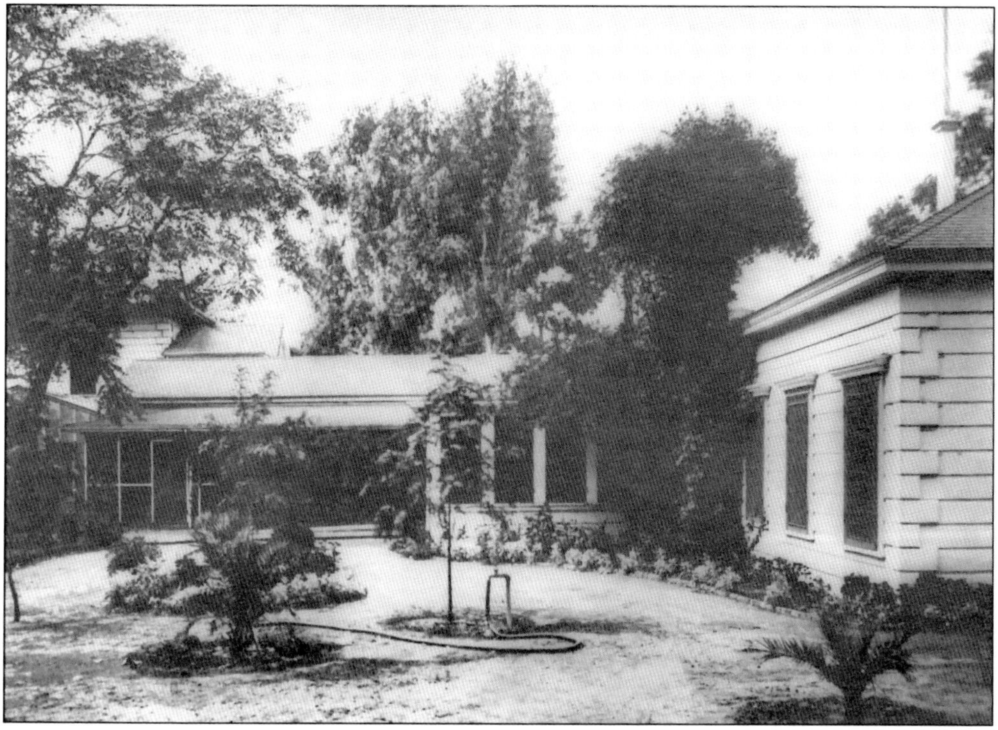

The ranch was located very near the San Joaquin and Sacramento Rivers.

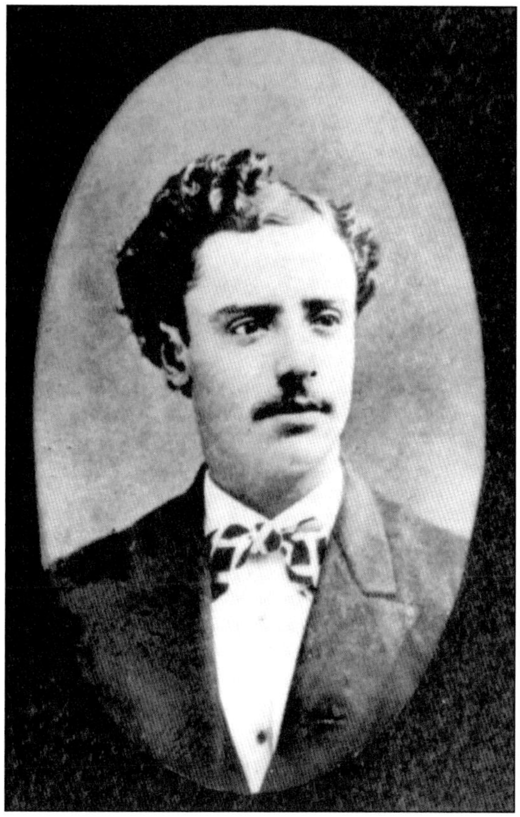

The names New York of the Pacific, New York Landing, Junction, Cornwall, Black Diamond, and Pittsburg were all associated with this area at one time or another. Pictured at right, Charles Appleton Hooper was a land baron and industrialist during the time when Pittsburg was known as New York Landing.

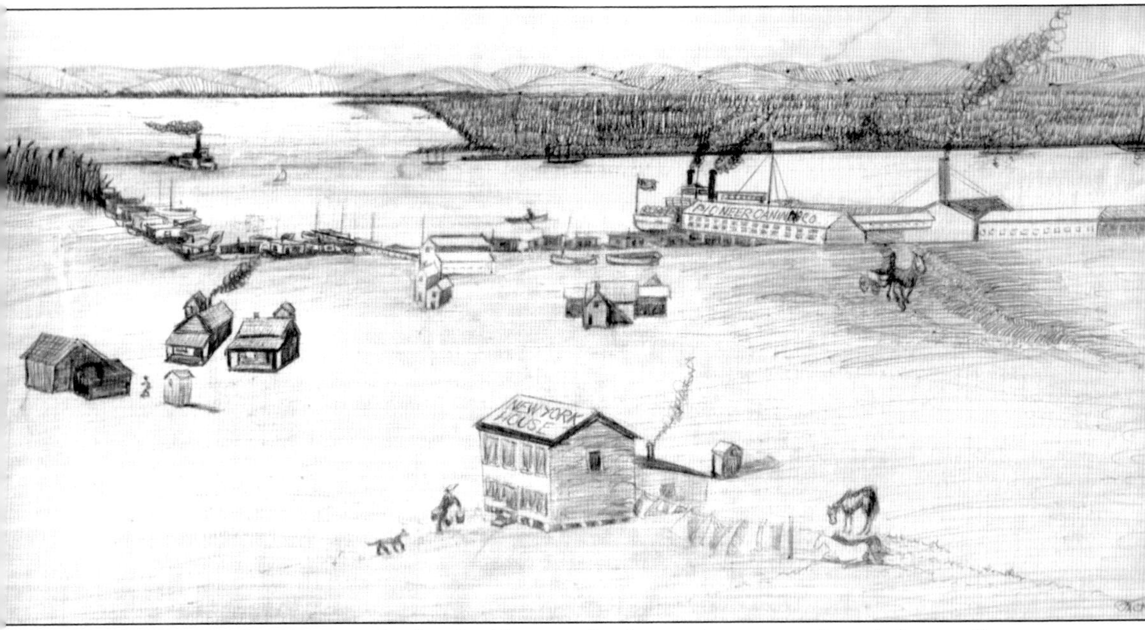

The New York House was the first building used to house the new settlers. A few small structures were added to serve as a kitchen and storage. Later the structure became the first stop-over for those headed to the gold county, serving as a sort of bed and breakfast with an outdoor oven and sleeping accommodations.

INDIANS

The Costanoan Indians, who lived in the western part of the county, and the Ompins of the eastern part displayed similar cultural characteristics, although detailed accounts of their way of life are scarce. They were described in 1879 as being small in stature, broad shouldered, with long, straight black hair, and possessing considerable strength.

The men wore no clothing at all and the women wore two narrow strips of cloth in the front and back made of tule, deerskin, or bark fiber. Early historical accounts mention that it was a common practice among the men to coat their bodies with thick layers of mud until they were warmed by the sun. In winter both men and women wore rabbit skin blankets for additional warmth.

The Indians constructed homes from native materials consisting of a framework of willow stakes covered with thatch made of tule and dried grasses. A common dwelling was conically shaped with a six- or seven-foot diameter.

Among the Indians of Contra Costa County, the sweat house was a cure-all for illnesses. A typical sweat house was made of tree branches and poles covered with layers of earth resembling an inverted bowl about 40 feet in diameter with a vent at the top to allow smoke to escape. Each tribe erected theirs near a stream or creek, and after building a fire and perspiring for several hours while sealed inside, they would jump into the nearby stream. The sweat house was also used as a kind of council room and, at times, a burial site for the dead.

The land provided early inhabitants with an abundance of food, including fish and water fowl, as well as large herds of antelope, deer, and elk. Ducks and geese were reportedly so numerous that they could be knocked over the head with a stick and taken home to be eaten. Acorns were leached and ground into flour for flat bread.

Instead of canoes, the Indians made balsas out of bundles of tules that were rolled and tied in ten-foot lengths. The balsas were tapered, with a wider diameter in the middle and narrow ends. In calm weather the interior would remain dry, but in rough weather, water would seep in, causing the boat to fill. According to written accounts, the Indians still used these balsas as late as the 1840s.

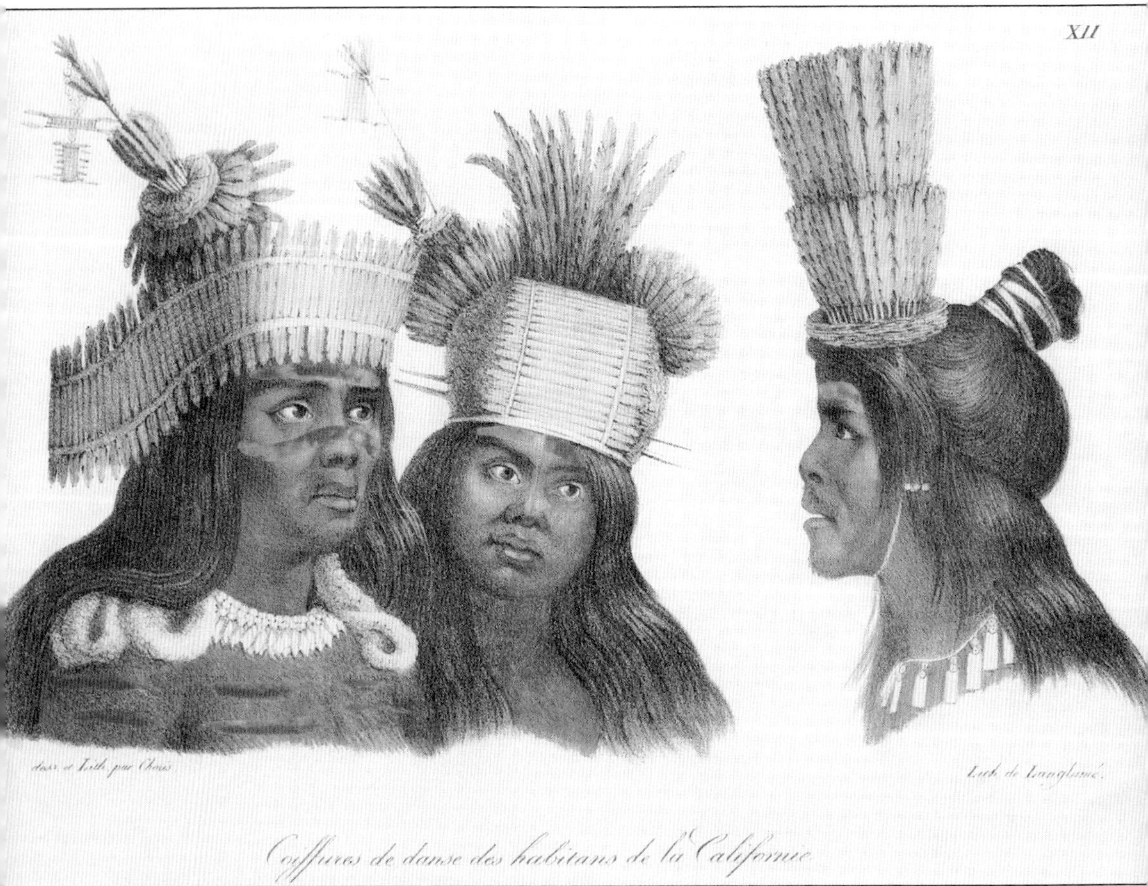

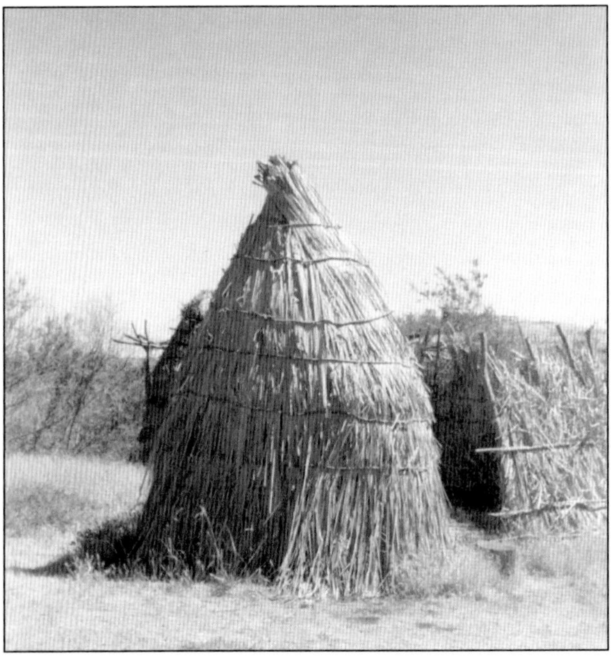

The Ompins were one of the many tribes of the Bay Miwok people. Living in small groups of around 30, they regularly came together with other Bay Miwok tribes to barter their goods for baskets or trinkets.

Huts made of bundled tule and swamp grasses formed the conical houses of native tribes.

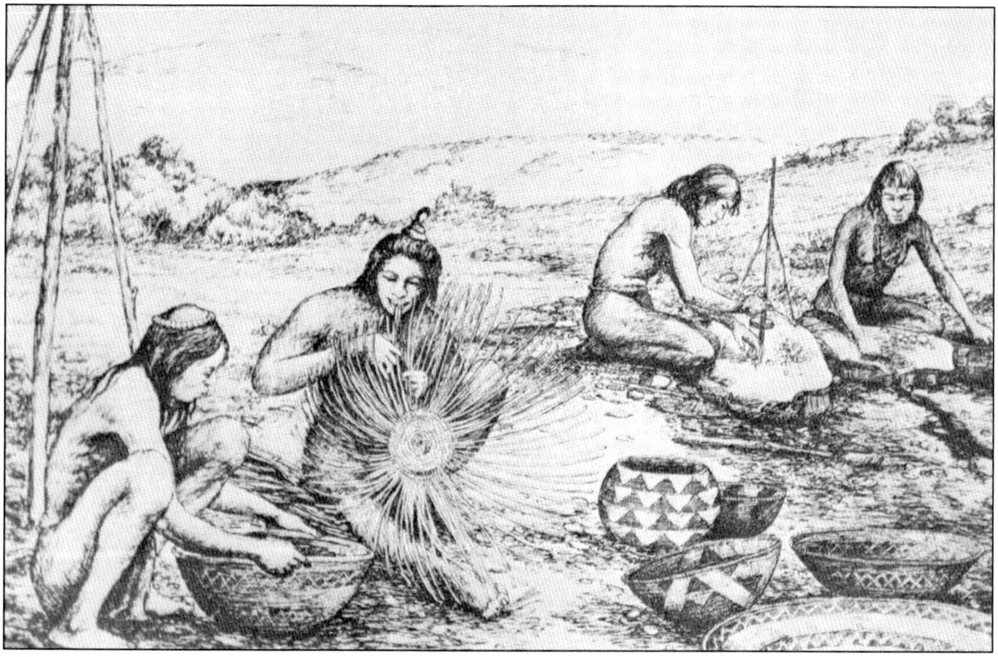

The Indians created colorful woven baskets with unique designs and shapes from dried grasses. Women filled their days with this kind of artistry.

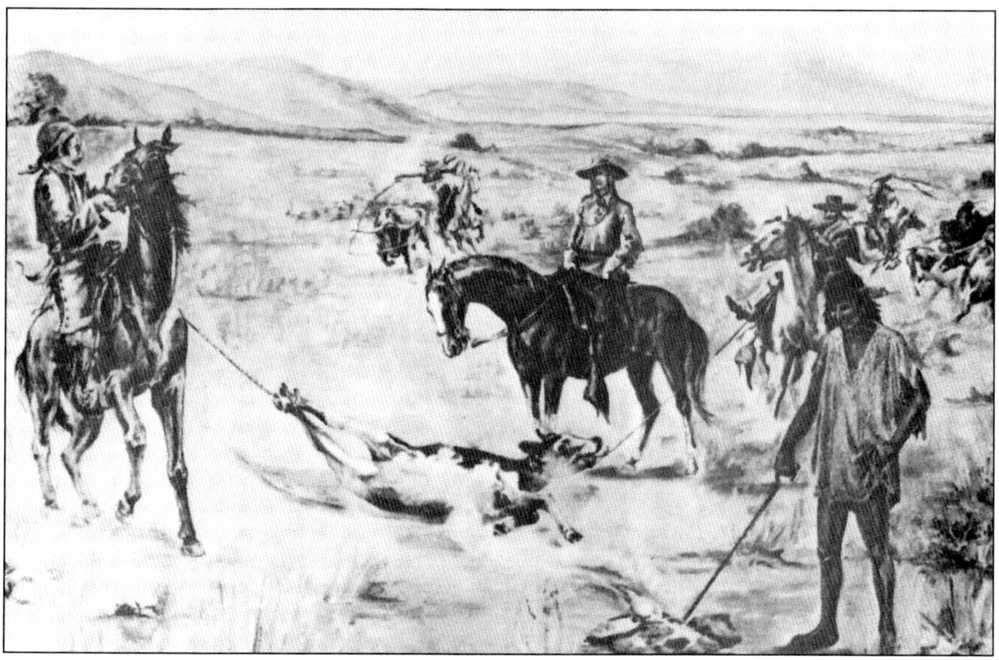

Indians worked for settler Dr. John Marsh in exchange for food and lodging. Running the cattle, branding, and farm work was an endless task. The women performed the household chores.

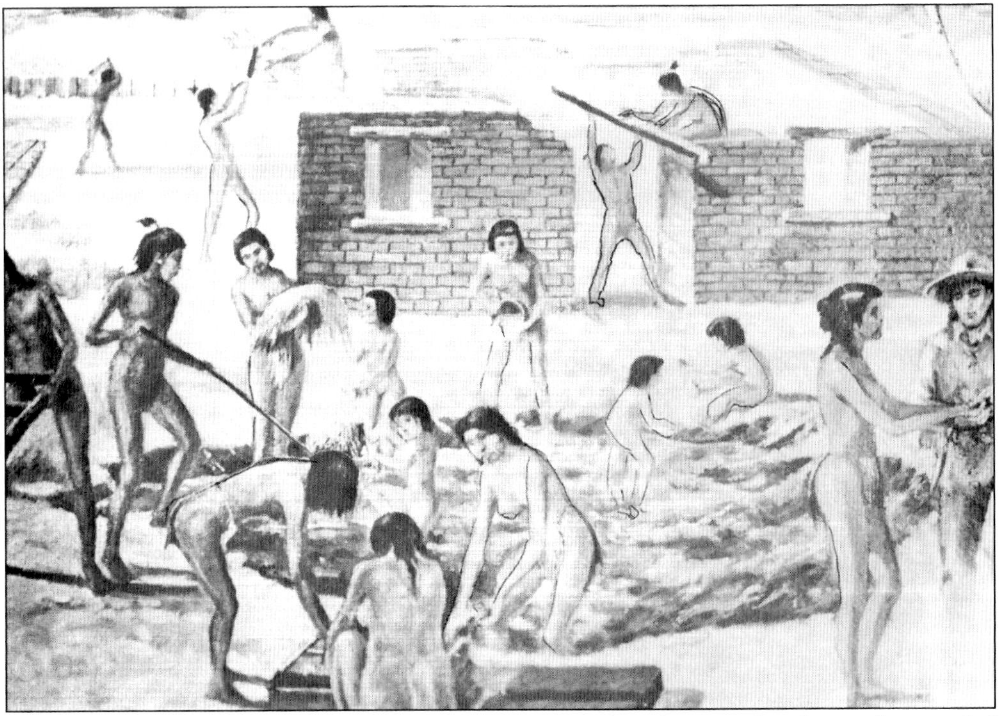

John Marsh used native labor for building his house and performing the chores that needed doing on the ranch. Because the natives had always lived in small communities and worked together for the good of the whole, Marsh easily persuaded them to work for food and shelter.

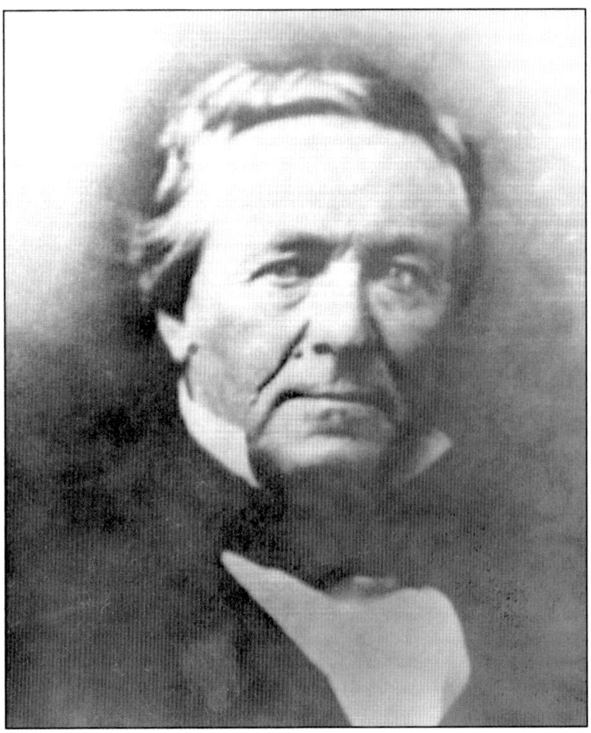

John Marsh came to California in 1846, leaving behind a wife and son of French-Indian extraction to start a new life in the unclaimed lands in Contra Costa. With the help of Mexican Vaqueros and the Native American tribes inhabiting the area, he established a large ranch and set up practice as the county's first doctor.

JOHN MARSH

In the 1800s, California was still considered "the wild and wooly West," with mercenaries, marauders, and murderers living on the shadowy periphery of civilization. One of the best known early settlers was Dr. John Marsh. Historical data collected about Marsh reveals a man gifted with intellect, generosity, and many of the finer qualities. He was a shrewd businessman but capable of actions that may have led to his untimely death. In a letter penned by Marsh in 1846, he referred to "some ill-disposed neighbors of mine [during the time he lived in Monterey] who have entered into a conspiracy against me."

Marsh's letter to the New Orleans Picayune*, on the other hand, sought to encourage Easterners to come to California to witness the "remarkable climate, the agricultural capabilities" and other assets that set the area apart from the rest of the United States. During his lifetime, Marsh entertain, as well as provide food and lodging, to many early travelers who had occasion to pass through the area.*

Marsh met his fate at the hands of some Mexicans caught stealing cattle from his ranch. Marsh was en route to catch the night boat to San Francisco when he was ambushed by three vaqueros—Felipe Moreno, Jose Antonio Olivas, and Juan Garcia—who reportedly had long nursed a grievance against the doctor. Marsh was viciously stabbed to death with knives. The assassination caused a commotion in California, where there had been a number of similar incidents, and Gov. J. Neely Johnson authorized a $1,000 reward for the capture of Moreno.

After his death, attorneys who had been friends of Marsh arrived at the ranch to search for the $5,000 in gold that Marsh had received from a cattle sale several months before the attack and which, as had been his custom, he had hidden somewhere on his ranch. They also looked for his will, which would help them to determine the distribution of his vast estate, although it seemed likely that his long-lost son Charles Marsh would inherit, considering that the two had recently been reunited and shared the stone manor house located near the town of Brentwood.

Determined to avenge his father's murder and bring the culprits to justice, Charles had himself deputized, learned to speak Spanish, and began following clues wherever they led. After ten years they led him to a ranch near Santa Barbara, where Olivas was captured and brought before the grand jury in Martinez. He was later released on a legal technicality. Following another lead regarding the whereabouts of Moreno, Charles took a futile trip to Mexico, but finally spotted Moreno partying at a honky-tonk bar in Sacramento. Charles took him prisoner and brought him back to Martinez, where he was convicted of second-degree murder and sent to San Quentin for life.

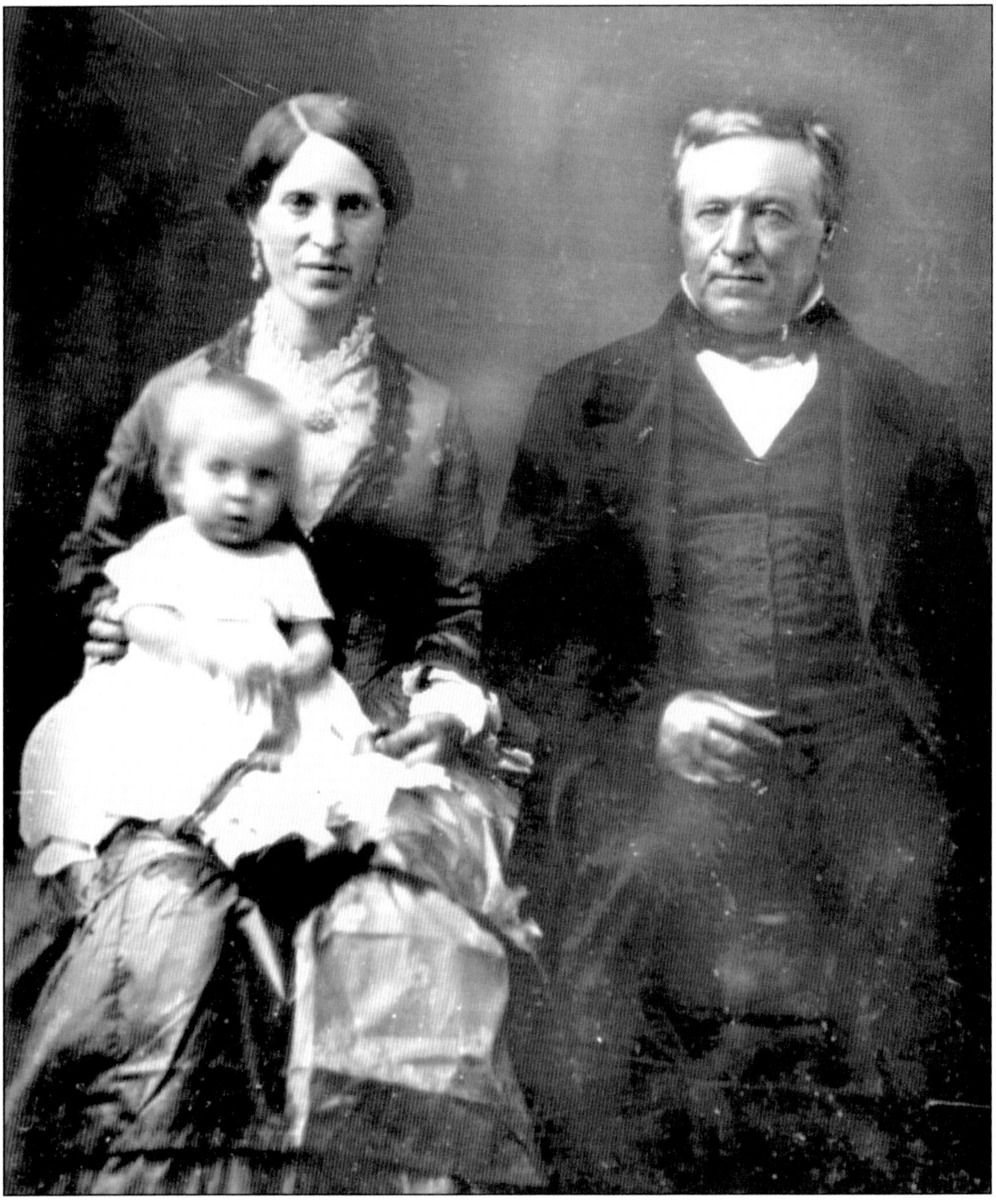

Abby and John Marsh were married in 1851 after a whirlwind courtship of two weeks. Daughter Alice was born just a year later in 1852. Shortly after Alice's birth, Abby's health began to decline, and in August 1855 she died of tuberculosis.

In 1841 John Bidwell led the first party of settlers across the Sierra Nevada. Passing through the Contra Costa area, he staying with Dr. John Marsh and later moved on to the wilderness of Rancho Chico.

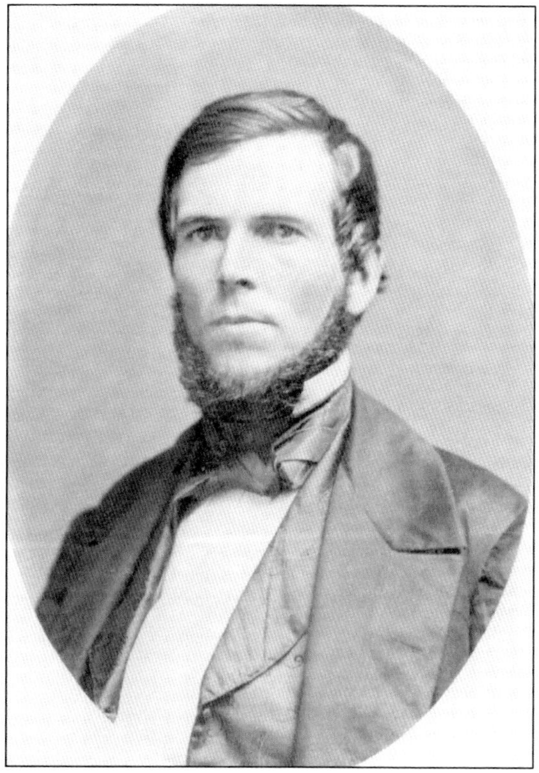

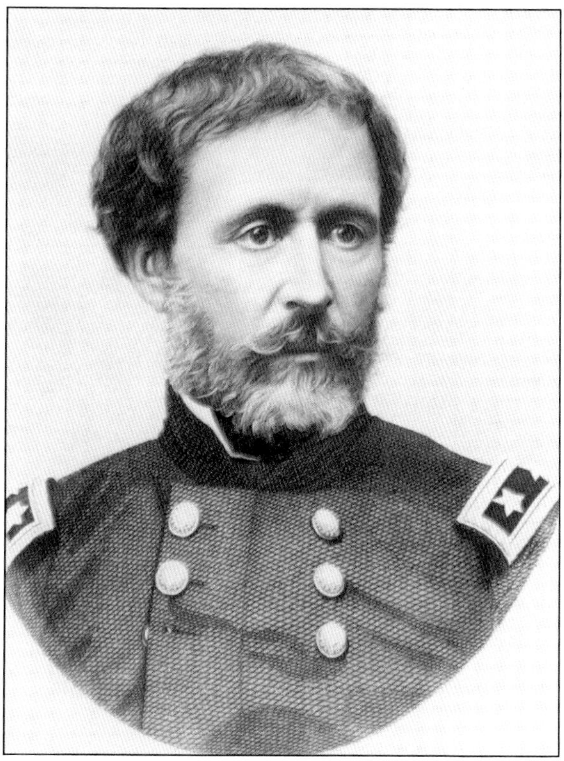

John Freemont was an explorer, naturalist, and a U.S. Army officer who came to the area as an engineer with the U.S. topographical service, mapping out trails in early California.

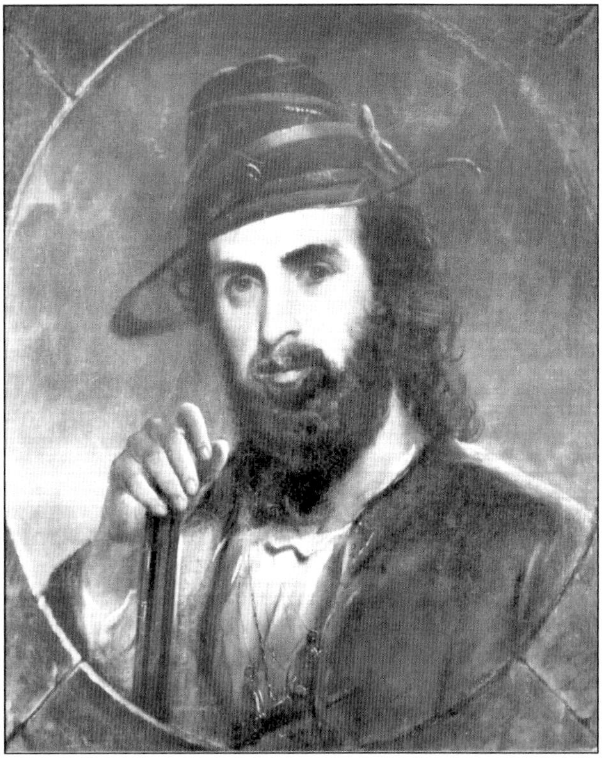

In 1833, Joseph Reddeford Walker arrived in Contra Costa and, after exploring the area, settled in Alhambra Valley, where he lived out the last ten years of his life. Schooled in topography, Walker was the first pioneer to follow the San Joaquin River to its mouth at Pittsburg's waterfront. Upon his death he was buried in Martinez.

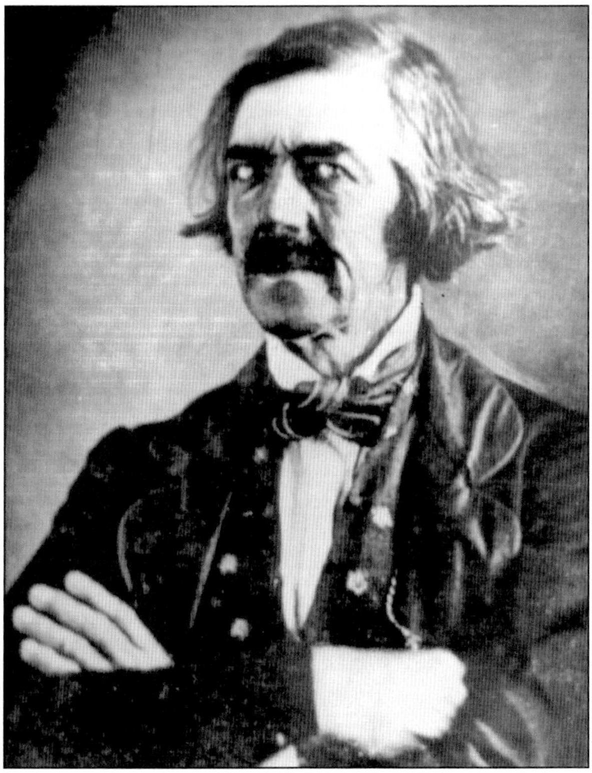

James Kirker was a soldier of fortune, running with the Indians, joining the Mexican army, then deserting and joining the American side when war with Mexico became a reality. Kirker later settled in the hills of Nortonville, south of Pittsburg, and was buried in Rose Hill Cemetery.

JAMES KIRKER

James Kirker was a fascinating and remarkable man called Don Santiago Querque by the Mexicans and the Shawnee and the Delaware Indians with whom he traveled. His photograph on the page opposite shows a man with piercing dark eyes and a brooding countenance. But who was he and what brought him to settle on the land south of Pittsburg?

Born in Ireland, Kirker immigrated to the United States in 1810 and engaged in commerce in New York, where he married and fathered children. In 1821 he went off to live as a trapper in the Rocky Mountains, where he traded with the Shawnee and Delaware Indians with whom he would later travel westward. The scene shifts, and by 1830, he was waging war against the Apaches, according to a book about his life called Savage Scene *by William Cockran McGaw.*

Kirker had been hired by the mining company in the state of Chihuahua to guard the supply wagons that were the targets of frequent raids. He was given the rank of colonel by the Mexican Army and was purported to have killed more than 500 Apaches. Later, when hostilities between the United States and Mexico escalated into a full-blown war, Kirker deserted and joined up with the Missouri volunteers of the United States Army. A $10,000 reward was offered by the Mexican government for the capture of this traitor. After the war ended, Kirker rejoined his Shawnee and Delaware companions and moved to California, leaving behind a wife and several children in Chihuahua as well as a wife and family in New York. Kirker began life anew in the foothills above New York Landing in 1849 with his Indian friends and died in 1853.

Perhaps the quiet life lost some of its luster for this energetic pioneer; he took a steamboat to San Francisco in October 1850 to engage in an all-day celebration of California's admission to the Union. While we was there, a startling thing happened after the celebration. Kirker had boarded a new steamboat, the Sagamore, to purchase a ticket for his return voyage when the boat's boilers exploded. The force of the blast blew him 15 feet into the air. His life was spared by two dead bodies that cushioned his fall. Fifty people were killed in the blast; many were hospitalized. It seemed that Kirker, in some ways, led a charmed life. He lived until 1853 and then died of unknown causes.

Vincent Neary, who was nearly 90 years old in 1965, told how his father, who worked in the mines at Somersville, described Kirker as a "strange old man" and a "bad man" who had not made friends with the whites, but had lived with the "red skins" too long.

Kirker was buried by a faithful Shawnee friend in the Rose Hill Cemetery above Nortonville. The Indians who had buried this interesting, colorful man rode away from the cemetery, never to be seen again in that part of California.

According to county records, the original road from Cumberland Mines to New York of the Pacific was established in 1861 and was later named Kirker Pass.

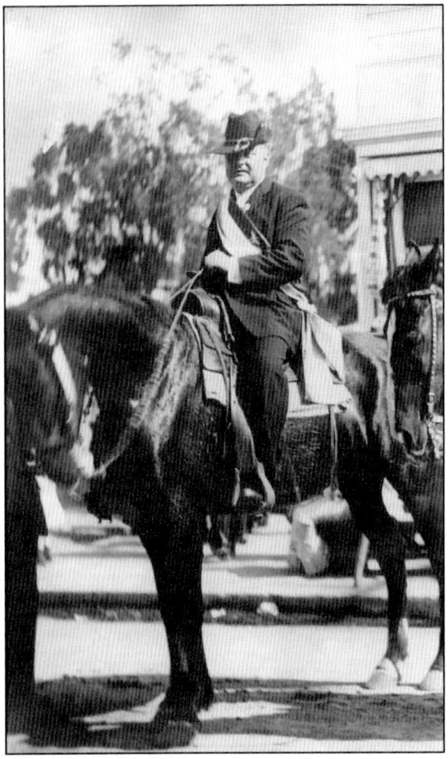

James Edward Fahy, the son of William Fahy, was born in 1873 on the Fahy ranch. He attended the New York Landing schools and became marshall in the city of Black Diamond, an office he held until 1916. After getting married he opened a saloon in partnership with his father-in-law.

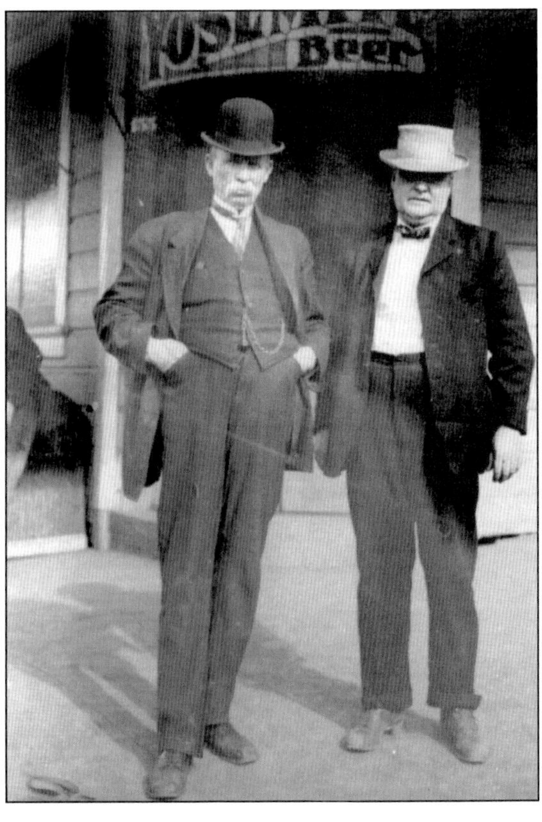

Town marshall Jim Fahy (right) and Con Griffin (left) were partners in the tavern visible behind them.

Two

THE LAND

California agriculture is largely responsible for changing the eating patterns of most Americans and of many other countries in the world thanks to the development of its production practices. The variety of food now accepted as commonplace in grocery stores both here and abroad was influenced by distribution methods developed in California less than a century ago.

The average diet for Americans 100 years ago consisted of homegrown wheat products, potatoes, beans, and seasonal vegetables, as well as fruits such as apples, pears, and peaches when available. Beef, pork, poultry, and dairy products supplied needed protein, and Port Costa and Sears Point became the destination for hay barges that shipped these products by water to California's burgeoning population. As the importance of rail and water transportation became clear, farm produce shipping increased, and a wide variety of new foods found their way into the average diet of the American consumer.

Further productive experimentation in agriculture, horticulture, and viticulture changed the landscape of Contra Costa County as the Great Depression took hold and thousands of impoverished people seeking work came west to California, by then a widely acclaimed leader in the production of fruits, vegetables, olives, walnut, and almond crops.

Camps were set up to accommodate the migrant workers during "picking seasons" in various parts of California. As new agricultural industries developed, however, many of these itinerant workers chose to go into the labor market or commerce and began making their homes in the area.

H.P. Garin opened his headquarters in Brentwood and became a pioneer in the growing, packing, shipping, and distribution of fruits and vegetables of the San Joaquin–Sacramento Delta area. Balfour, Guthrie and Company of Brentwood and the Fontana Produce Warehouse of Oakley in the eastern part of the county supplied the country with produce from the many truck gardens of the delta. California Packing Company, Hickmott Canning Company, and Western California Canneries of Antioch, as well as F.E. Booth of Pittsburg, were among the expanding list of growers and canning operations in the county.

As refrigeration systems for shipping produce by rail to eastern markets were developed, Americans were introduced to new and exotic items such as asparagus, artichoke, different varieties of lettuce, cauliflower, eggplant, honeydew melons, cantaloupe, apricots, nectarines, almonds, and walnuts. Until now, oranges, tangerines, and lemons had been a rarity in most households. Europeans were also beginning to experience these new foods as oceangoing vessels were outfitted with refrigeration systems. An added bonus was the fact that people became healthier as out-of-season food became more readily available.

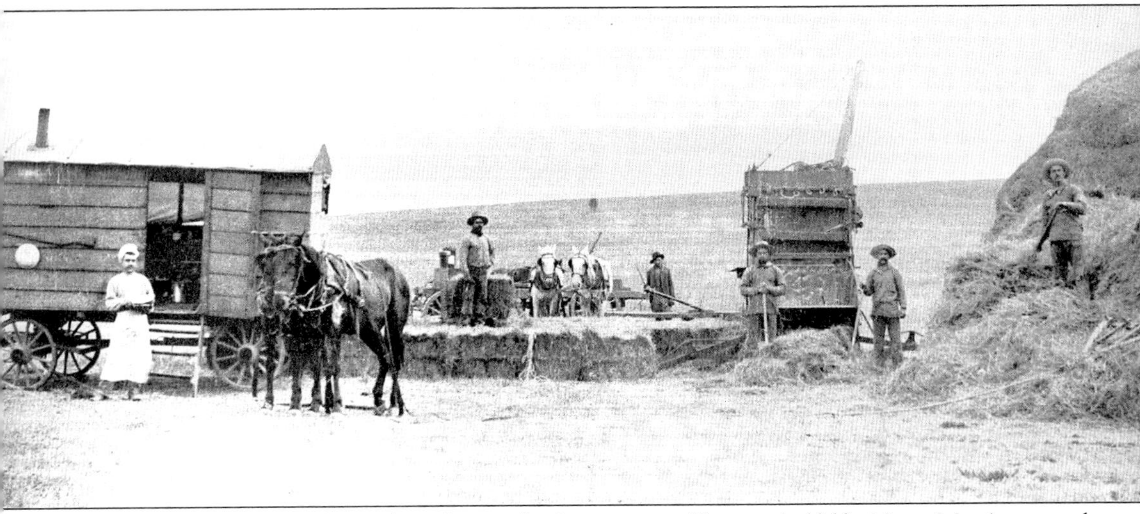

Hooper Ranch was a busy place during the harvesting of hay and alfalfa. Here, Mr. Arata and his crew are working the hay bailer. Notice the cook's chuck wagon where he is waiting to feed the crew.

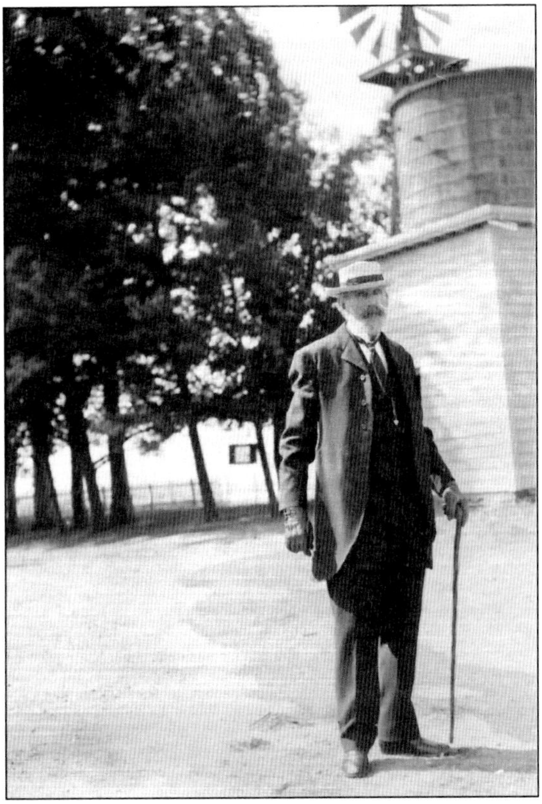

Charles N. Wight is believed to be one of the first American settlers in the West Pittsburg area with a ranch located near the river. In 1847 Wight met and married Sarah E. Huntington, a schoolteacher at Bay Point, now the site of the Port Chicago Naval Weapons depot.

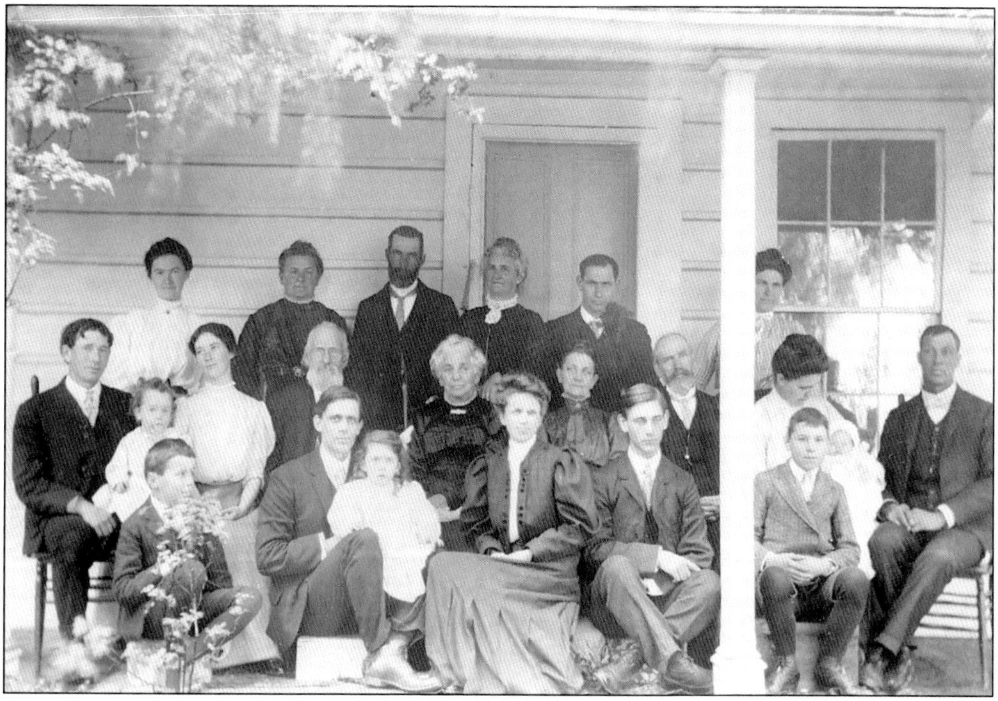

The Charles N. Wight family included Charles and his wife Sarah (sitting, front and center). Charles is credited with being the first American settler in the vicinity of New York Landing, also called New York Valley by the people who lived there at the time.

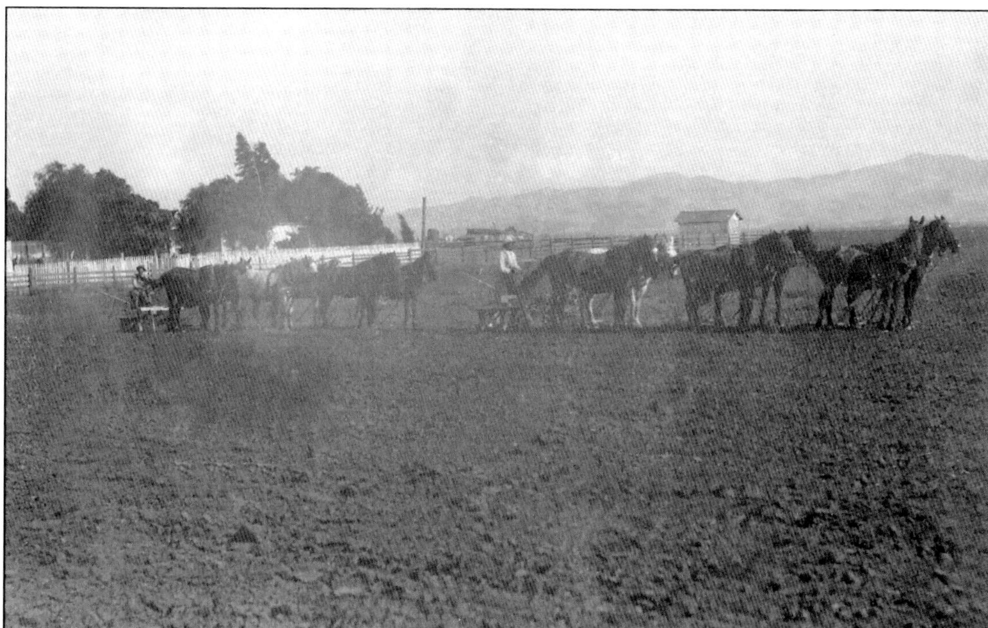

Ramus Hansen and his son William are shown here at Redding Ranch, north of the Buchanan Ranch homestead. The Hansens were another prominent ranching family running cattle and growing wheat and other grain products.

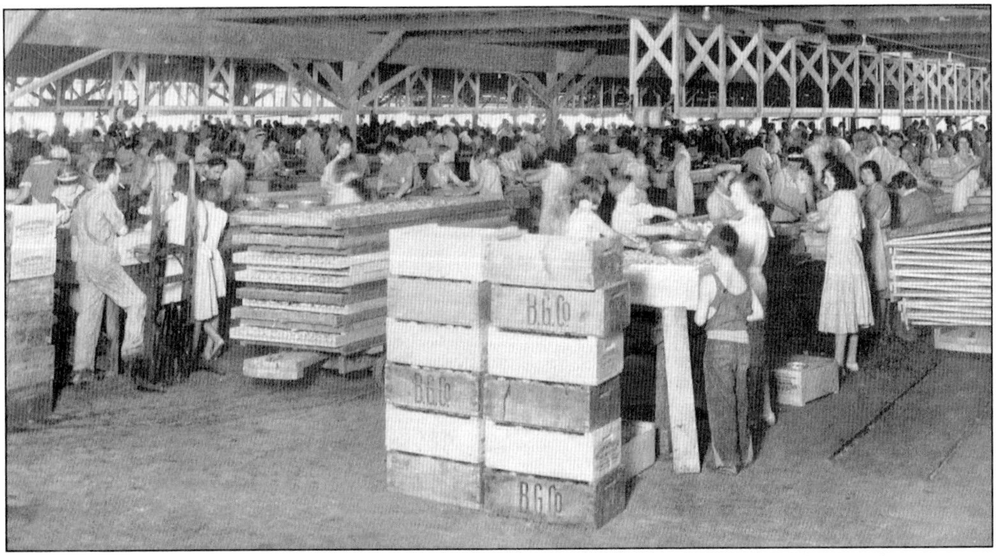

More than 600 hands were employed at the fruit cutting shed of Balfour, Guthrie and Company at Brentwood in East Contra Costa County. Boxes of peaches and apricots were cut, dried, and canned at the company's facilities.

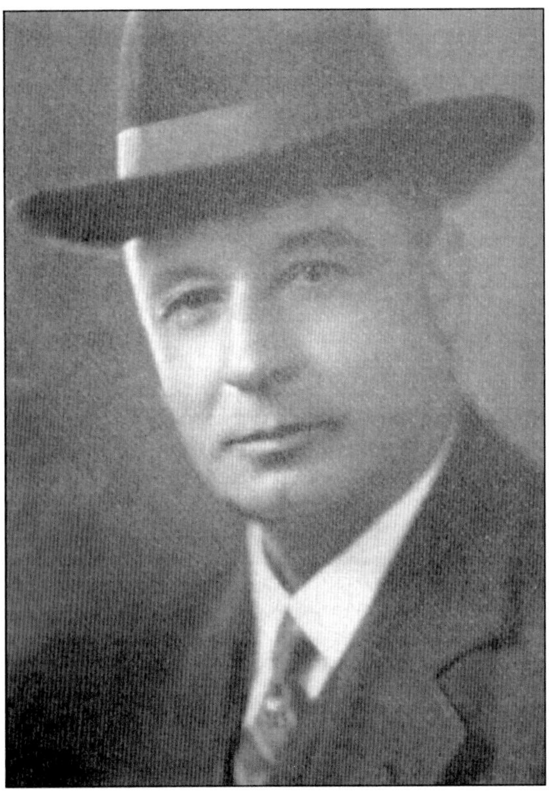

Company President H.P. Garin invested in the Brentwood area after a few short years in the agriculture business, where the rich delta soil produced large crops of vegetables and fruits. Grown from seeds, the yields were plentiful.

Coal Mining

Nora Norton, founder of the town of Nortonville, was 74 years old when he filed claim on the Black Diamond coal vein discovered in the hills south of Pittsburg. Norton was not the first to lay claim to the site. Francis Somers and his partner Jim Cruikshank prospected the area in 1859. After their efforts to borrow money on the property failed, they became discouraged and neglected to secure title to the land. Norton, a Welsh miner, came into the area looking to buy in on the new find and promptly filed claim on the property. He was able to induce some investors to advance money for development of the mines and the laying of a roadbed to the area.

The Black Diamond Company was incorporated with a capital stock of $500,000. Within a few years the coal fields were supplying the city of San Francisco with 45 percent of its needs. Norton built a fine house close to the mine, and a settlement sprang up around the hills of the town bearing his name. Except for coal, natural resources for energy were sparse. The climate was hot in the summer, with coal dust and smoke constantly sprinkling the little town. Muddy dirt roads during the winter rains made walking difficult. Nevertheless, miners from Wales, as well as Italian and Irish immigrants, began to populate the five small settlements that had sprung up in the hills with the discovery of coal.

Welsh people, accustomed to heavy work in the mines of Wales and Pennsylvania, began to increase in numbers until they reached about 1,000 inhabitants. They were hard-working, instinctively clannish people, standing together and helping one another out after mine accidents and disasters, as well as the deaths from typhoid and diphtheria that decimated many families with young children.

The Welshmen continued to observe the joyous celebrations of their homeland. A biennial patriotic national celebration of Eisteddfod featured poetry recitations, singing, and music competitions. A Welsh chorus was formed and carried on the traditions of their ancestors. Despite alternatives to many "watering holes" that opened up for the menfolk, drink seemed to offer an evening enticement that was difficult to discourage. Problems with public drunkenness and brawling were common. An effort was made by the concerned board of trustees of the Black Diamond Coal Company to improve the town's image by subsidizing schools and exerting their influence against intemperance, "the curse of the age."

A public debate ensued, and the decision was made to bring temperance laws to the people for a vote. After much discussion, the influence of the board and the "ladies" of the town prevailed, and a law was passed to prohibit drinking in public. A popular establishment, the Black Diamond Exchange, sold its last drink on a Friday night, as soon as the polls were closed. The other six saloons in Nortonville opened to a full house, saying they were going to continue on, regardless of the law. Suggestions that "Song Books to be traded for shooting-irons; community singing for gambling and dancing, a fine town chorus and band instead of jail and an organized police force" were promoted.

Not all ghost towns were beyond redemption in the early days, for the above is a short, yet true picture of Nortonville, a once-thriving coal mining community of Contra Costa County. It seems that Nortonville literally sang itself free of a crime wave in the early days.

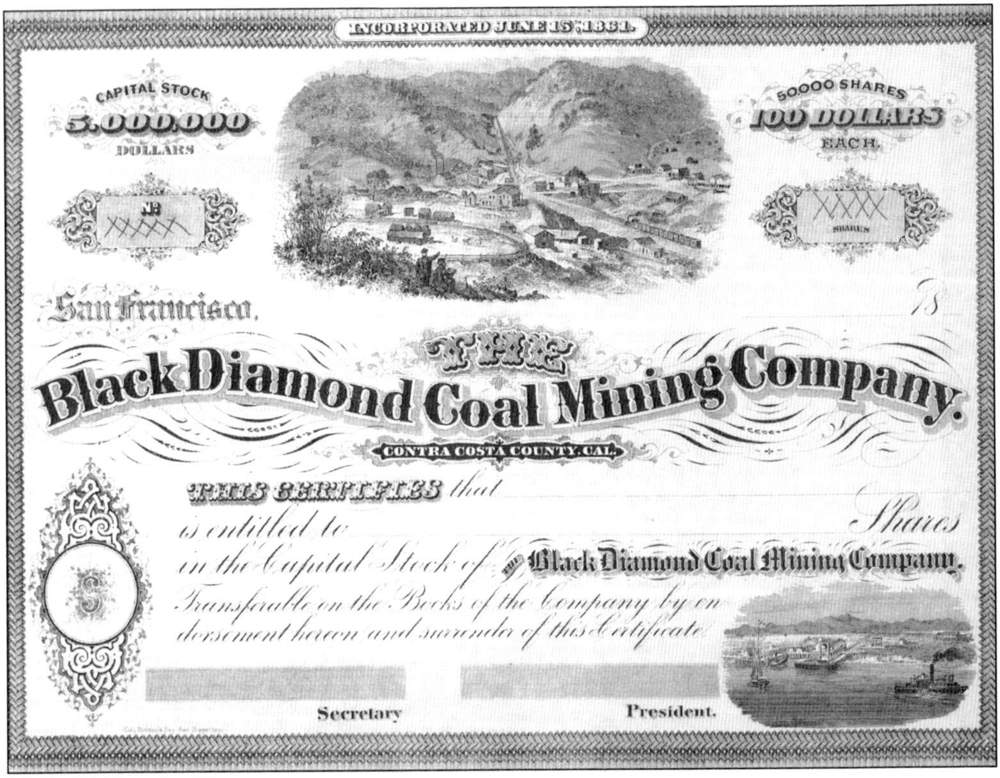

The Black Diamond Coal Mining Company issued coalmining certificates, selling 500,000 shares for $100.

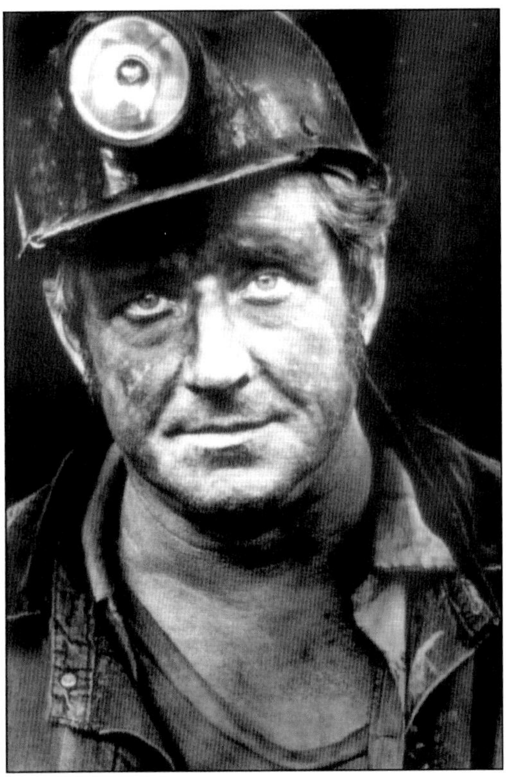

Coal mining was difficult work. Miners faced danger from on-the-job accidents as well as from the lung disease that often affected them in later years.

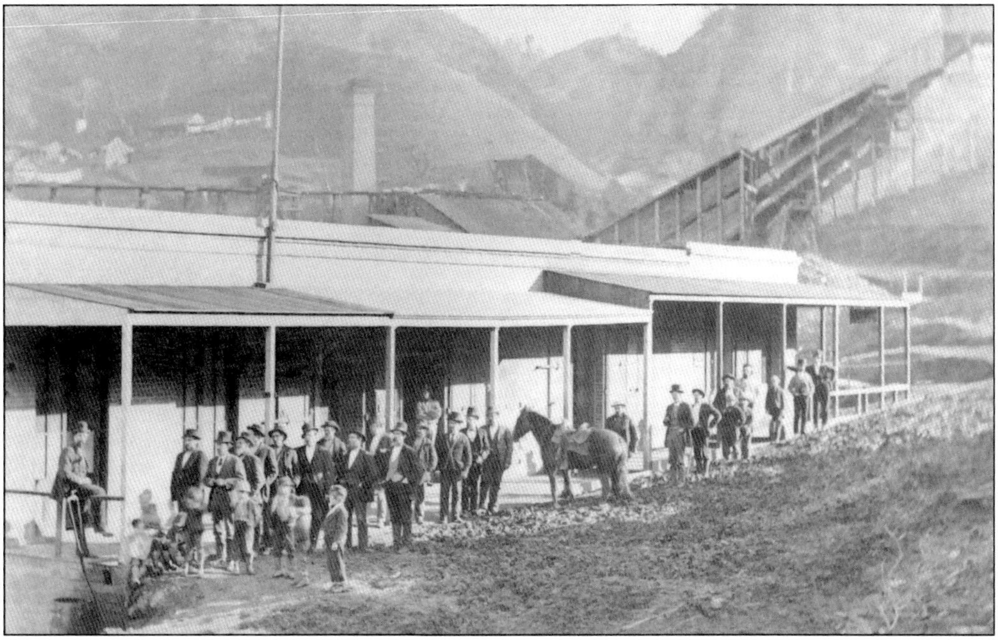

Nortonville in 1883 was a busy little town that included the Nortonville Department Store, commonly known as the Brick House or main office of the Lasedel Company. Note the smoke house and mine equipment in the background. Mount Hope is the left slope and Cumberland Hills are on the right.

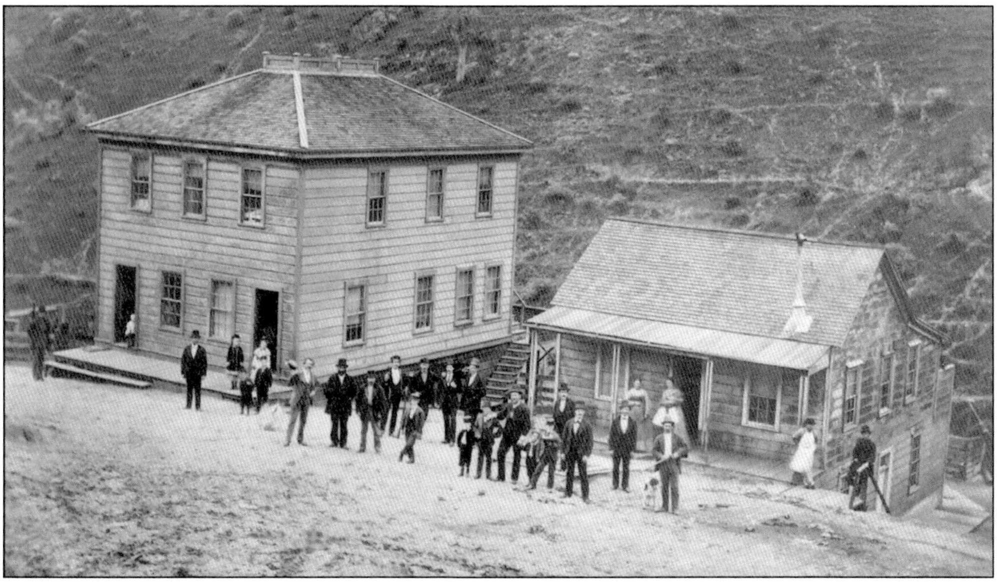

The boarding house and a candy store were also part of Nortonville. The neighboring building is a one-story boarding house. Note the cook dressed in white at the left-hand corner of the building.

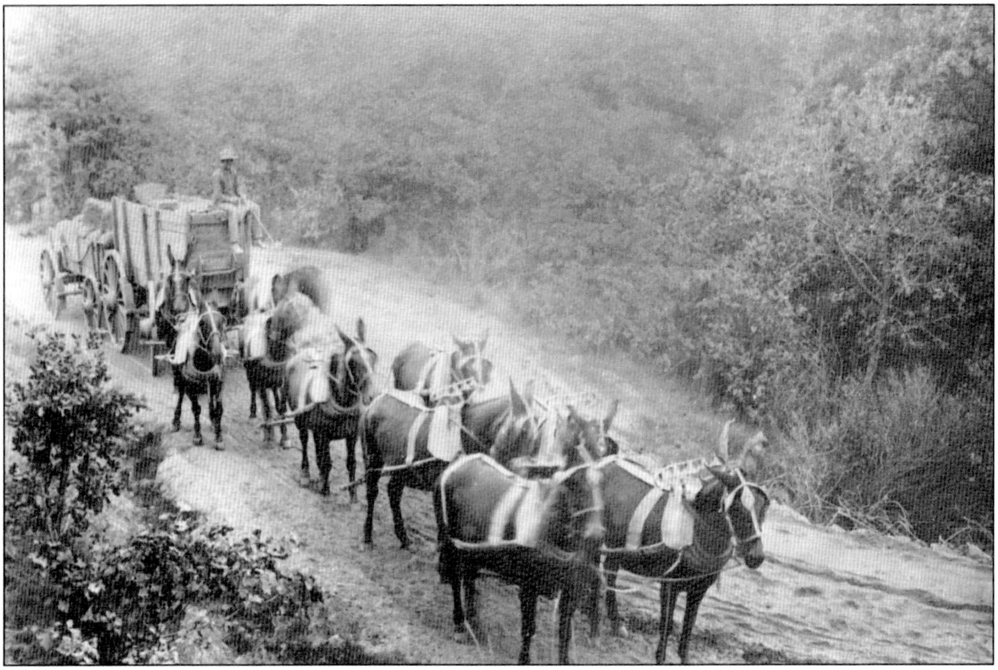

A wagon and a team of eight horses climb the steep hills of Nortonville delivering freight to the storage sheds.

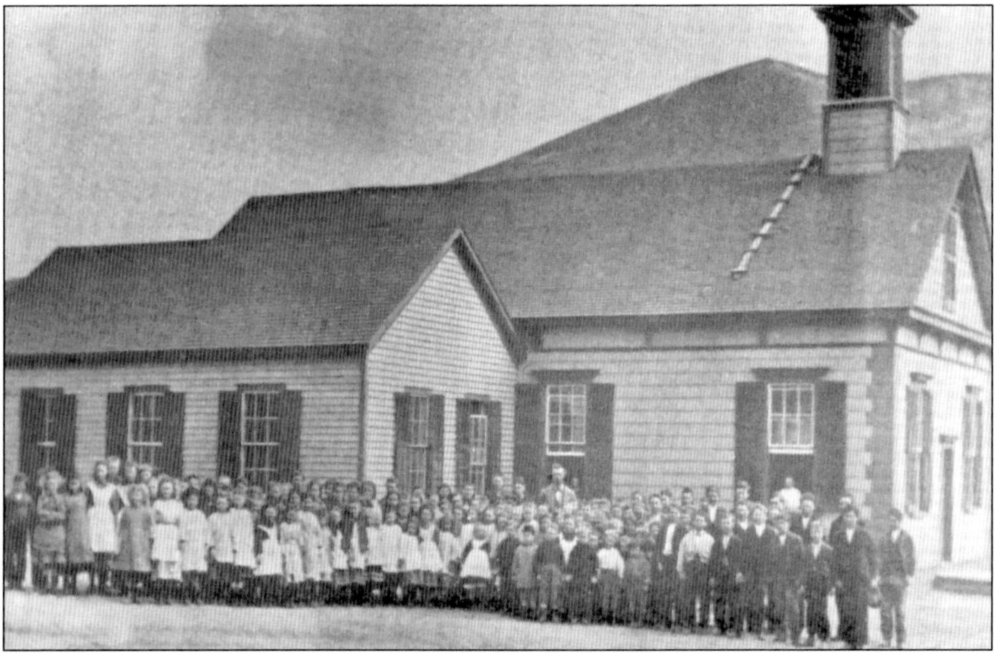

This photo of Nortonville's little old schoolhouse shows the students standing in front with teachers and parents posing to the left. This single schoolhouse held all of the classes, from primary to elementary grades.

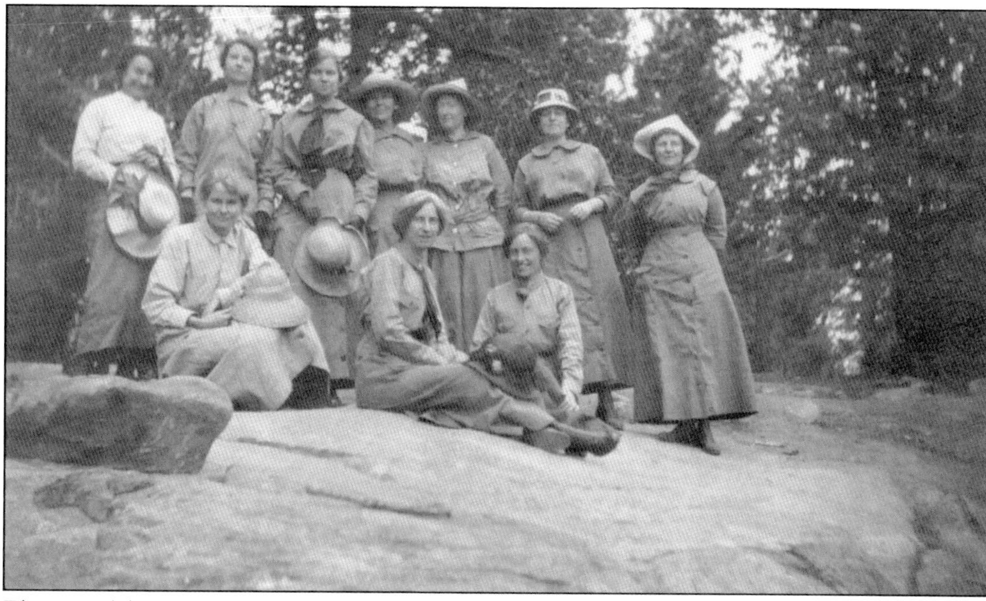

These Welch women on a ladies picnic in the hills of Nortonville dressed simply but with the proper hats and a festive air about them.

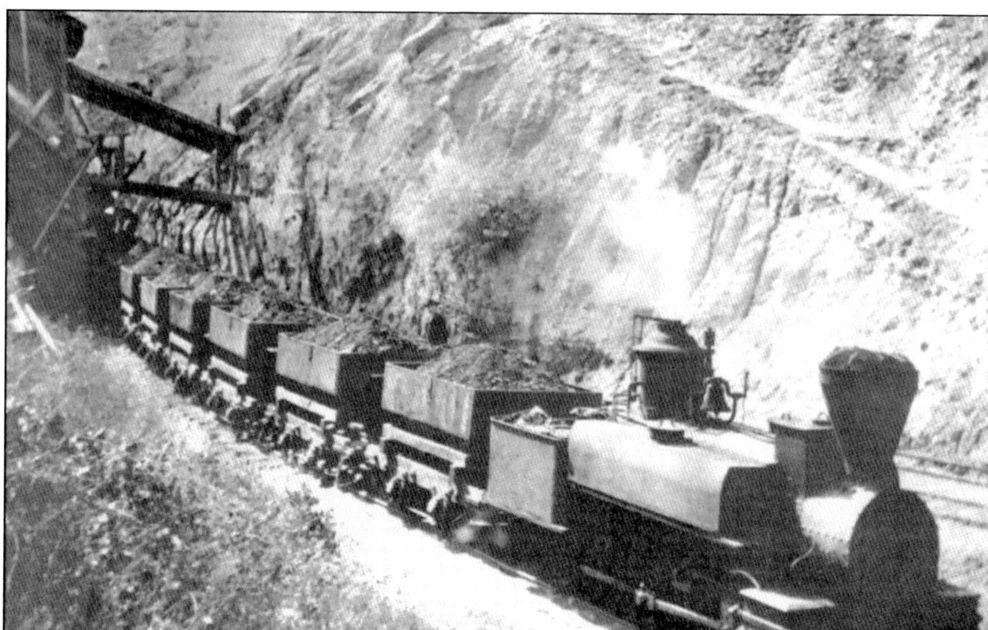

Black Diamond Coal Company cars come down the hills en route to the New York Landing docks where they loaded the barges with coal to be delivered to San Francisco.

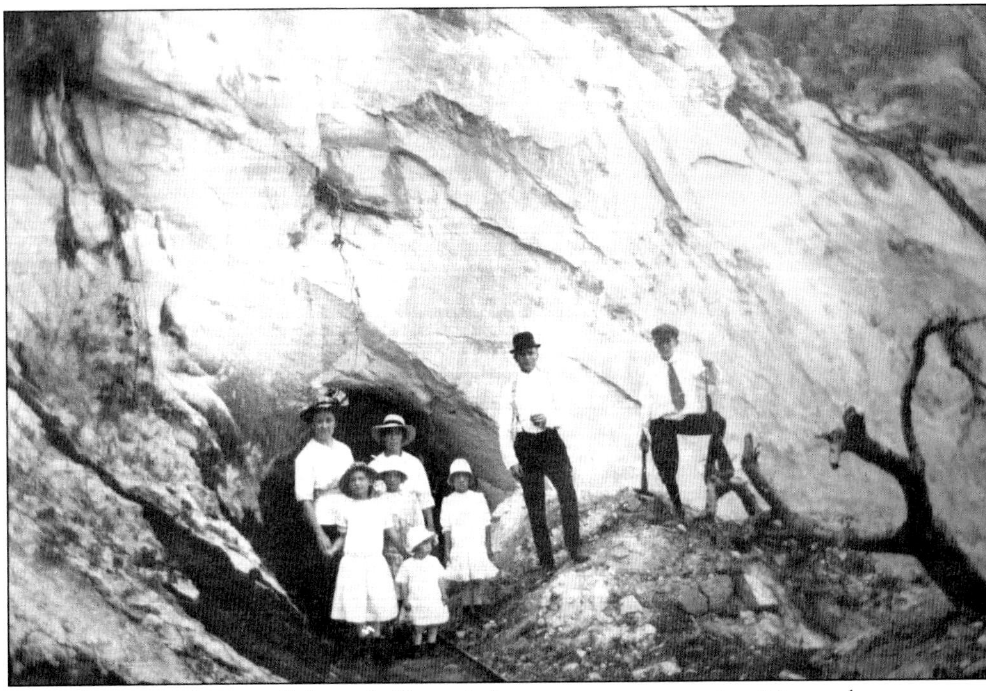

A Sunday trip to the mine "where daddy works" was a common practice. Men and women spent long hours day after day in hard labor, and a day off was a treat for the whole family.

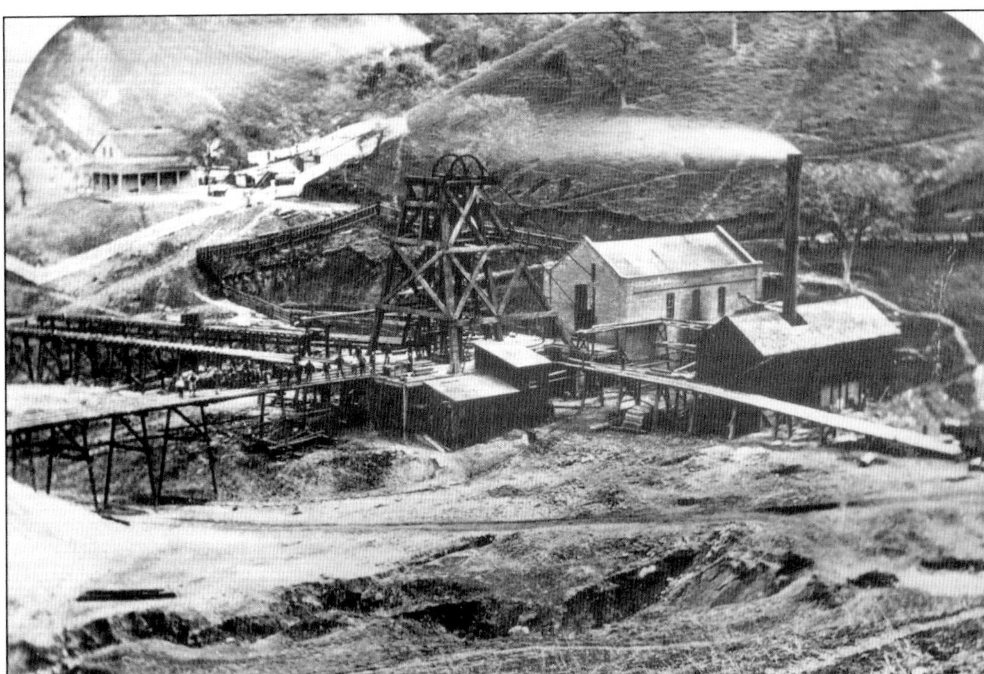

The Black Diamond coal vein was mined via this hoisting derrick and shaft. The trestle to the left was used to carry the one-ton coal cars to the bunkers. The home of Morgan Morgans, the superintendent of mines, is on the left side of the picture.

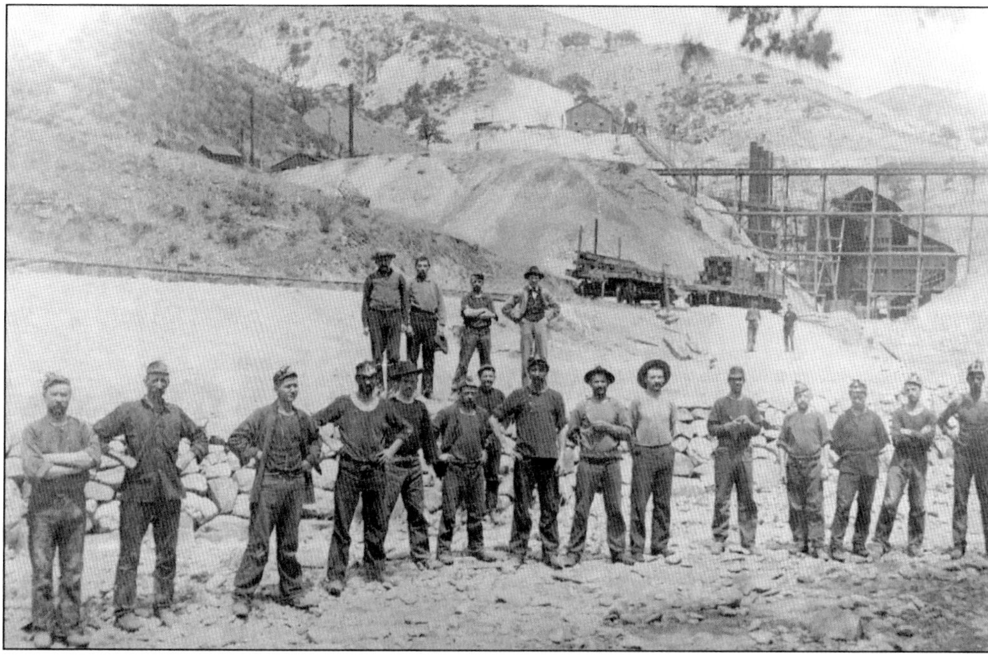

Miners ready for another work day are dressed in work clothes that will soon be covered with another layer of coal dust. Note the lanterns worn on their heads. The trains in the background are loaded with coal to be carried down to the waterfront for shipping to San Francisco.

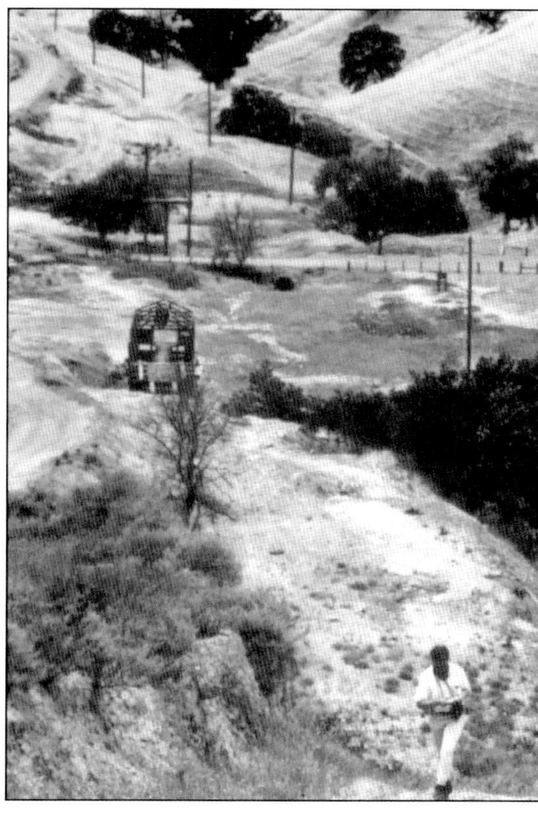

The rolling hills of Nortonville provide a backdrop for the mineshaft at center.

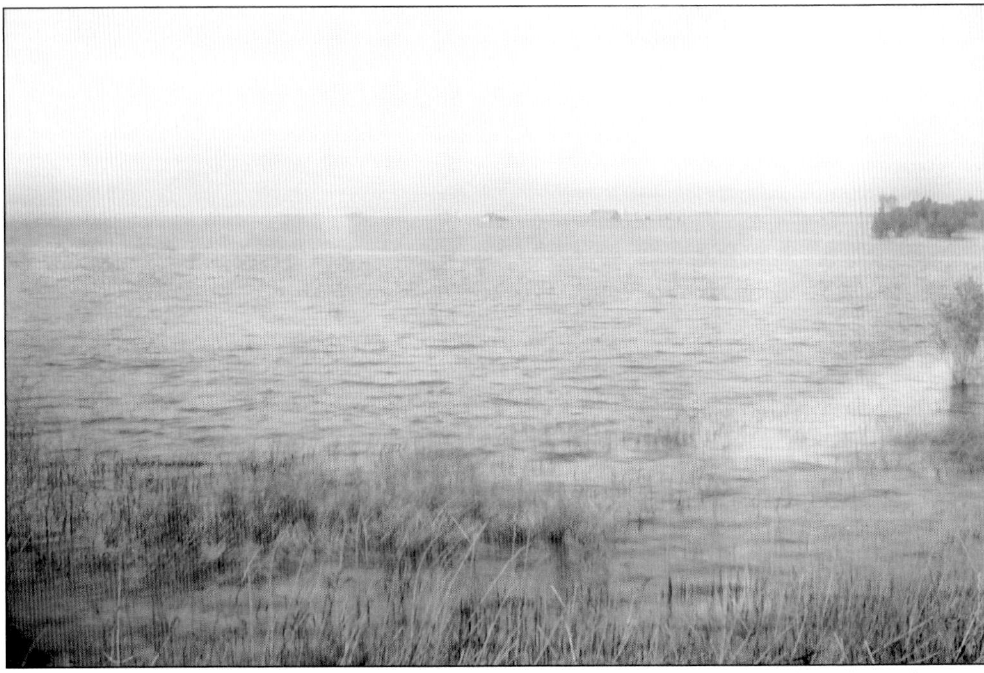

Although the river appeared calm and peaceful it could be deceiving. Many have been drowned here, taken by the eddy that lies beneath the surface of the water. Fishermen have struggled against the storms that frequently capsized their small craft in unexpected rough weather.

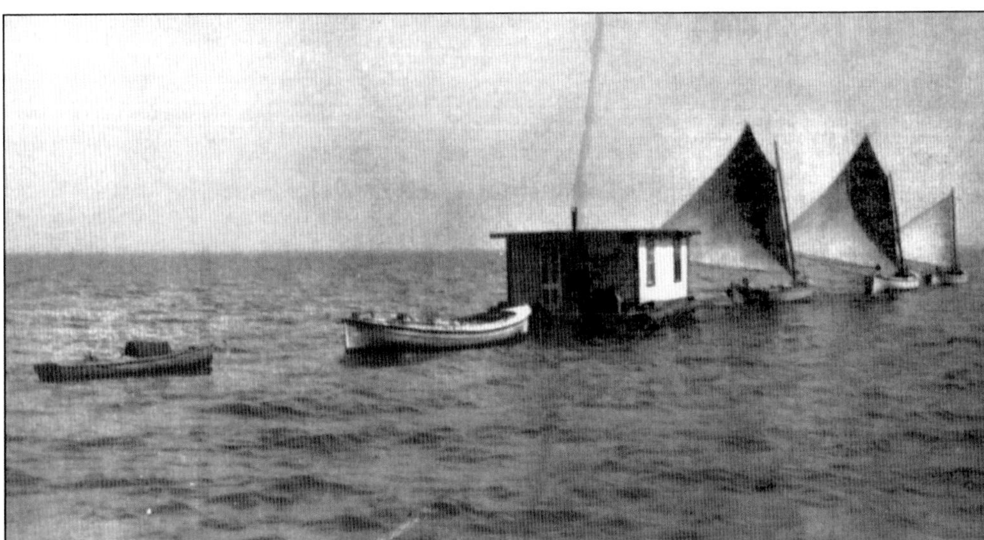

Houseboats, like the one shown here, were often the first living quarters for fishermen. Felucca sailboats are pictured alongside.

Three

The River

Travelers en route to the gold county crowded the Bay of San Francisco and the gateway to the delta as a tide of immigration made its way to destinations beyond the booming city. In 1849 and 1850 a commander in the U.S. Navy was requested to execute a survey of the bay and the rivers' many pathways.

The anchorages of the inland bays were crowded with ships laden with goods awaiting transport to the mining regions through the unexplored mazes of the rivers flowing north. Thousands of men and women sought transportation in open boats ill-suited for carrying passengers to the interior, with sometimes tragic results.

Overwhelmed with the responsibility of human lives at stake, the lack of authentic navigational charts, and the necessity of an immediate survey of the area, skilled hydrographers carefully prepared the documented work. Beginning the surveys with a system of triangulation and true azimuths, the chart makers established a reference point on the plan. Two trees were used as a base meridian for this survey at the site of New York Landing situated on the south bank near the mouth of the San Joaquin River.

To the south was a mountain range, with Mount Diablo rising from the center and its spurs branching off in all directions. To the north was another mountain chain, with the Montezuma hills in close proximity to the Sacramento River. This junction was the fountainhead of the expanse of water embracing San Francisco Bay to the Farallones. It was not until 1851 that Mount Diablo's northerly pinnacle was established as a point of base meridian for all surveys in California.

Buoys were assigned to the various points along the way, and the newly formed town of New York of the Pacific was again considered the starting point for a thorough exploration of the channels. The time spent exploring the San Joaquin and Sacramento Rivers was well worth the effort, as the extensive report helped to illustrate the most advantageous sites for future cities. In fact, the halfway point and the stopover for passengers heading upriver was the New York House hotel, where the future city of Pittsburg would be located.

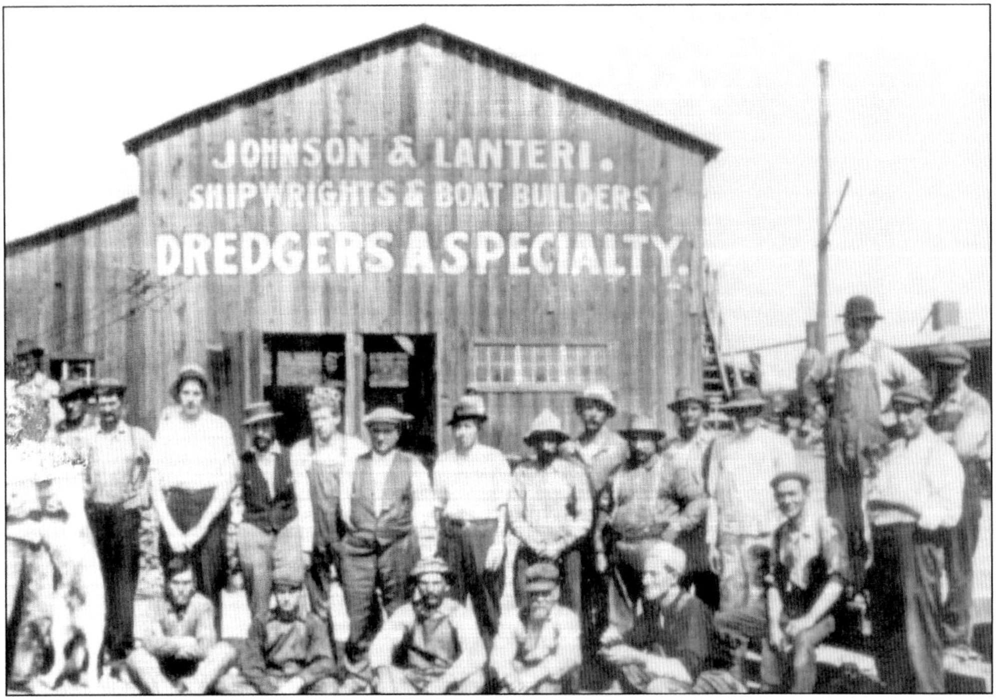

Barney Lanteri, a boat builder, and Lan Maupin, a dredge captain, were instrumental in building an early biplane at the shipyards. The plane, named the Diamond, was flown in an air meet in Los Angeles in 1912 and won first place.

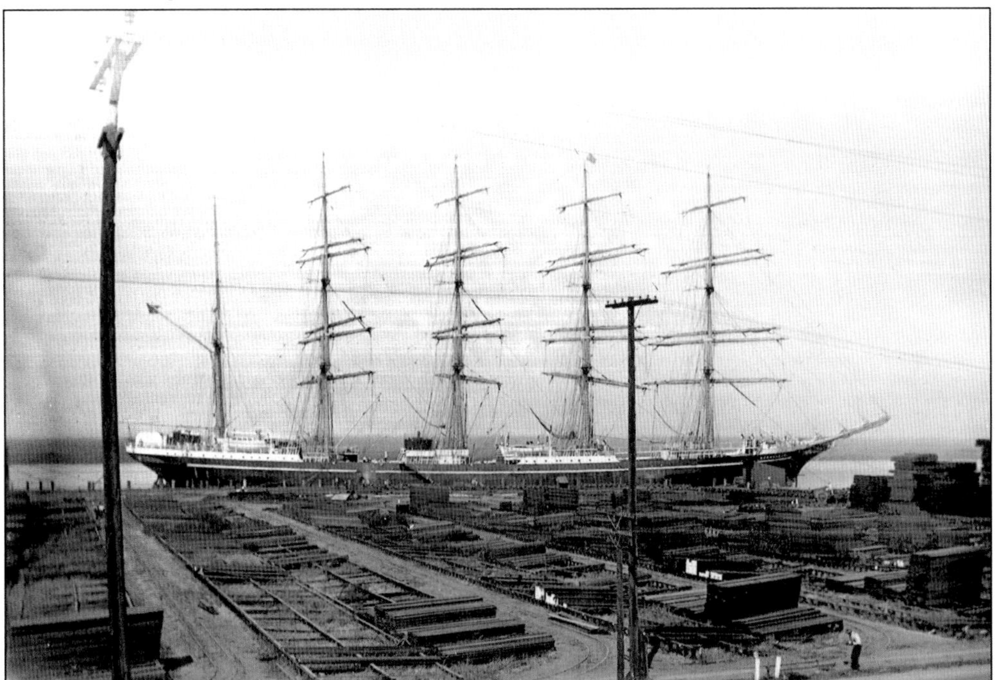

Sailing ships were used by the Redwood Manufacturing Company to bring in the raw logs that were manufactured into lumber and then shipped out to various users.

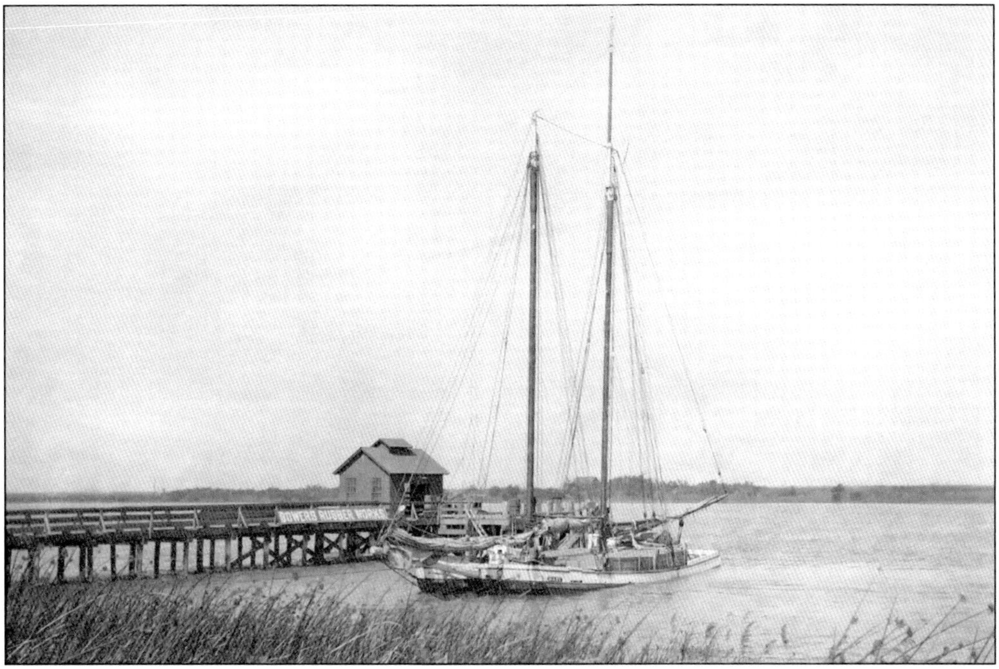

A cargo ship docks at Bowers Rubber Company loaded with raw rubber from Jakarta, Indonesia. The raw material was then processed into rubber products such as hoses, tires, and other manner of rubber goods.

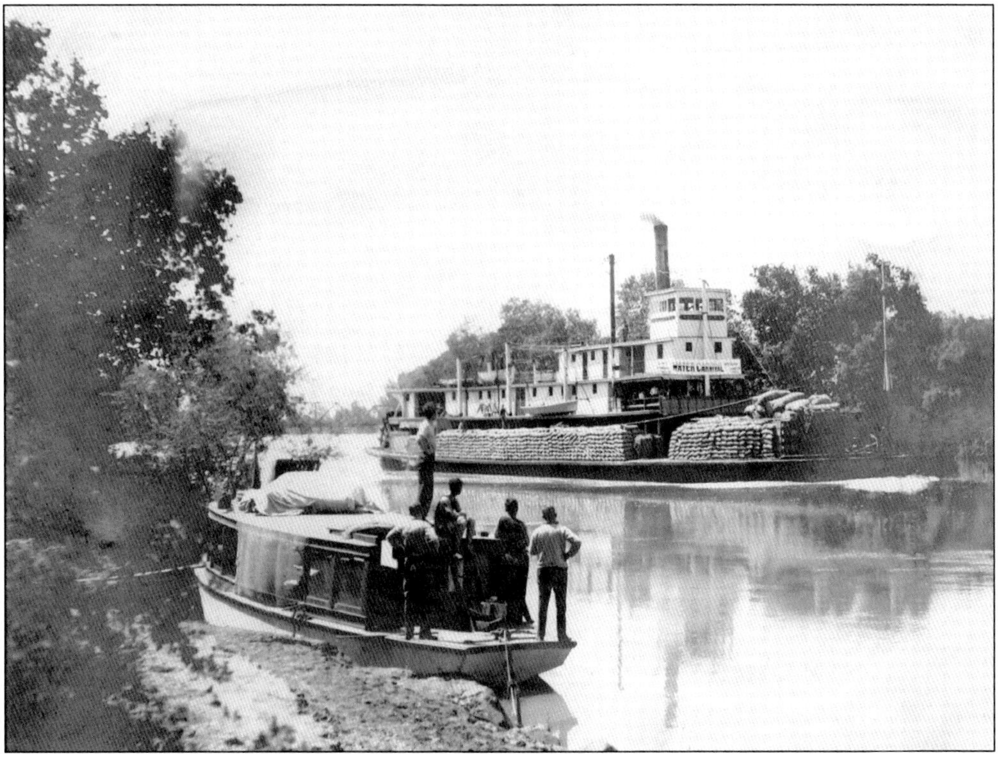

Early sternwheelers carrying passengers and freight were a common sight at the local waterfront.

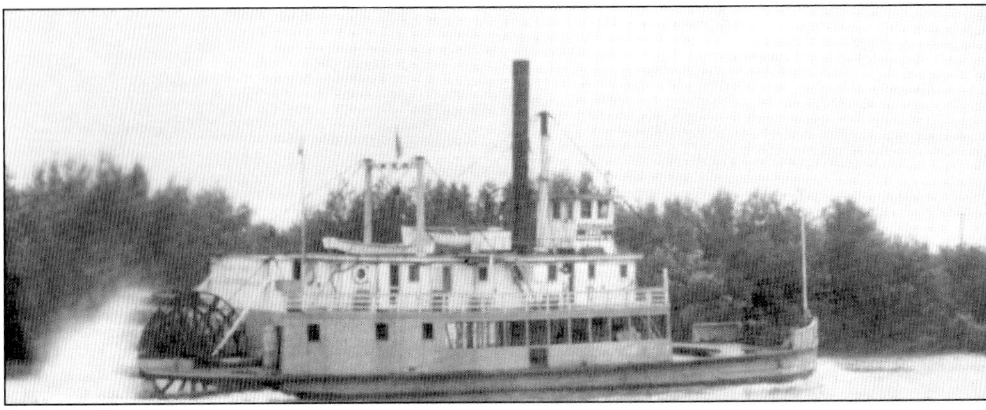

The delta cargo boat, a paddle-wheeler, provided transportation for both passengers and agriculture products in the late 19th and 20th centuries. The Napa City of San Francisco was one of the many vessels that sailed into the delta.

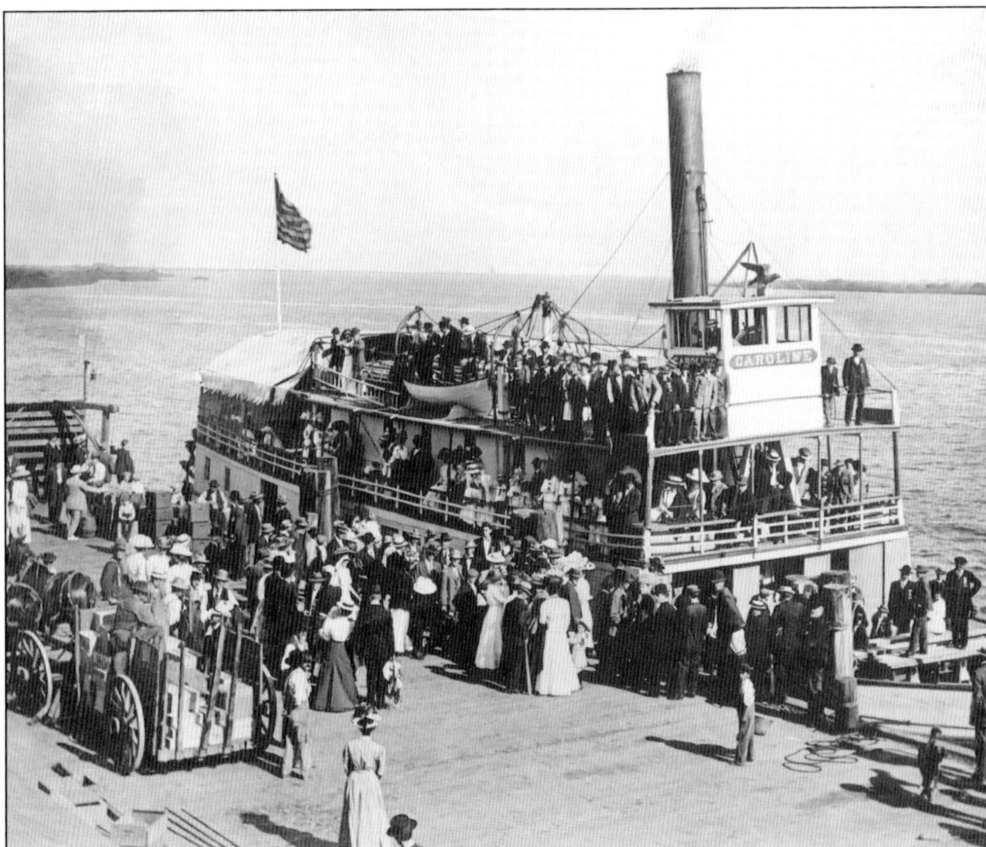

Bowers Rubber Company employees take a picnic on the Caroline, a ferryboat carrying passengers up the river for the day.

FISHING

The enterprising Italian, Greek, Portuguese, and Asians who came to New York Landing in the 1860s found the twin rivers of the Sacramento and San Joaquin teeming with fish. Those who previously lived and fished near the waters in their native countries began to make a life for themselves in America by continuing to work in commercial fishing. For nearly 100 years fishing was one of the major industries along the California coastline. Sicilians from Italy who had fished the Mediterranean for generations were naturally drawn to the mild and sunny climes of the area, and Italians would ultimately shape the town now called Pittsburg.

The business of catching, processing, and selling salmon, bass, shad, and other fish-food became the major industry for the first 50 years after the founding of the town. Commercial fisheries began along the rivers from here to Sacramento, and California river salmon found a ready sale in almost every market in the world.

Some of the first immigrants from Isola Delle Feminine in Sicily to arrive in the small village of what was then New York of the Pacific were Pietro Aiello and his brother Russell. The brothers had first fished on the Columbia River in Oregon before settling here. The move turned out to be advantageous for the brothers, and soon, large numbers of other Sicilian fishermen left wives and families behind to make their way to America. Some came by ship to New York, then journeyed to California on the transcontinental railroad. Others landed in New York and then sailed around Cape Horn and up the Pacific coast.

After settling in, many of the immigrants found accommodations on the water, where they lived in simple houseboats or shelters near the shoreline. When they could afford to send for their families, permanent houses were built near the wharves. As the town grew and the Italian population dramatically increased; a more stable life brought commerce, schools, and churches. The immigrant artisans began shipbuilding operations and used quaint sailboats extensively throughout the delta waters. Jack Del Monte, Ramey Seeno, Gaitano E. Seeno, Andrew De Stefano, and Barney Lanteri were some of the early boat builders of the era.

The first commercial fishermen used a unique fishing boat to gather the fish harvest of the river. The craft, called a felucca, was equipped with a sprit-rigged sail, and measured about 26 feet in length. The boat had an eight-foot beam and a retractable keel that allowed it to enter very shallow water. It also had a removable rudder that permitted the net to be hauled over the stern. The felucca was a local adaptation of the lateen-rigged sailing ship that was used in the Mediterranean for centuries and had originated in ancient Egypt. Fishing was performed with long narrow gill nets, which were played out in a line across the water, causing it to drift with the current and snagging the larger fish in its diamond-shaped mesh, while allowing the smaller ones to pass upstream to spawn. Gillnetting along the Sacramento River became the favored method because of the number of fish caught and the ease of their delivery into the boats.

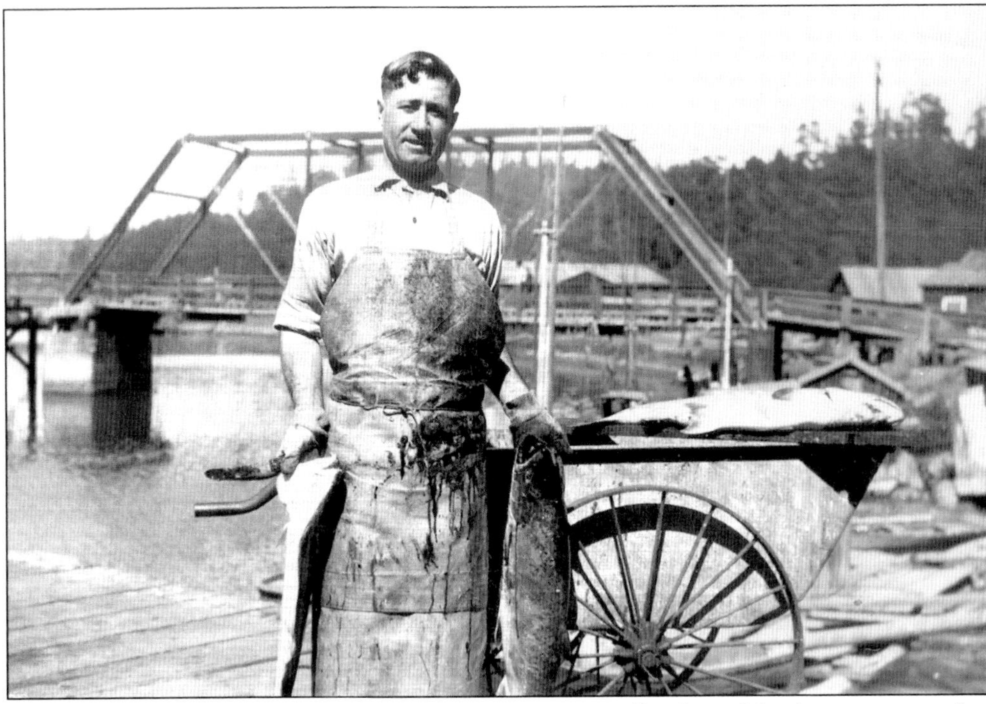

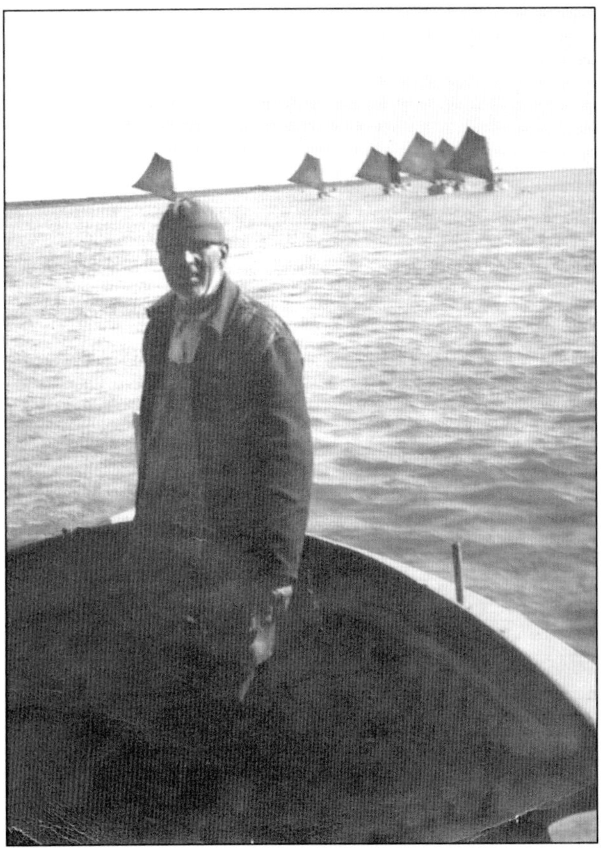

Catching fish, then cutting and canning them was all part of the industry that brought many Italians to Pittsburg. Anthony Davi and his family came in 1890 and distinguished themselves in the business of processing fish.

Joe Viscuso, a veteran commercial fisherman from Pittsburg, spent time in Alaska for the salmon fishing season and is shown here coming into the harbor at the Diamond J. Cannery. The felucca sailboats were used in Alaska in the 1940s.

Sal Russo and Vince Bruno are shown in their boat while the man at the scale is Paul Aiello, who worked at the Paladine Fish Company.

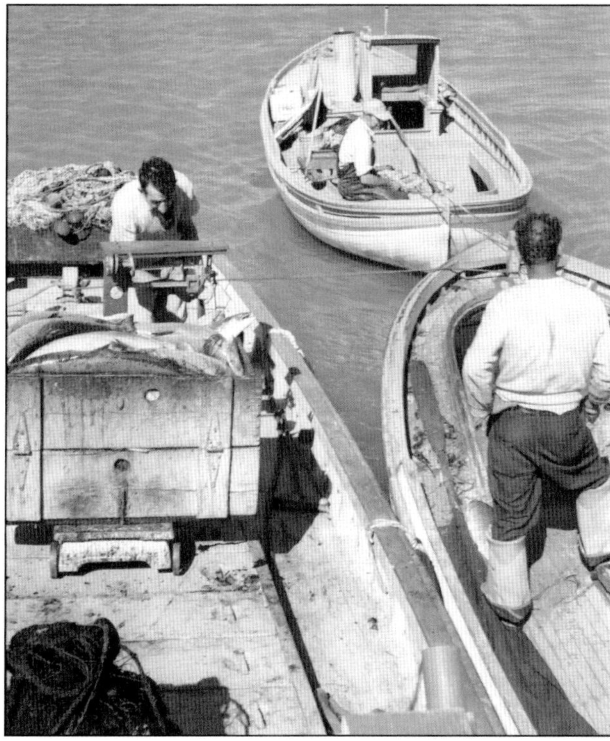

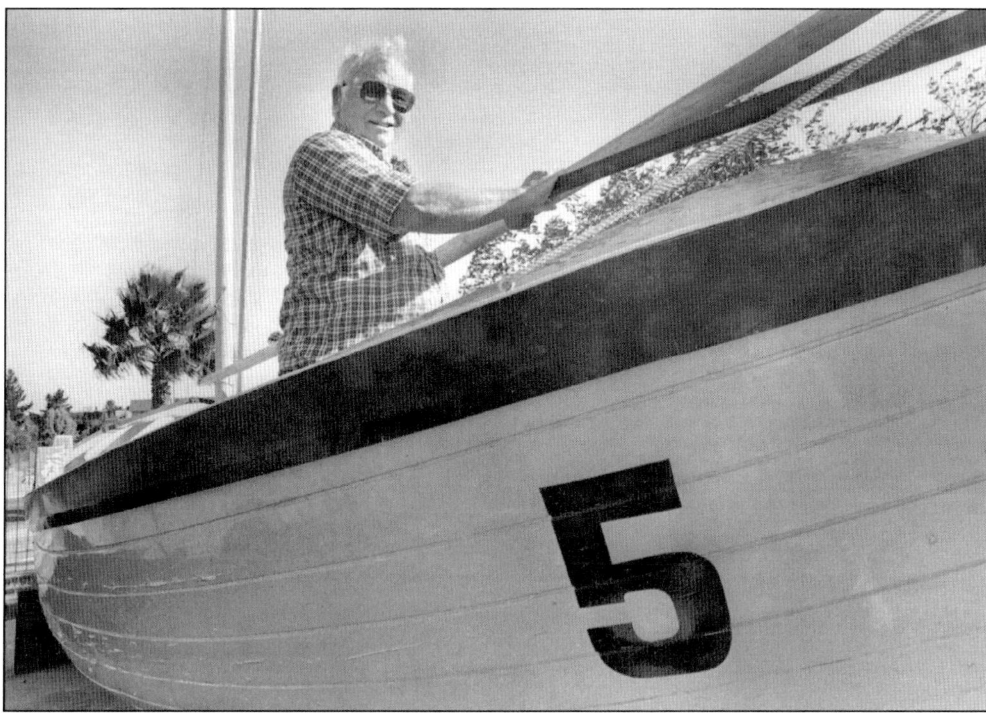

Joe Papetti is shown here with his 1928 boat, the *Red Salmon*, which is now on display at the Pittsburg Marina. Jack Aiello, Pittsburg's historian and curator for the museum, restored the boat in 1970.

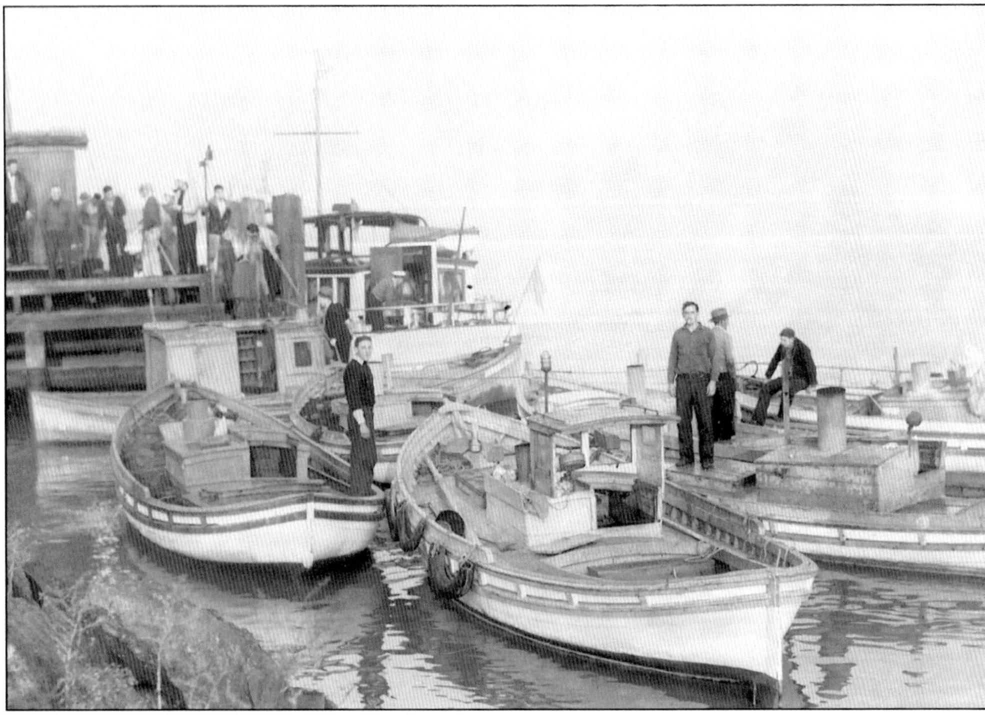

Local fishermen and their boats are active on the Pittsburg waterfront in 1943. The waterfront was always bustling with men tending their boats, fishermen mending nets, and children playing near the water.

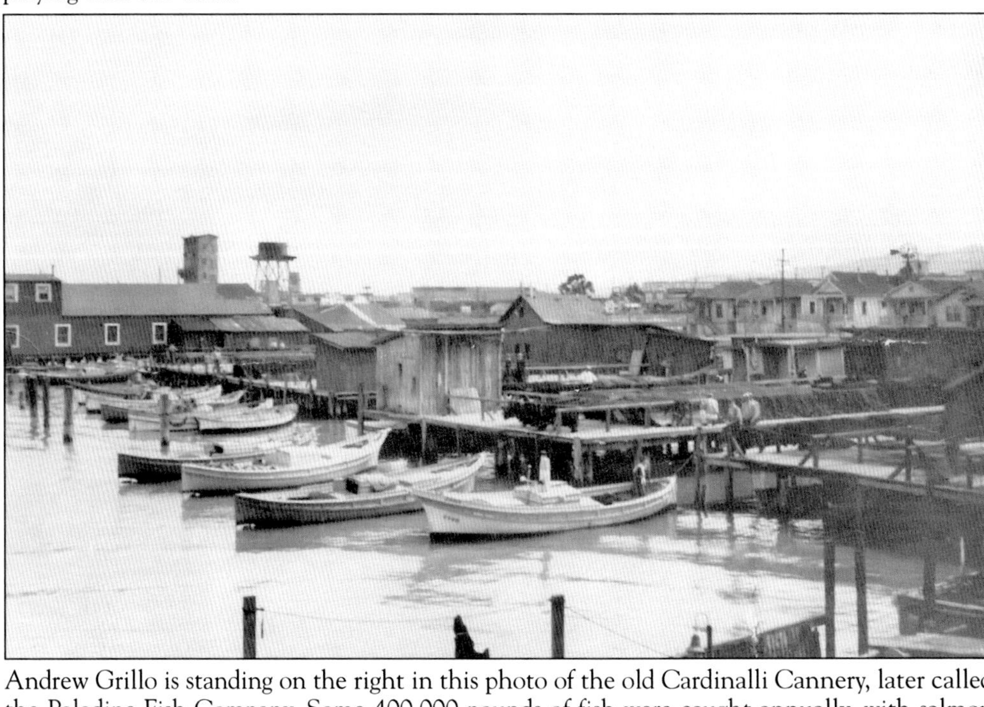

Andrew Grillo is standing on the right in this photo of the old Cardinalli Cannery, later called the Paladine Fish Company. Some 400,000 pounds of fish were caught annually, with salmon and shad mild-cured in large quantities.

MORE FISHING

Nets were woven of linen and were soaked in tanning vats to preserve them. Fishermen kept their nets in excellent condition and spent many hours at the wharf repairing them draped across wooden sawhorses, while spending time with other fishermen sharing stories and other town gossip. Either at the wharf or at home, busy hands continued in an endless pattern of work. Women and children were involved in mending the nets with handmade shuttles and making new nets.

Large numbers of salmon, shad, bass, and sturgeon were caught in local waters and required a different sized mesh in the nets used for catching them. Catfish was caught in a cone-shaped "fyke" net, a purse-like net with a large opening at one end, introduced by area fishermen. This method of netting helped in the development of the sardine industry in California

Fish buyers, who were often employees of the canneries or independent workers, used launches to pick up the catch directly from the boats while the men continued to fish the rivers. It was economically beneficial to continue to harvest the fish uninterrupted while the buyers unloaded the catch at the cannery or packing sheds.

As the fishing industry prospered, fishermen traveled north to Alaska in the summer months after the local season had ended. The trek to Alaska began as early as 1886, with men spending up to three months on sailing ships bound for the fishing grounds. By 1893 the Alaska Packers Association had launched their own "Star Fleet" with cargo capacities of up to 50,000 cases of salmon per vessel. By the turn of the century Italian immigrant fishermen were doing 80 percent of all commercial fishing in the State of California. The lateen sailboats, modeled after those in Italy, dominated the Pacific coast waters as far north as Alaska and were a common sight in the San Francisco and Monterey Bays.

With the advent of the Industrial Revolution at the turn of the 20th century, the familiar felucca sailboat was replaced by the "double-ender," and boats became longer, with higher bows to accommodate rougher waters and larger catches. Gasoline engines were added and the "clipper bow" shielded the boat from the water spraying over the bow. A "duck back" was later added to the stern, meant to keep the propeller from fouling the nets.

Builders of the Hicks and Standard engine launched the so-called "one-lunger," a single-cylinder, two-cycle marine engine that appeared shortly after 1900. Known for its ruggedness, reliability, and ease of repair, it was amazingly efficient and powerful, and technically very simple. The motor could be run by gas, kerosene, or coal oil, and since many lacked a muffler, the "chug, chug" sound gained it the nickname "potato engine." There were more than two dozen marine engine builders in California, but the Hicks and Standard engines continued to be the favorite among local fishermen.

As the state's population increased, so did competition for the river as a resource, resulting in an end to the delta commercial fishing era. Numerous ferryboats and larger vessels plying the rivers destroyed the nets while increased pollution from factory and agricultural run-off fouled the waters. Damming and diverting the waterways also caused a dramatic decline in the fish populations as their habitats were destroyed. Heavy catches and inadequate fishing regulations, coupled with successful lobbying efforts by the sports fishermen, finally led the government to place a ban on commercial fishing in 1957.

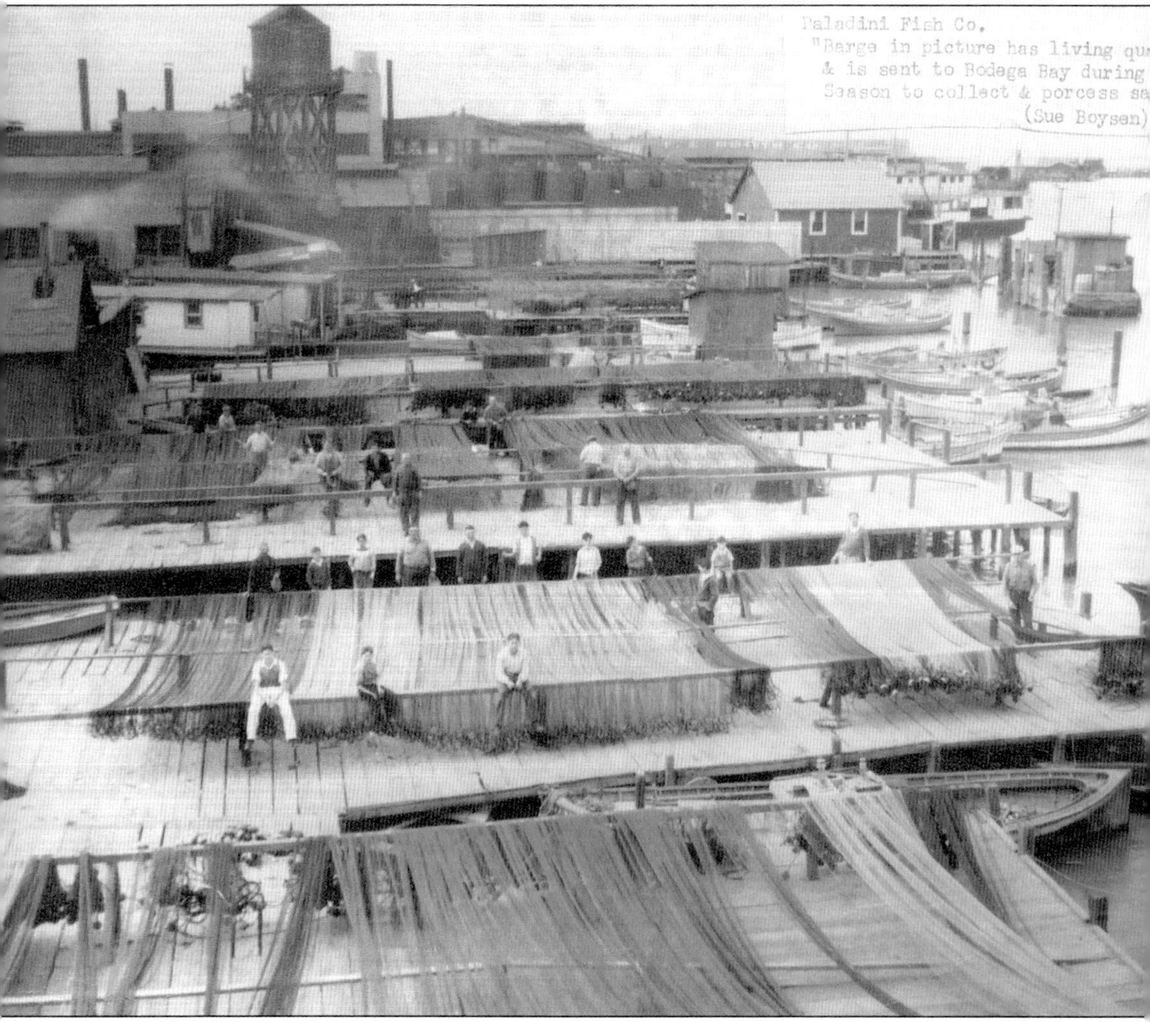

Nets dry on the wharf at Paladini Fish Company. The barge to the right is equipped with living quarters and was sent to Bodega Bay during the salmon season to pick up the salmon for processing in Pittsburg. Fishermen spend hours mending nets and preparing them for the next trip out.

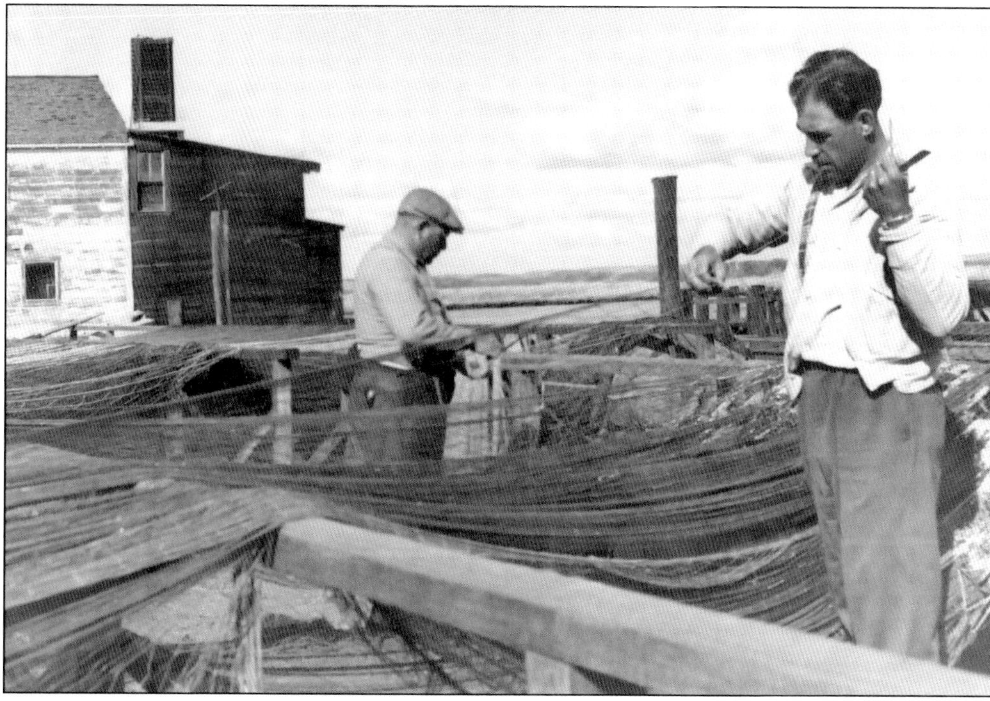

Sal and Joe Mercurio mend nets at the wharf. Net making or repairing was part of the everyday duties that kept equipment in good working order. Many fathers and sons and other relatives worked together in the fishing business.

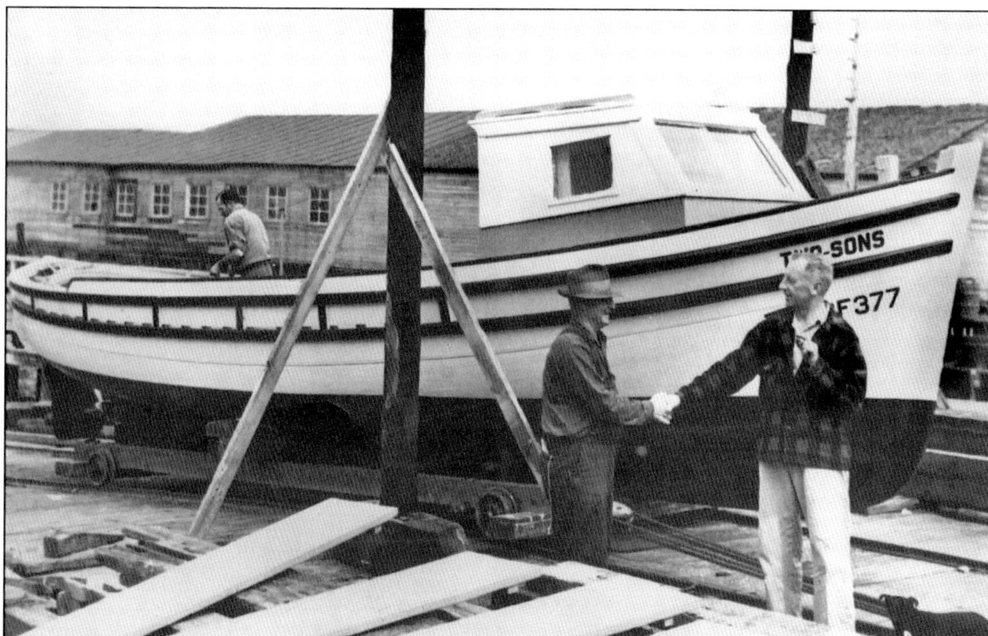

John De Stefano (center) built the last boat in 1955. Commercial fishing ended in 1957. De Stefano built boats for both Pittsburg and Monterey fishermen. Vincent Bruno is in the stern of the boat and Henry Nuttman is on right.

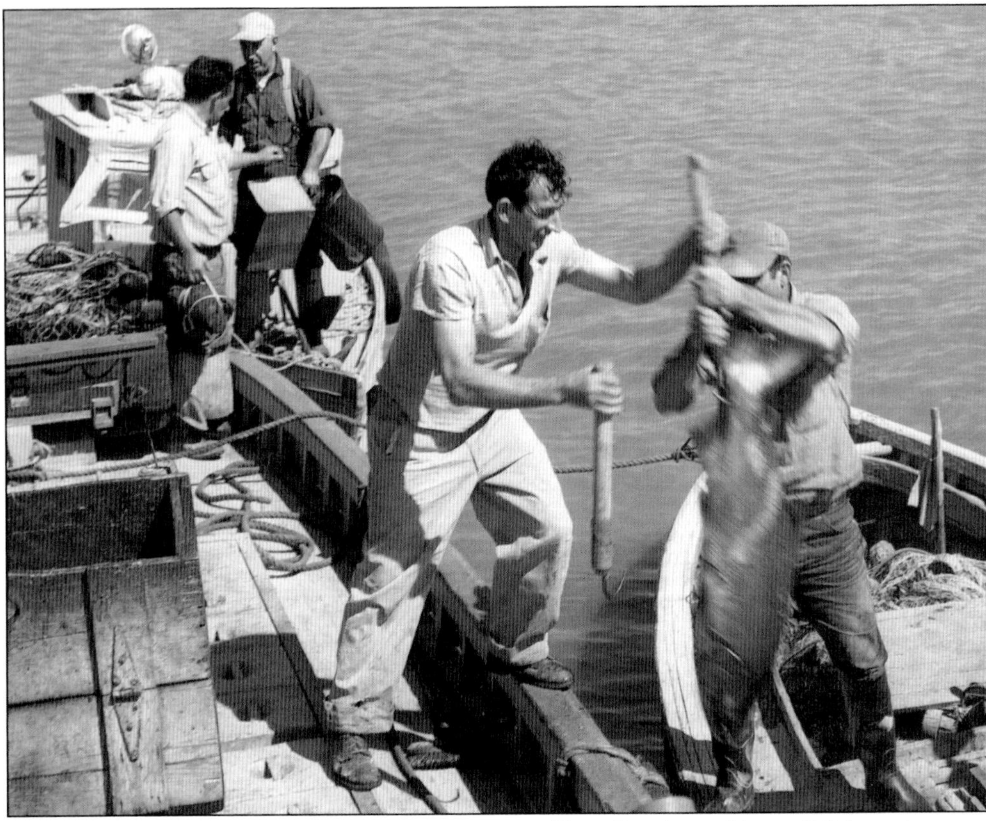

Tony Randazzo, Tonno DiMercurio, and Dutch Belleci are back from a salmon run. Paul Aiello accepts the fish for weigh in.

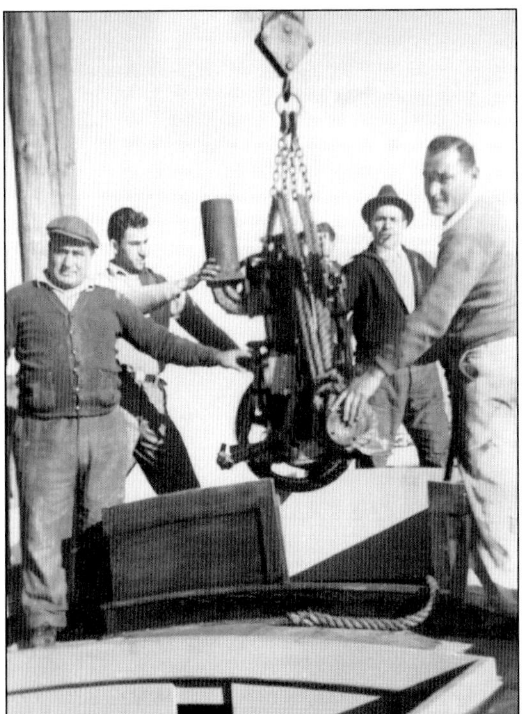

Mr. Fontera, Vince Seeno, Frank Seeno, and an unidentified man on the side are installing a one-lunger, a single-cylinder marine engine built either by California-based Hicks or Standard. The model appeared shortly after 1900 and was well known for its ruggedness, reliability, and ease of repair.

CANNERIES

In 1852, as gold fever continued to draw hoards of fortune hunters to the Sierra foothills, the more sober-minded men of vision sought a different path. California was a new frontier, and enterprises that would supply work for eager immigrants making their way to this new land with something other than gold in mind usually proved successful. Three men from the East Coast—William Hume, his brother George, and a friend named Andrew Hapgood—were the first in California to open a cannery.

The company, founded by the Hume brothers and Hapgood in 1864, was responsible for the beginning of one of the world's greatest fishery enterprises that developed on the Sacramento River. The rapid growth of this new industry soon began to encompass riverside sites running north and west into Oregon and Washington.

Here in Northern California, Black Diamond was recognized as a canning center by the year 1882. The J.D. Haller Cannery was a pioneer in the industry. Frank E. Booth, son of Robert Booth, president of the Sacramento River Packers, bought up this promising business, employing about 400, in 1909. It had the distinction of being the most successful in the 50 years of local canning operations.

During the history of canning in Pittsburg, companies such as the Paladine Fish Company, Pioneer Canning Company, Black Diamond Canning, Sacramento River Packers, Lindenberg Canning, the San Joaquin Fish Company owned by Arasimo and Frank Cardinalli, and the King Morse Canning Company were in operation. Ben Sendermen and the A.B. Davi enterprises were also among the many canning and packing companies that lined the riverfronts to mild-cure and sell fresh and frozen fish to the ready markets of California and other states.

In the beginning, processing was performed by hand. Chinese labor was used to economic advantage. Terms between the cannery superintendent and the Chinese boss or spokesman were worked out and the laborers hired. Barracks were set up on the grounds near the cannery. Cans were fashioned from metal using tin snips. The salmon was then packed into the cans, and other teams of workers would solder on the lids, then tap them with a wooden mallet to assure a tight fit. However, because the Chinese were presumed to be taking jobs away from the white settlers, Congress passed the Chinese Exclusion Act in 1882 forbidding the Chinese to enter the country.

At the turn of the century and during the peak of the Industrial Revolution, the Chinese laborers would be replaced by an invention called the "Iron Chink," invented by Edmund Augustine Smith of Seattle, Washington, who found a way to mechanize the cleaning step in the processing of fish. Canneries bought up these machines that helped revolutionize food preservation technology.

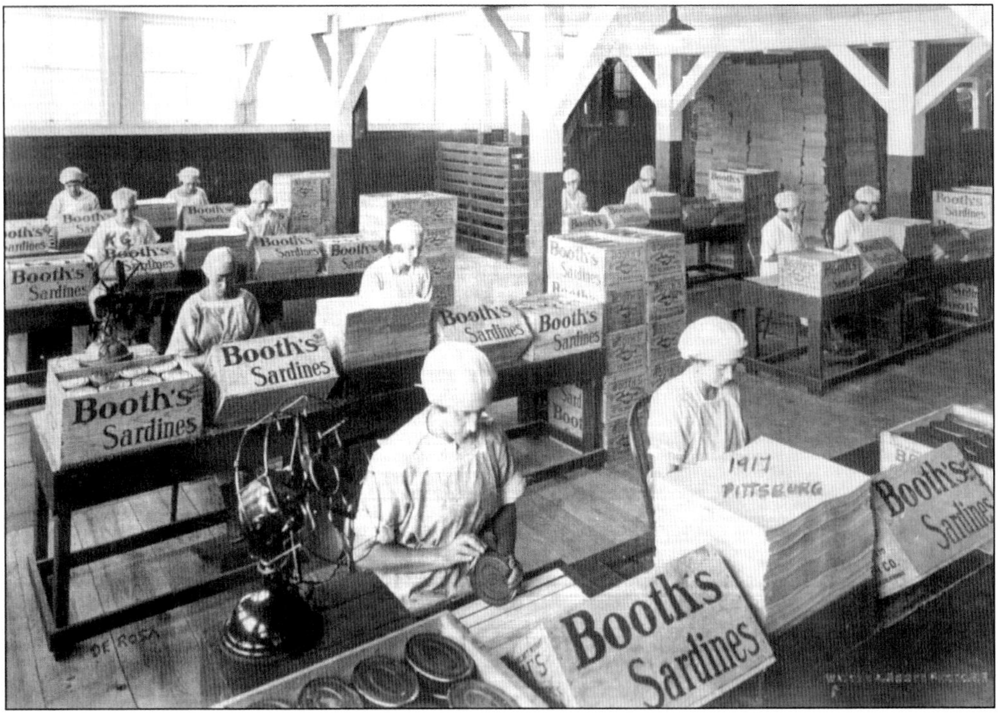

In 1917, the workers at F.E. Booth Canning Company consisted mainly of women who worked on a seasonal basis. When the fish came in during salmon season, the whistle blew, bringing the cannery ladies to the cannery where fish was steamed and placed in cans. Labels were then placed on the cans in another department.

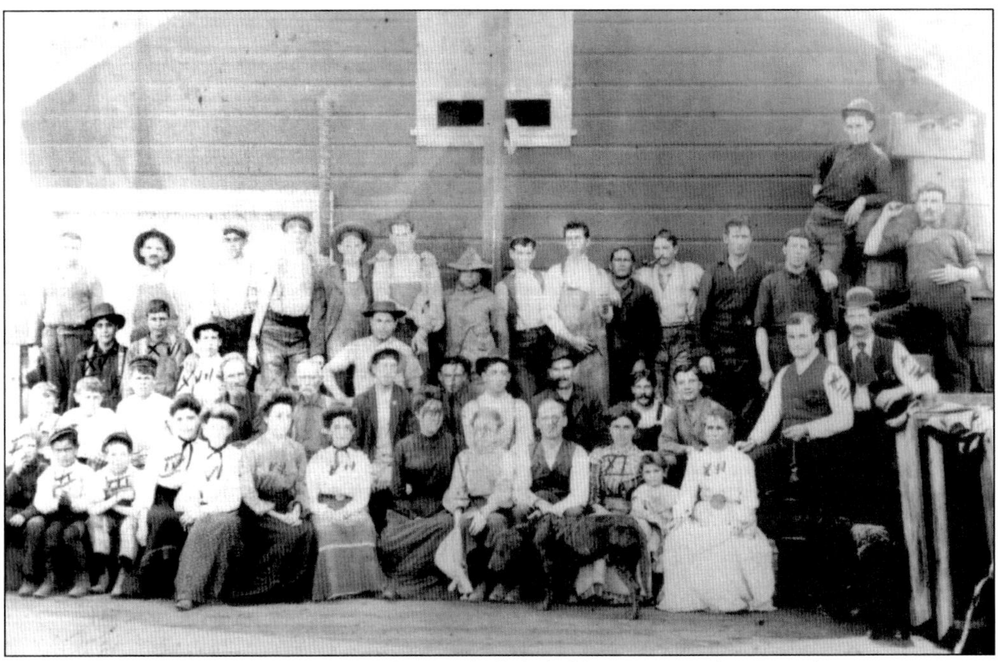

Cannery workers of the early 1900s often included children among their numbers.

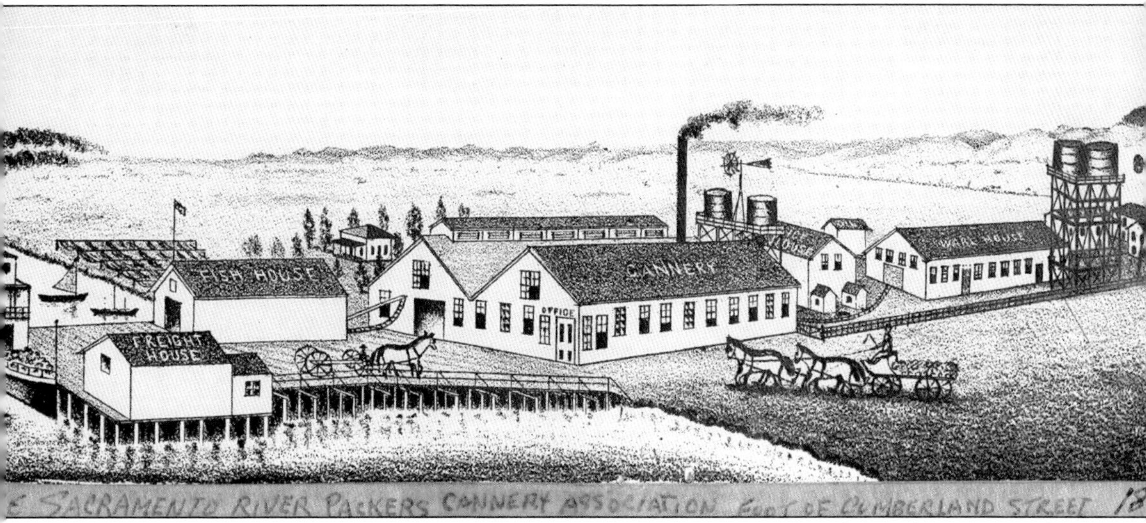

Sacramento River Packers Cannery Association built two canneries, one located in New York Landing and the other across the river on Chipps Island. J.P. Haller, an early pioneer in the industry, managed both of the canneries.

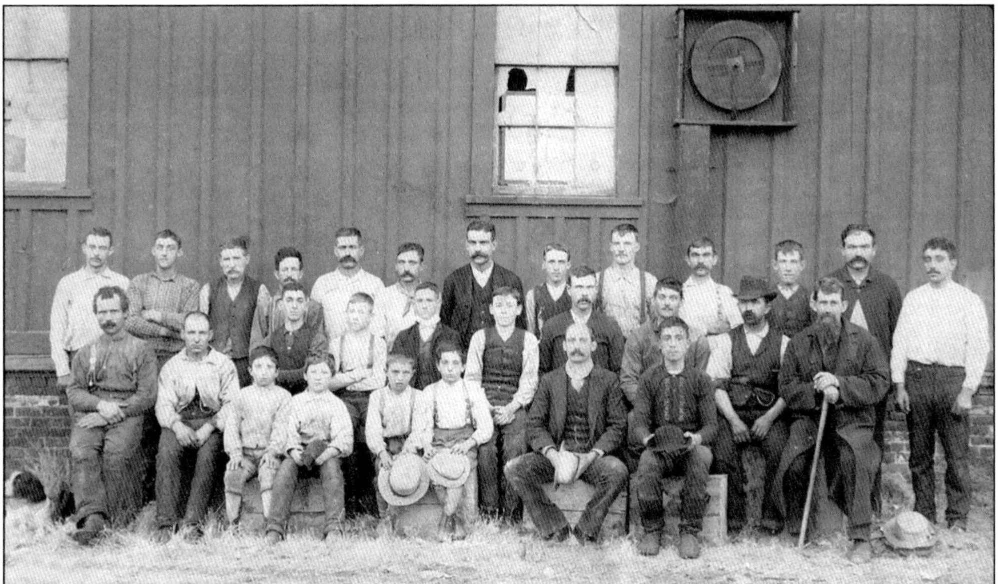

This photo of the F.E. Booth Company's first cannery crew shows that young boys and older men were employed in the canneries.

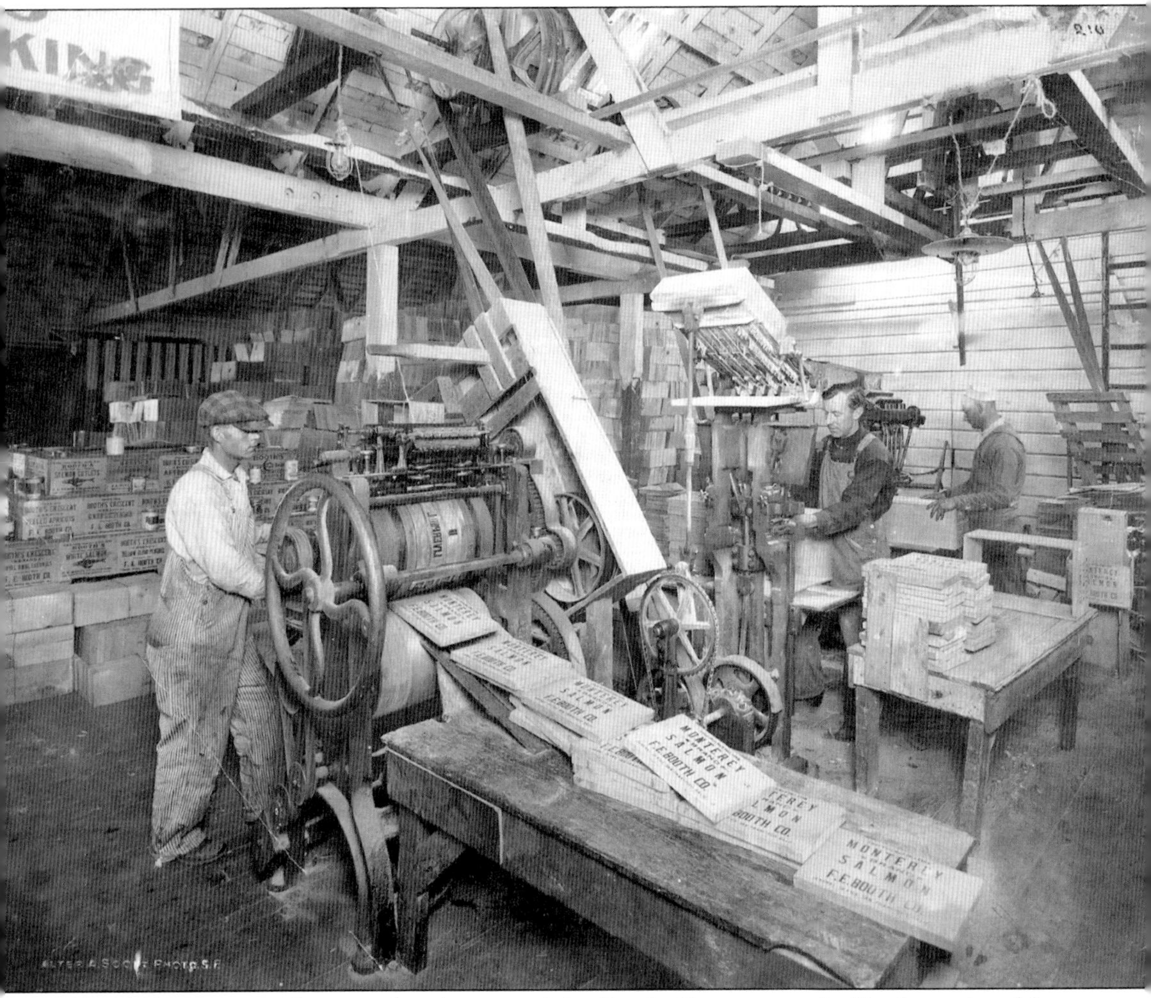

Labels were turned out in this division of the Booth Company and affixed to printed boxes made of wood that held the cans of processed salmon.

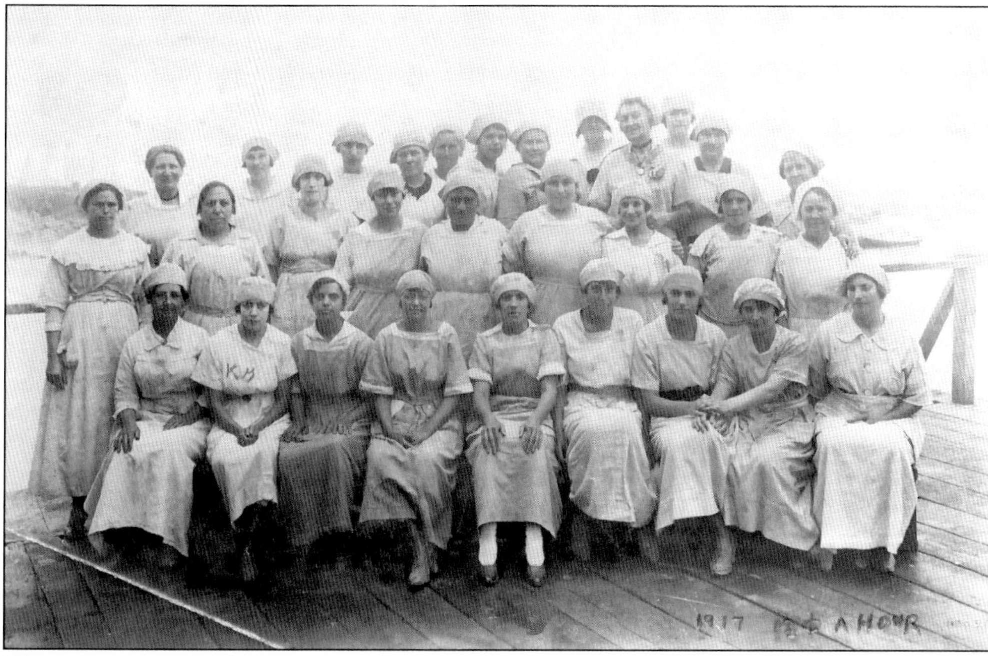

The wages in 1917 when this photo was taken was a mere 12¢ an hour. The ladies in this packing plant all wore white uniforms, but of different styles. Those in the darker colors were the "floor ladies," who ran the crew.

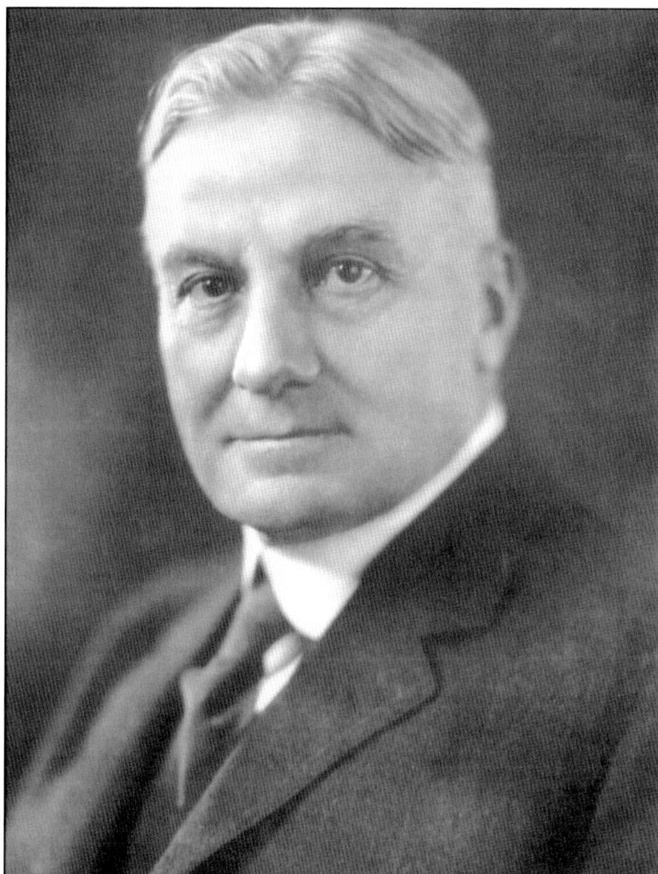

F.E. Booth (1863–1941) was a pioneer in the California canning industry whose integrity and fair dealings with employees earned him great respect. His first cannery was purchased from the Sacramento River Packers Association in 1892.

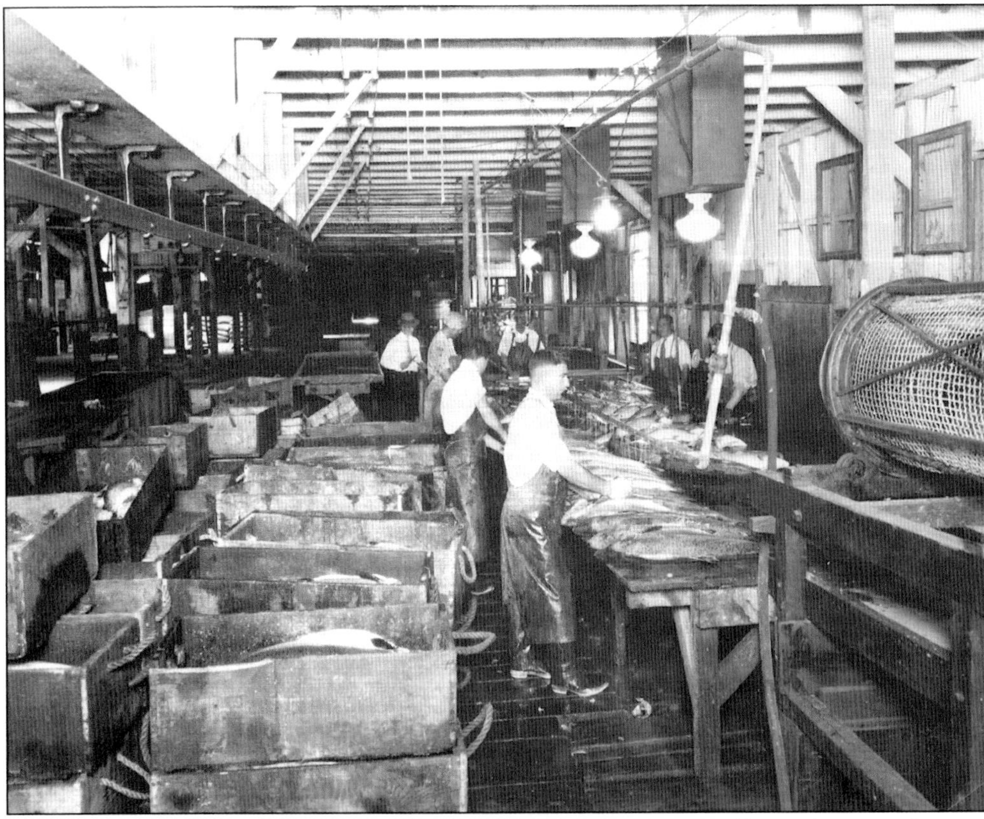

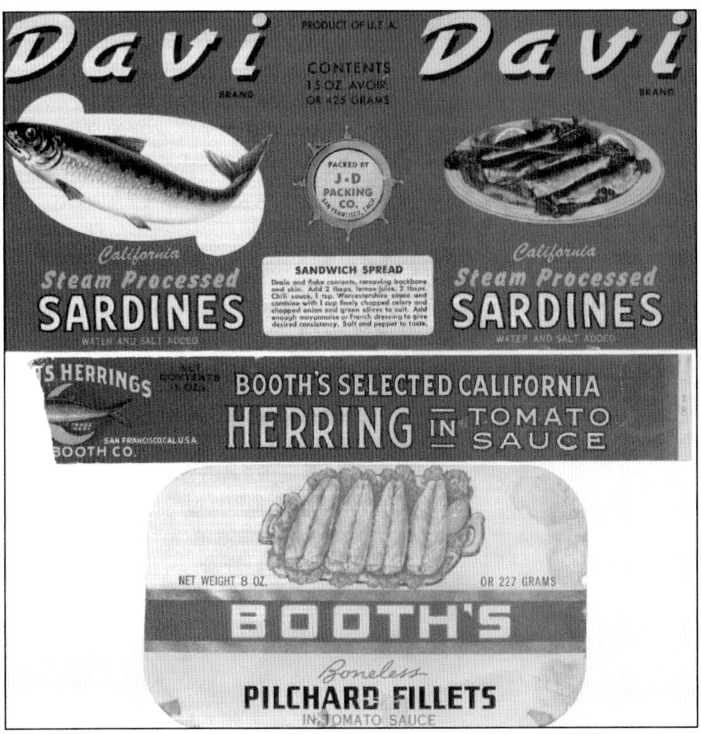

Shown here are the salmon packers of the F.E. Booth Company. The fish were first washed and then scaled in the wire drum in the right foreground. Next they were sent to the cutters to be sized for the cans and then steamed for a short time before processing was complete.

Labels used in the packing process included those for herring in tomato sauce, pilchard fillets in tomato sauce, Bernice Sardines, and Drysol, a fish byproduct. The Crescent Brand was also a popular brand.

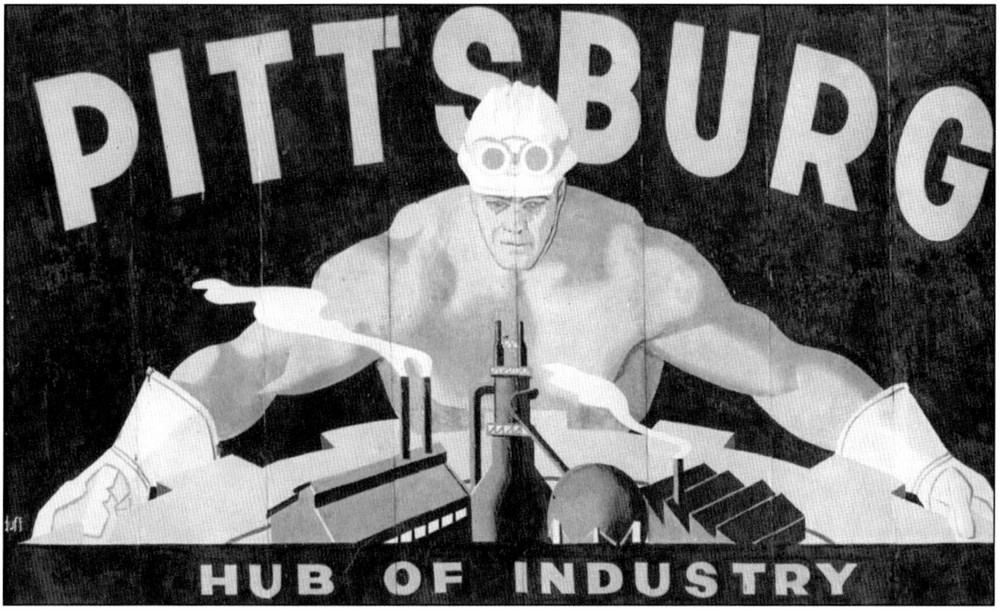

Pittsburg has long been tagged the "Hub of Industry" and was certainly the engine that drove the city's economy for over 100 years. At the beginning of the Industrial Revolution, this small town embraced the concept of building factories in this ideal setting, with both water and rail transportation permitting the raw materials to be efficiently shipped in and the manufacturing products to be efficiently shipped out.

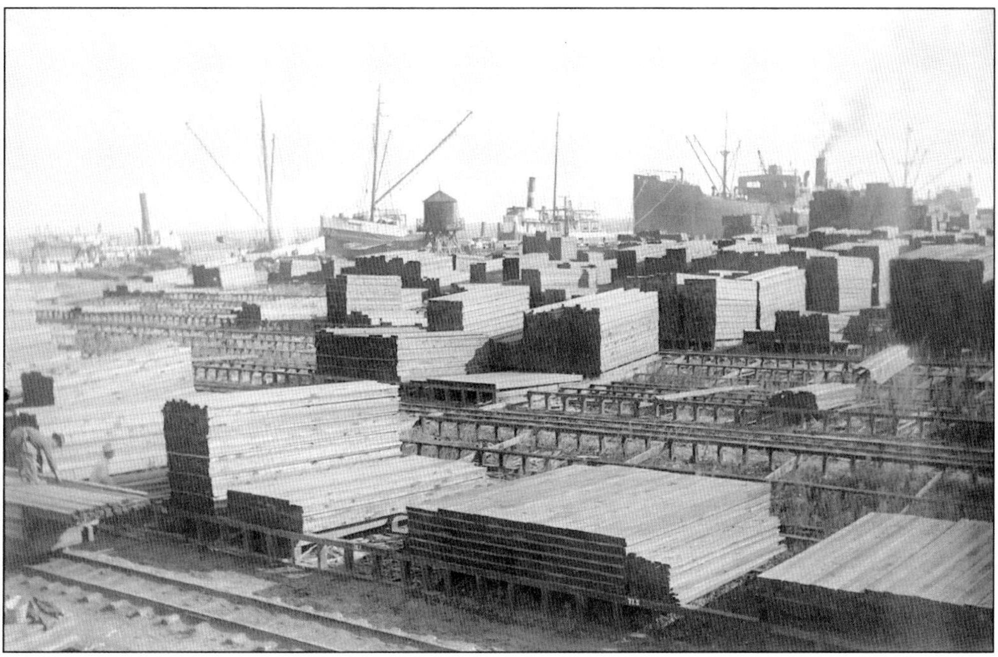

The Redwood Lumber Company was build in 1903. Finished lumber was stacked and then loaded onto the waiting ships to be barged away to other cities in California. Raw lumber was brought in from the Eureka area and manufactured here.

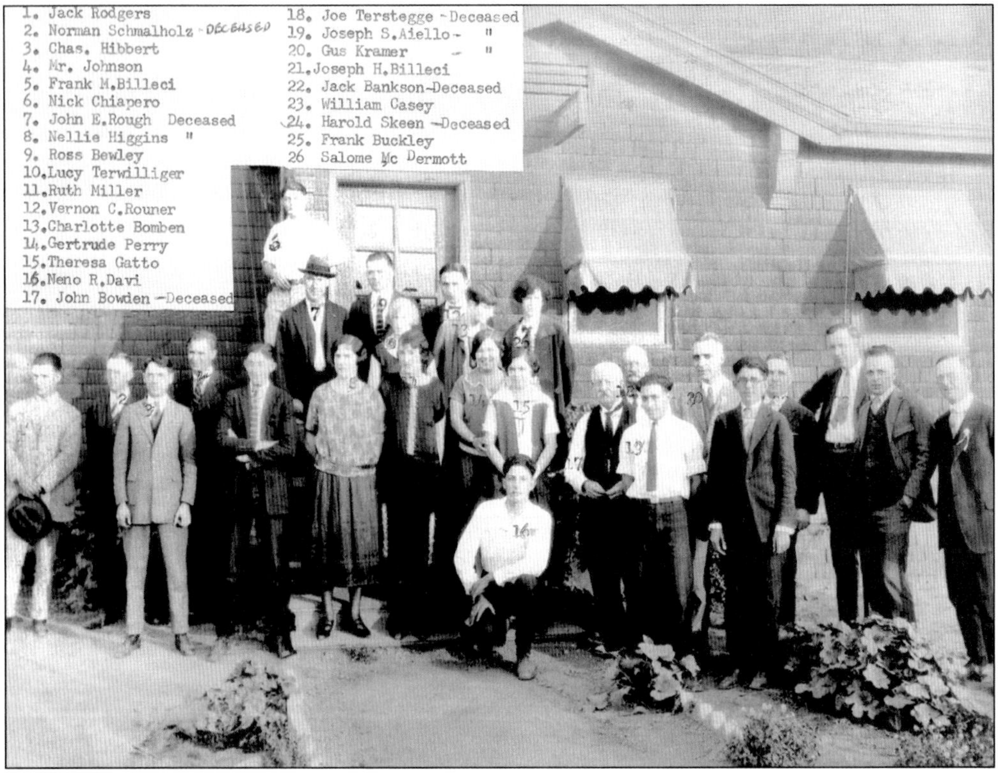

The office crew from the Redwood Manufacturing Company, pictured here *c.* 1925, included Jack Rogers, Norman Schmalholtz, Charles Hibbert, Mr. ? Johnson, Frank M. Billeci, Nick Chiapero, John Rough, Nell Higgins, Ross Bewley, Lucy Terwillinger, Ruth Miller, Vern Rouner, Charlotte Bomben, Gertrude Perry, Thersea Gatto, Neno Davi, John Bowden, Joe Terstegge, Joe Aiello, Gus Kramer, Joe Billeci, Jack Bankson, William Casey, Harold Skeen, Frank Buckley, and Salome McDermott.

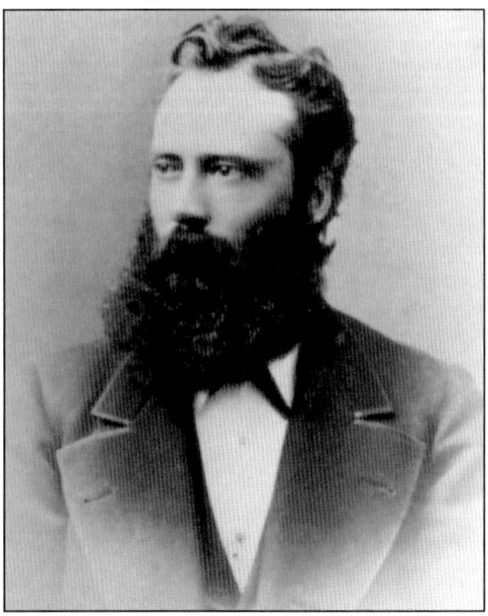

Charles Appleton Hooper was an important leader in Pittsburg's early industrial life, establishing several different businesses over the years.

Four

INDUSTRIES

In 1901, Charles Appleton Hooper purchased the Los Medanos Ranch and developed it into one of the most outstanding ranches in California. Born in Bangor, Maine, in 1843, Hooper came to live on the West Coast in 1863. He organized several lumber companies and invested heavily in California ranch lands and timber tracts, showing faith in the future of the state. In 1903, with interest earned in timber, he established the first industry in Pittsburg.

The Redwood Manufacturing Company, located on the land Hooper had purchased just two years prior, would be the beginning of a thriving "Industrial Empire" in New York Landing. Hooper created the area's first electric power company after the turn of the century so that power could be provided to his manufacturing plant. Hooper also proposed that the town's board of trustees install electrical lines throughout the small town of Pittsburg. The board discussed rates regarding street lighting, but no action was taken. Town clerk T.M. Donovan was instructed to write to nearby towns using arc lamps to ascertain the rates charged per month. On May 17, 1904, the town accepted the lowest bid, from D.L. Henney, to perform the work of constructing the lighting system that Hooper's company would power. Hooper sold his power company to Great Western Power Company in 1910; it later merged with Pacific Gas and Electric.

Hooper built a flour mill called the Diamond Milling Company, as well as the Diamond Brick Company, the Pioneer Dairy, and the Bowers Rubber Company. In 1910, he was also instrumental in bringing the Columbia Steel Mill to Pittsburg. Hooper became a philanthropist to the two neighboring towns of Pittsburg and Antioch, providing the financing for a high school, donating property to the Catholic Church, and making other generous donations. Before he died in 1914, Hooper had already achieved the honor of being called the "Father of Industry" in Pittsburg and was responsible for establishing the town as the "Industrial Capital of the West." With the establishment of factories by Hooper, many other industries saw the advantage of building their companies in the area.

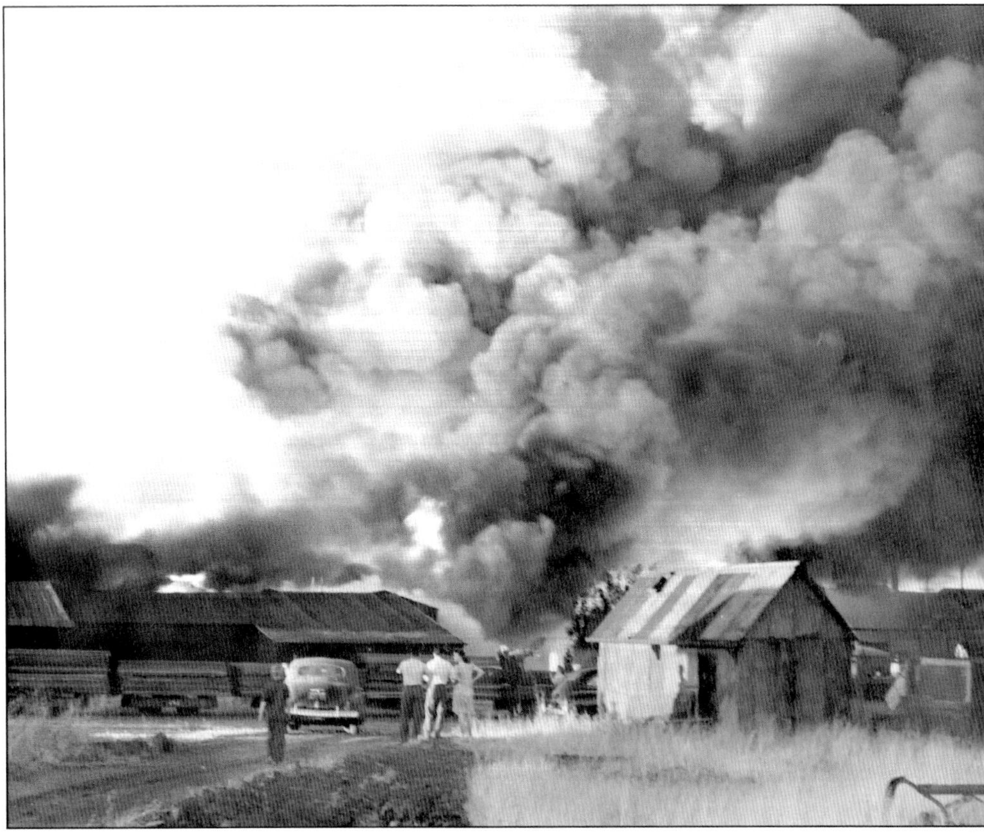

In 1944 a disastrous fire destroyed the Redwood Manufacturing lumber company. The community mourned the loss of an industry that had been part of the town for over 40 years.

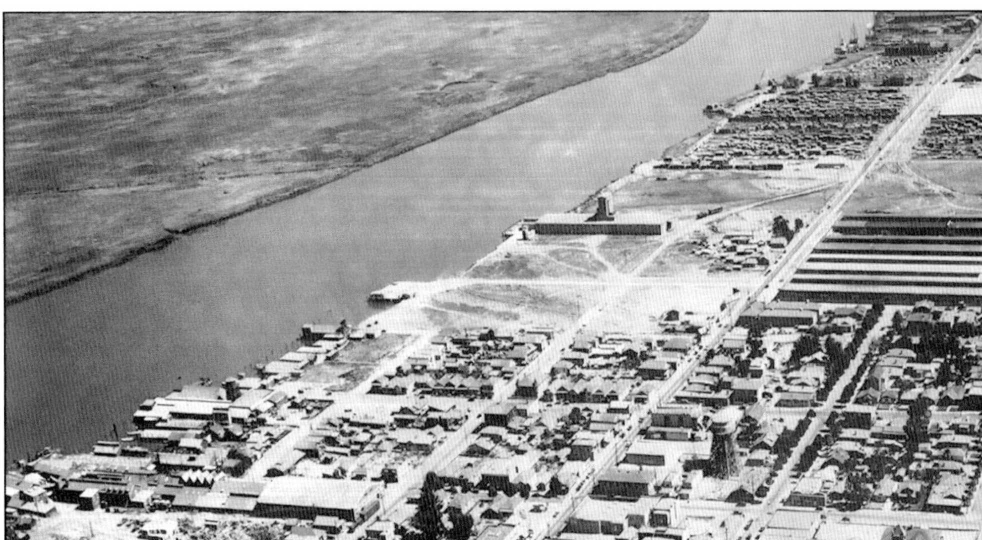

From its beginning in 1910, the Columbia Steel Company continued to grow, and in 1927, another factory building was added. The company worked to satisfy the needs of railroads, automotive, mining casting, hydroelectric casting, and the marine and construction industries.

Columbia Geneva Steel

No phase in local history was ever so glorified or so packed with romance as that of Pittsburg's industrial growth. The development of electricity made industry possible on a large scale thanks to the application of steam in transportation and, most important to Pittsburg, the Bessemer process, which made it possible for the United States to produce more than one-third of the world's steel supply.

The Pittsburg plant was one of the city's principal industries. When the steel company first built the industrial complex in 1910, the rapidly growing concern immediately began employing men from all parts of the United States to produce steel casting, commercial bars, sheets wire, nails, and various other commodities. The setting for the mill was very similar to Pittsburgh, Pennsylvania.

By 1938 the community was comprised of more that 12,000 persons—enterprising, energetic, and solidly situated on the industrial foundation that was Pittsburg at the time. The annual payroll of approximately $8 million from more than 25 manufacturing and industrial concerns drove the economy.

Largest of these industrial payrolls was the Columbia Geneva Steel company, employing nearly 2,700 workers with an annual salary output estimated in excess of $350,000. Founded in 1908, Columbia Steel employed only about 60 men by 1910, but it best serves as a barometer of the tremendous industrial growth of Pittsburg. In 1910 the entire plant was located on 20 acres. But as the demand for steel products on the Pacific Coast grew, so grew the company. In 1919 the first unit of the rolling mill was constructed and in 1923, when the company was reorganized into the Columbia Steel Corporation, two additional open-hearth furnaces were built and a wire and nail mill, sheet mill, and rod mill were added. In 1928 the plant added a tin plate mill. An independent entity until 1930, the Columbia Steel Corporation then became a subsidiary of the giant United States Steel Corporation. Since that time more that $3 million has been spent on improvements and additions, until it ranked as one of the leading industrial plants and the largest steel manufacturing concern on the West Coast.

By 1938, it grew to 400 acres, of which approximately 150 were occupied by buildings. As originally designed, the foundry had a capacity of 250 tons per month, increasing over the years to 1,350 tons per month.

During the 1940s the company grew in payrolls and profits due to World War II and the Korean conflict. The wartime economy outpaced anything that went before it in terms of the number of men and women employed and the production of steel-related materials. With the end of the wartime boom and the increased worldwide marketing by foreign competition, as well as new technology that allowed the manufacture of goods without a large work force, production of steel as well as other commodities decreased radically.

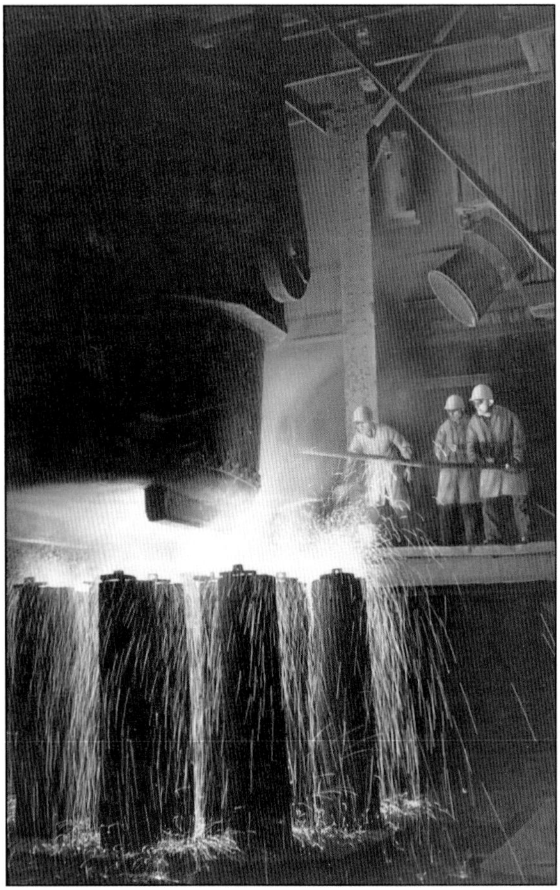

Open Hearth workmen pour molten steel at the Pittsburg works of United States Steel. The Open Hearth foundry opened in 1922 but is now closed.

The Diamond Brick Company owned by C.A. Hooper was one of the first industries to employ 80 men and produced 80,000 bricks daily. The company was located in the area where Johns-Manville now stands.

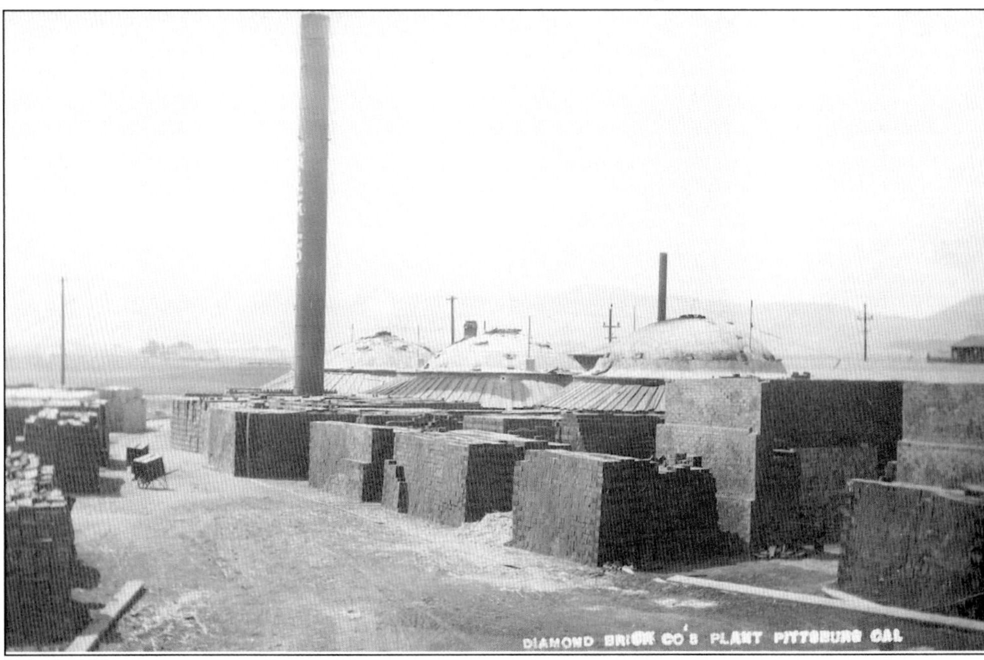

THE DAY THE REDWOODS STRUCK OUT

In 1938, the Redwood softball team nearly captured a national championship. Being on the wrong side of a 2-1 score was all that separated the boys who played in the Chicago finals from an unprecedented shot at the national title. Here is their story.

The Pittsburg Redwoods softball team was made up of young and talented men who held jobs in the local factories and was the closest thing to professional sports a small town could find. In 1938, the team qualified for the right to travel 2,000 miles by train to play for a national title after having beaten all comers for the California state title. Most people in town had heard of the "Windy City," but few had ever seen it. A trip to Chicago might well have been a trip to the moon for this entourage of men in their twenties.

In a twist of irony, the Redwoods opened against a team from Pittsburgh, Pennsylvania, and Harry Cowan, the team's ace pitcher, allowed only four Steeltown batters the chance to visit first base while pitching a no-hitter in the Redwoods' 6-0 win. The next day the team was pitted against a Florida team but lost 2-1 for the first time in nearly a year-and-a-half. Nevertheless, when the train carrying the team home from Chicago arrived in Martinez, a throng of residents escorted them in a caravan of 70 cars, many donated for the parade, into downtown Pittsburg for a celebration.

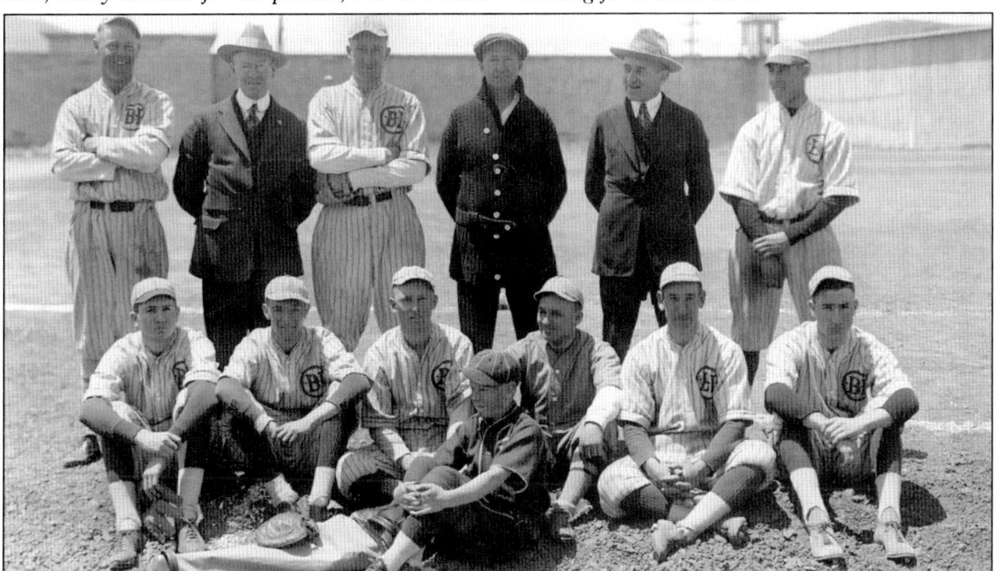

Pittsburg's baseball teams were all winners. As early as 1910, the Bowers Rubber Company was sponsoring a popular baseball team while many local merchants had teams like the Edmonton Togs, the Sunset baseball team, and the Sirs' team. Local businesses and industries participated in the community by being team sponsors and by encouraging their workers to play ball.

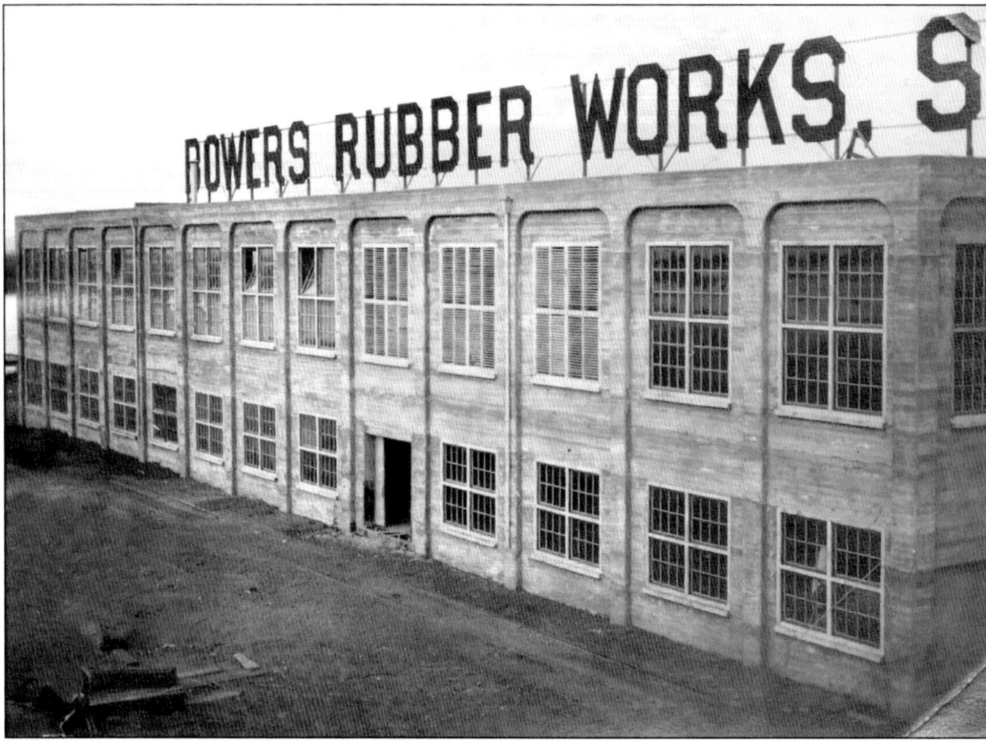

PITTSBURG IN FIGURES

INCORPORATED, 1903; age, 29 years; population, 10,000; many home-owners; waterfront, 6 miles long, 26-foot channel; railroads, 3 transcontinental; good-will prevails between employers and employes.

The enterprises listed following employ some 3560 people, disburse more than $6,000,000 yearly in payrolls, and exemplify the great diversity of the city's activities:

Name of Institution—	Number of Employees	Annual Payroll
Columbia Steel Company (U. S. Steel)	2200	$3,500,000
Redwood Manufacturers Co.	300	300,000
Pioneer Rubber Mills	450	600,000
Pittsburg Fishermen	250	500,000
Shell Chemical Co.	300	300,000
Stockton Fire Brick Co.	75	....
F. E. Booth Co.	375	425,000
Great Western Electro-Chemical Co.	185	300,000
Johns-Manville Inc. of California	150	225,000
Pittsburg-Alaska Fishermen	300	400,000
Pittsburg Schools	89	150,000
Railroads	80	145,000
Pittsburg Fisheries Co.	50	120,000
C. A. Hooper Co.	70	110,000
Standard Oil Co. (distribution)	50	100,000
Coast Counties Gas & Electric Co.	57	75,000
City of Pittsburg	50	75,000
California Spray Chemical Co.	00	72,000
Pioneer Dairy Co.	45	64,000
Ward & Weigel (W. & W. Garage)	18	....
Bundeson & Lauritzen Shipyard	45	45,000
Union Oil Co. (distribution)	15	40,000
Pittsburg Motor Co.	18	35,000
Diamond Building Material Co.	5	18,000

Pittsburg Extends You A Sincere Welcome

In 1903 Pittsburg began a time of unsurpassed industrial development. In 1904, Bowers Rubber became the second major manufacturer to locate in the city. The company made heavy-duty industrial hoses and fittings.

By the time the city incorporated, its population had reached 10,000. The enterprises listed in the *Byron Times* employed some 3,560 people. Payrolls were more than $6 million.

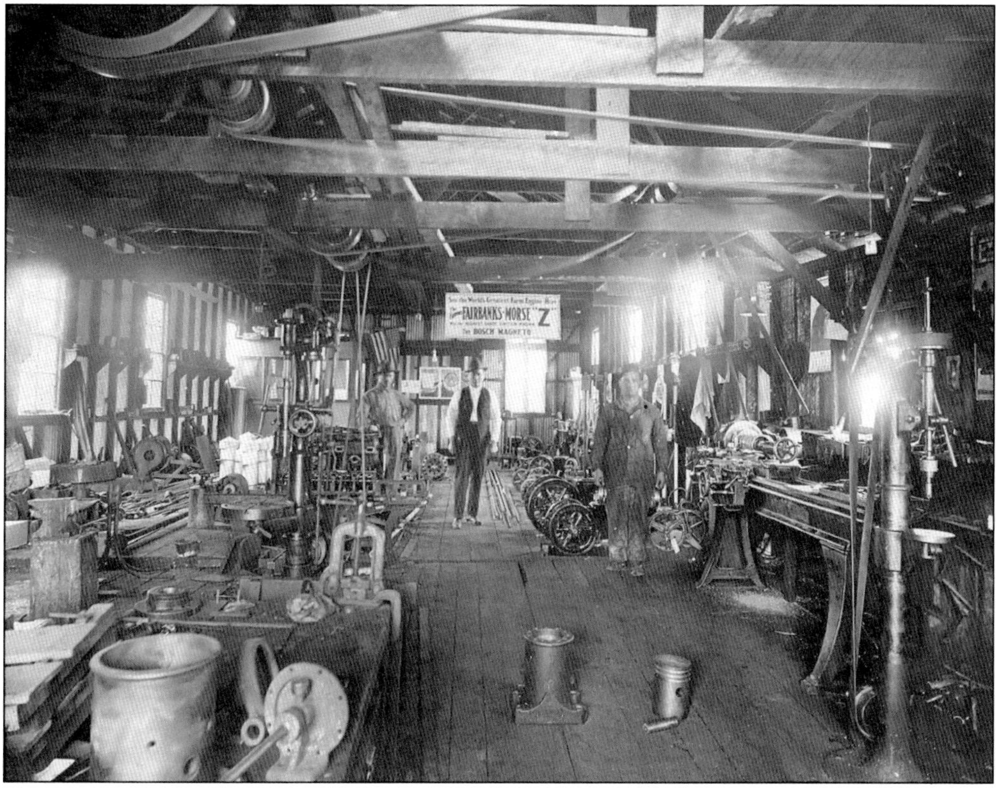

This machine shop was owned by Louis Solari (center), shown here with Tony Ferrante (left) and Bert Ventrice. Small, single-owner enterprises, such as this machine shop, added significantly to the economy.

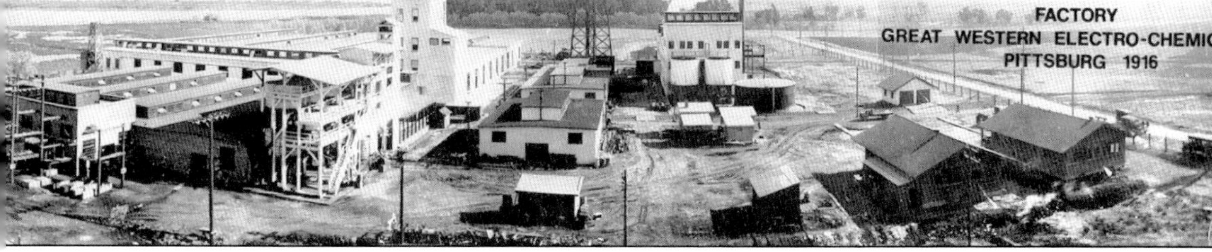

Established in 1916, Great Western Electro-Chemical Company merged with Dow Chemical in 1939, making it the largest chemical production complex in the western United States.

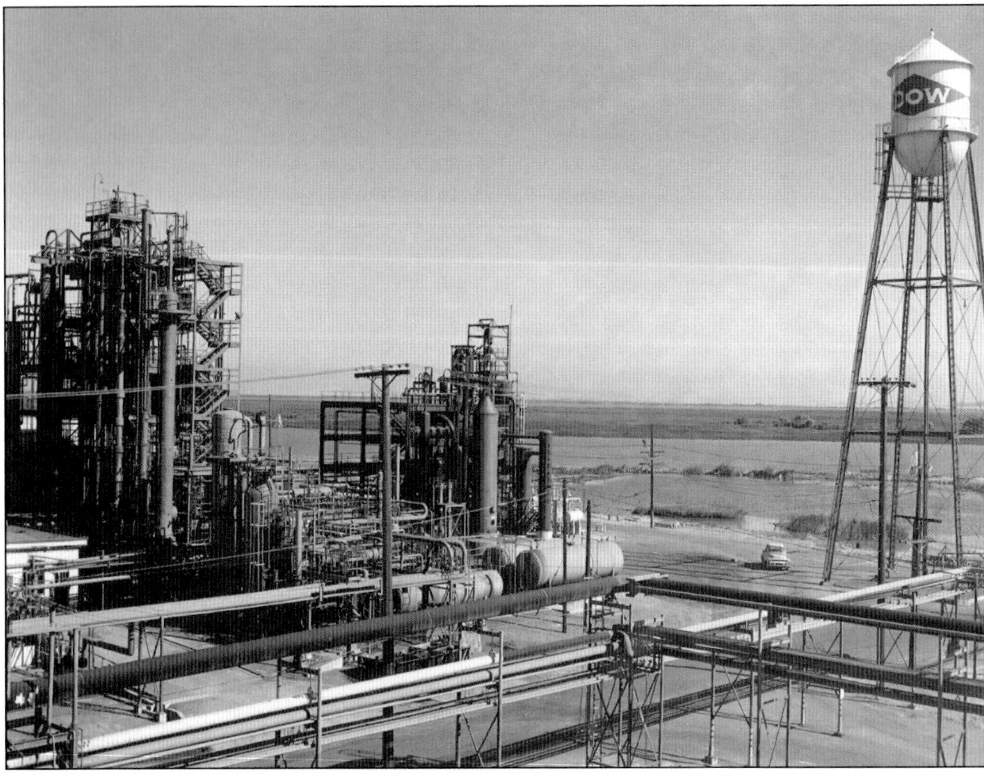

Great Western Electro-Chemical Company merged with Dow Chemical in 1939. Since that time the Pittsburg plant has been modernized an expanded several times.

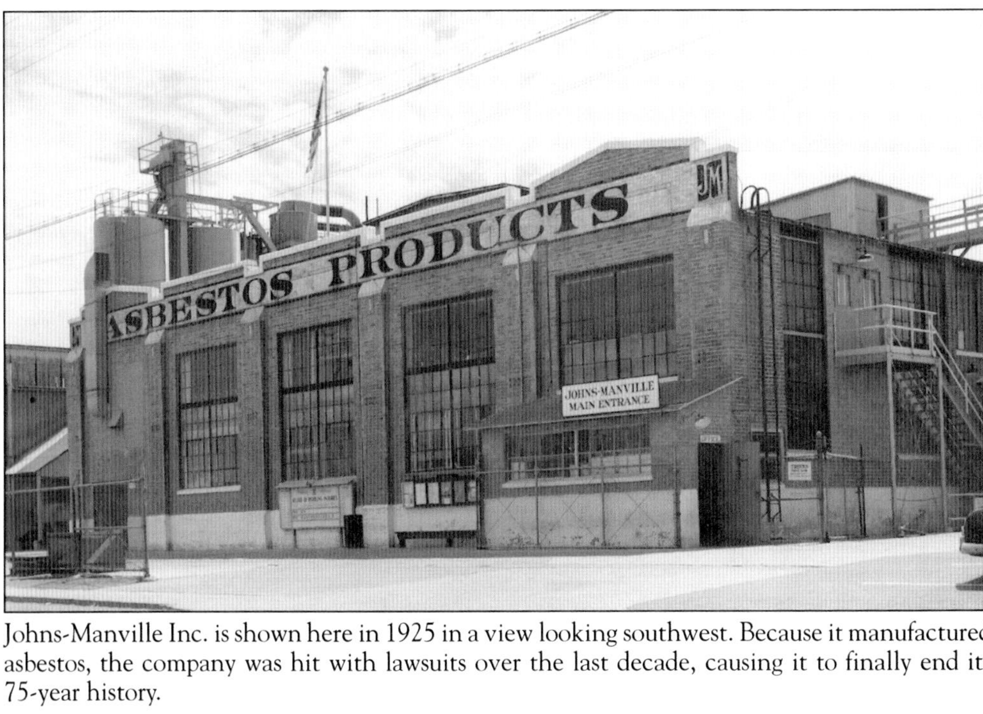

Johns-Manville Inc. is shown here in 1925 in a view looking southwest. Because it manufactured asbestos, the company was hit with lawsuits over the last decade, causing it to finally end its 75-year history.

Steel towers from the Pacific Gas and Electric Company can be seen from nearly anywhere in Pittsburg. Located near the river, the company's lights cast reflections on the water and bright dots of light against the night sky.

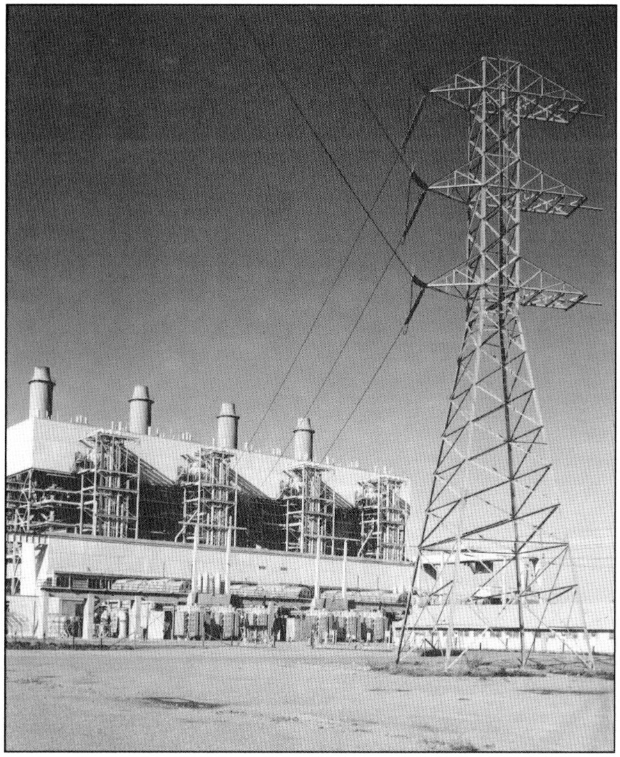

Since its beginning in 1910, Columbia Steel Company has continued to grow. "Forging steel for nearly every need" was the company's motto.

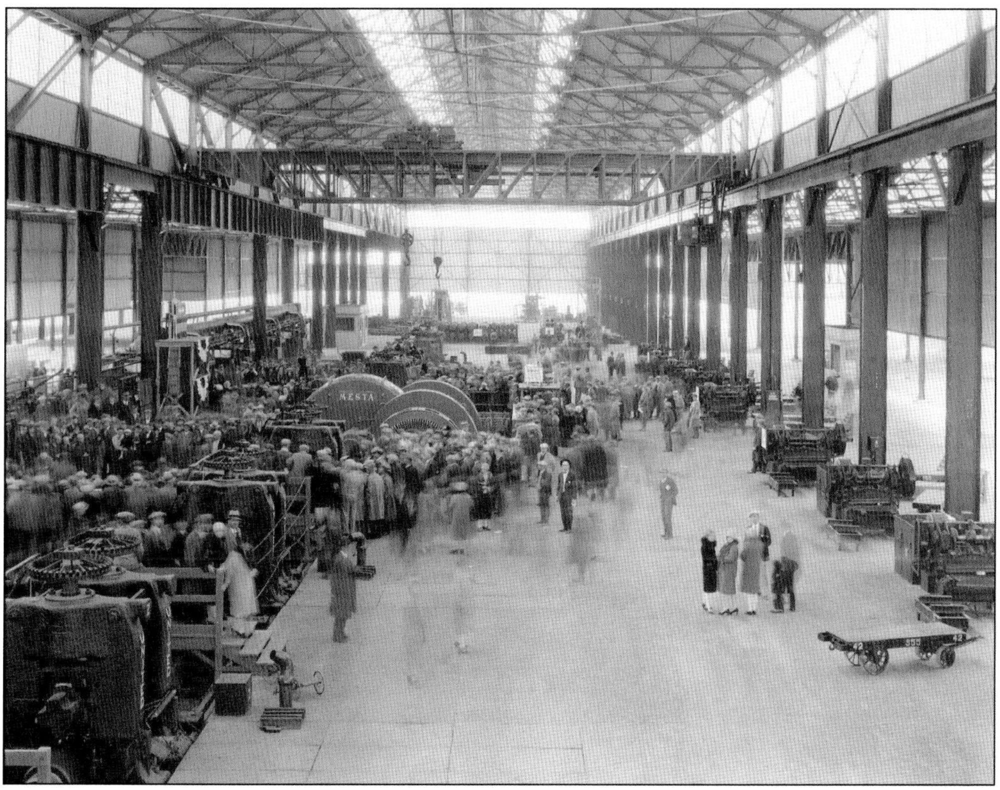

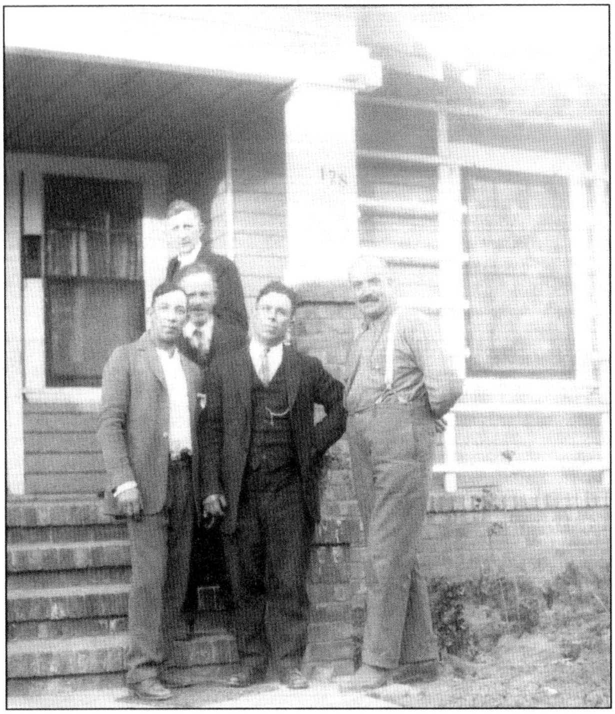

Workers of the Columbia Steel Foundry in this *c.* 1920 photo include Mr. Espinosa, Mr. Gonzales, and Mr. Columbo.

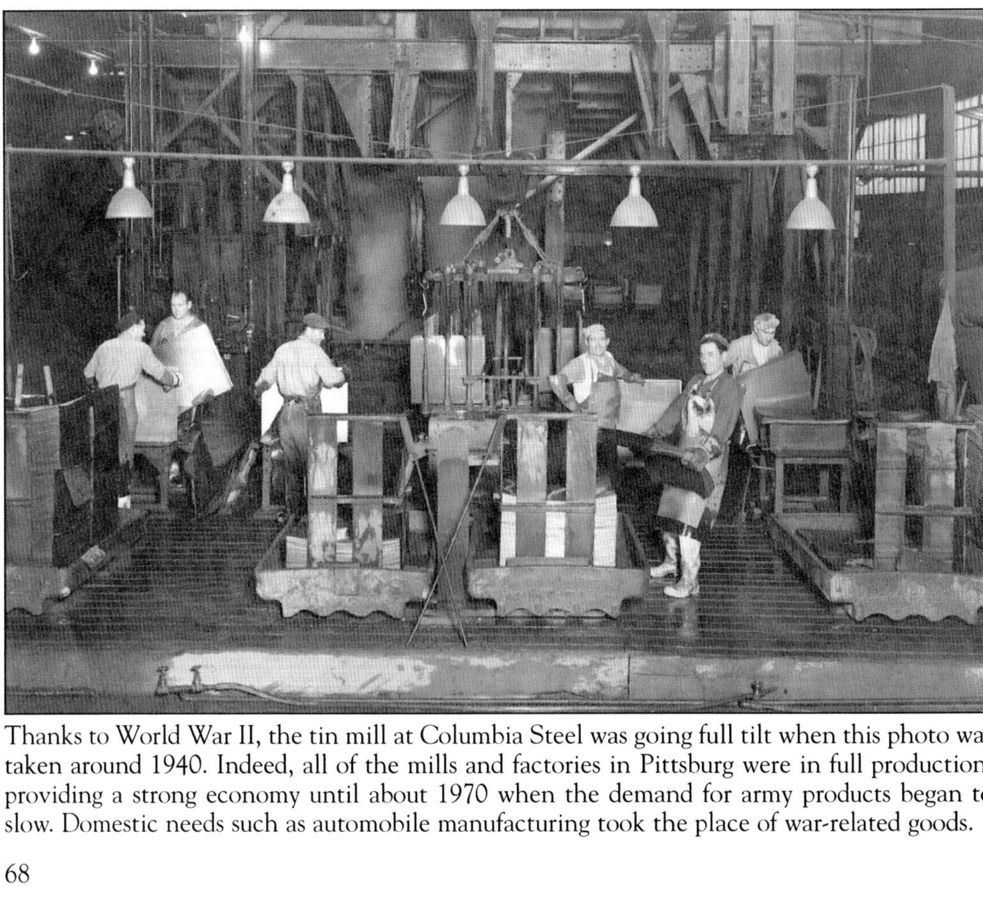

Thanks to World War II, the tin mill at Columbia Steel was going full tilt when this photo was taken around 1940. Indeed, all of the mills and factories in Pittsburg were in full production, providing a strong economy until about 1970 when the demand for army products began to slow. Domestic needs such as automobile manufacturing took the place of war-related goods.

Five

THE TOWN

As the newest state in the union began to increase in population, California experienced a proliferation of small towns struggling to come into their own and develop unique identities. East Contra Costa County towns developed according to the natural resources of the area. The rich delta soil proved ideal conditions for all agricultural products. Real estate was readily available and advertisements in newspapers and magazines like the *Byron Times* drew farmers from other states. In fact, farming was familiar work to many families of Middle America.

Soon the farmland of Oakley, Brentwood, Byron, and Knightson began to take on a picturesque beauty, with nut and fruit trees in bloom. Fields of tomatoes, lettuce, spinach, and carrots consumed large amounts of acreage. Canneries were built and spur tracks were laid to connect farms with railroads so that canned and fresh vegetables could make their way to markets throughout the United States.

The cities of Martinez and Pittsburg, however, depended on manufacturing industries as well as commercial fishing and canning—work that would drive the economies of both towns. Antioch was also considered an industrial city with both a cannery and paper mill operation.

In Black Diamond (Pittsburg), two separate social structures emerged as the little town developed. Immigrants from Italy, Mexico, Greece, and a few from China lived on the west side of Railroad Avenue. Businessmen in manufacturing or in managerial positions built better homes on the east and south sides of town. This was not to say that there was an elitism that excluded social intercourse, but the inevitable differences were apparent in the easy social skills of the more experienced English-speaking citizens who had the advantage of language and education. However, hard work and ingenuity, as well as natural intelligence, earned immigrants certain rights to material advantages, and as their children were educated and integrated, the differences became less noticeable.

By the 1900s Pittsburg's immigrant population was approximately 1,243. Of these, 1,079 were Italians, 36 were Irish, 26 were Jewish, and 101 were of other nationalities. Native-born and naturalized citizens came together in social organizations, the political arena, and city government positions, and worked to achieve harmony within an ethnically diverse community.

At the beginning of the 20th century, electricity and water were in place and utility companies were serving the community. City government included police and fire protection. Schools and churches brought a sense of permanence. Theaters and music became part of the budding culture, and several bands were organized. Sports teams were sponsored by the manufacturing companies, and competition between neighboring towns carried a sense of challenge. The town was becoming an important part of a growing East Contra Costa County.

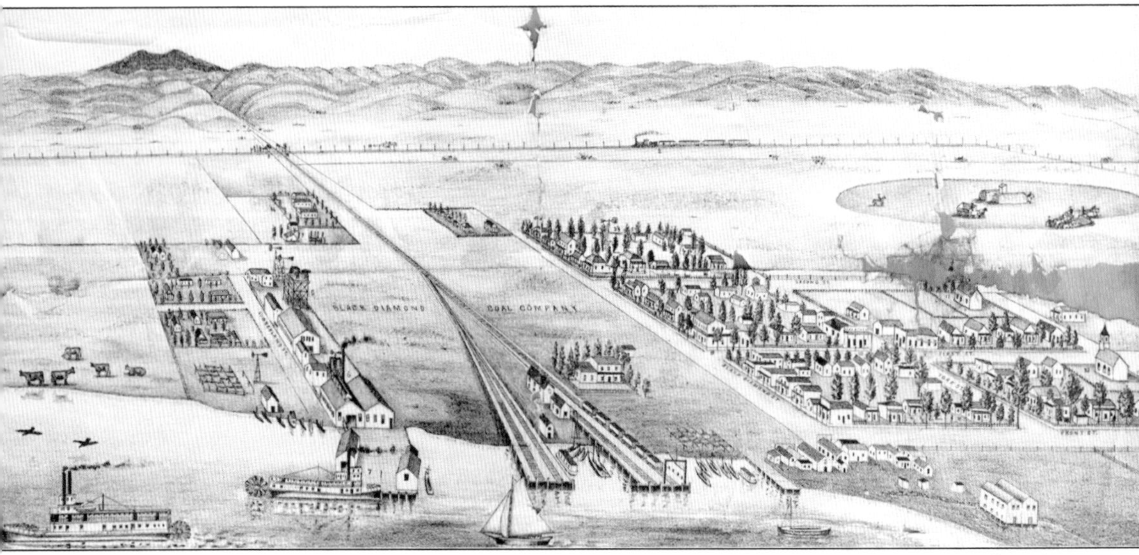

In this view of Black Diamond in Contra Costa County, train tracks can be seen extending from the hills of Nortonville, carrying passengers and freight to the waterfront. The Central Pacific trains ran east and west.

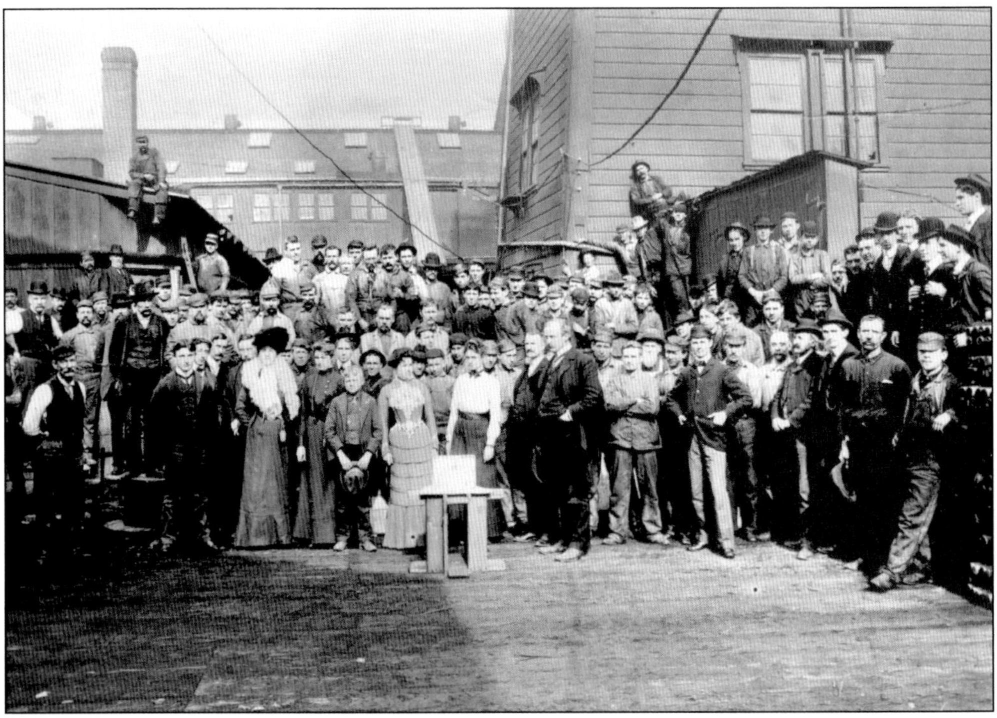

Workers of various nationalities worked at the factories in Pittsburg. Pictured here are the employees of Redwood Manufacturing Company.

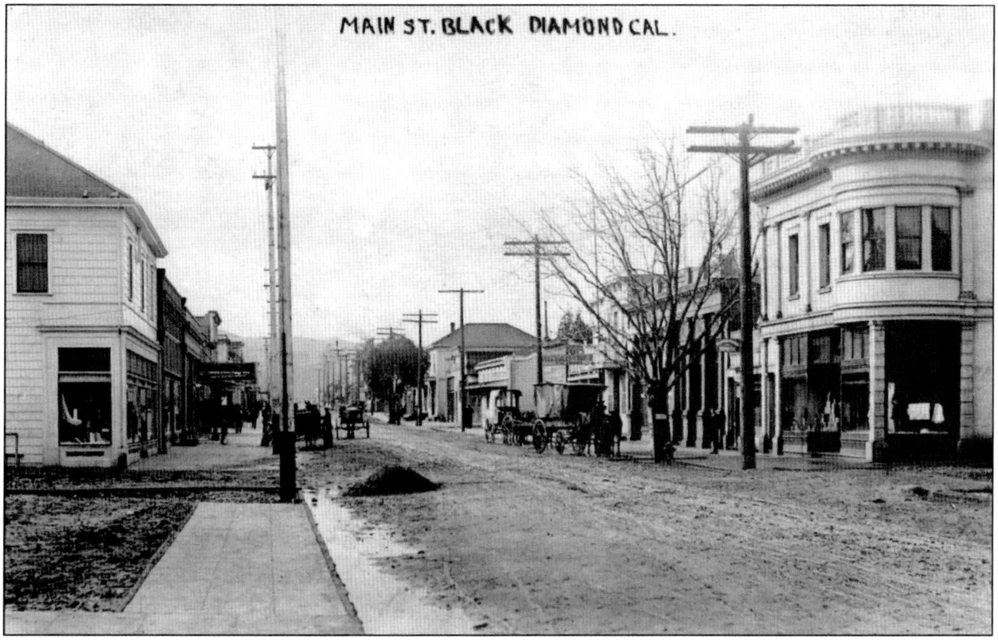

Black Diamond Street was the town's main shopping street. Shown here is the Buchanan General Store on Second and Black Diamond Streets. The store was owned by pioneers Nora and William Buchanan, who also ran a post office and offered telephone services.

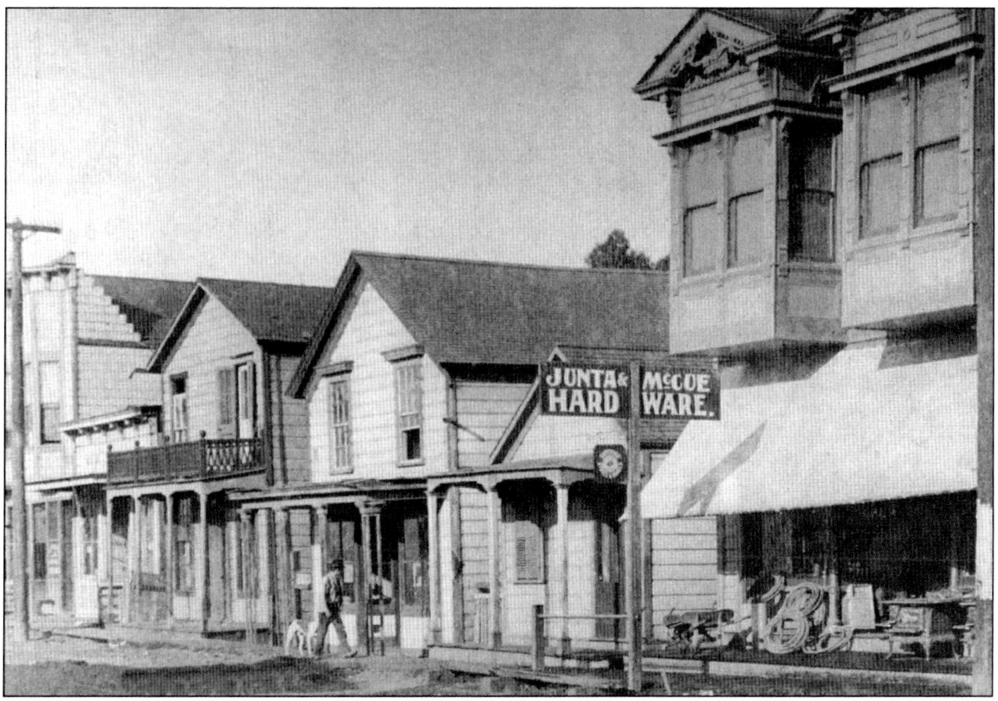

The Junta & McCue Hardwood Store displayed its goods in the front of the store. The city was still young and there was no need for protective measures against theft. A constable was hired for the occasional problems that arose.

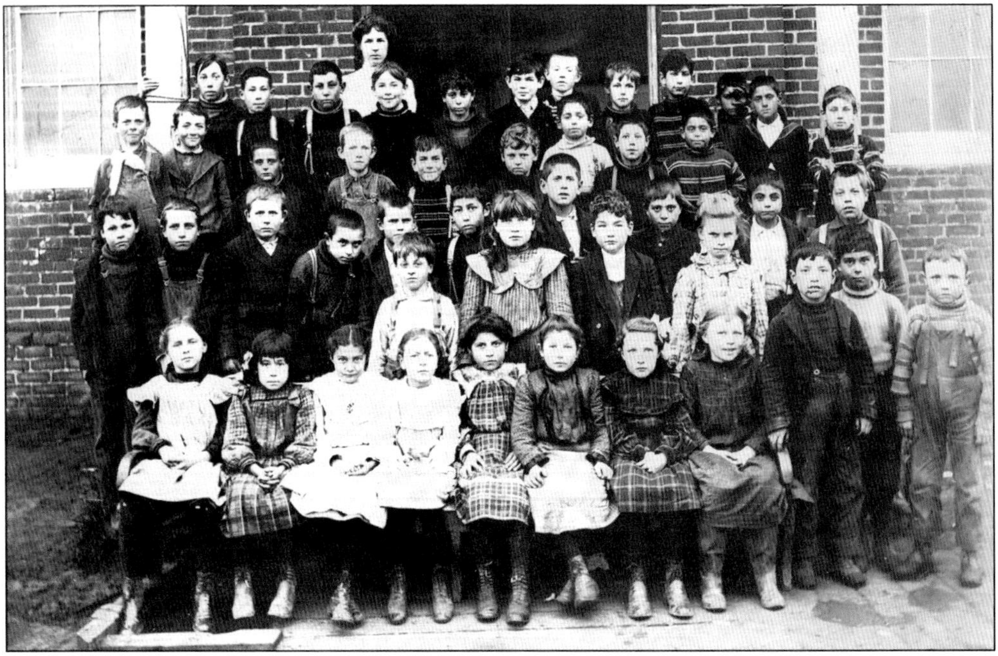

Students pose in front of the "Little Brick School House" in 1905. Built in 1874, the school was located at Fifth Street and Railroad Avenue, and the class accommodated all ages of children. It was a time when education stopped at the fifth or sixth grade, and the more fortunate students would continue school when the first elementary building was erected next door.

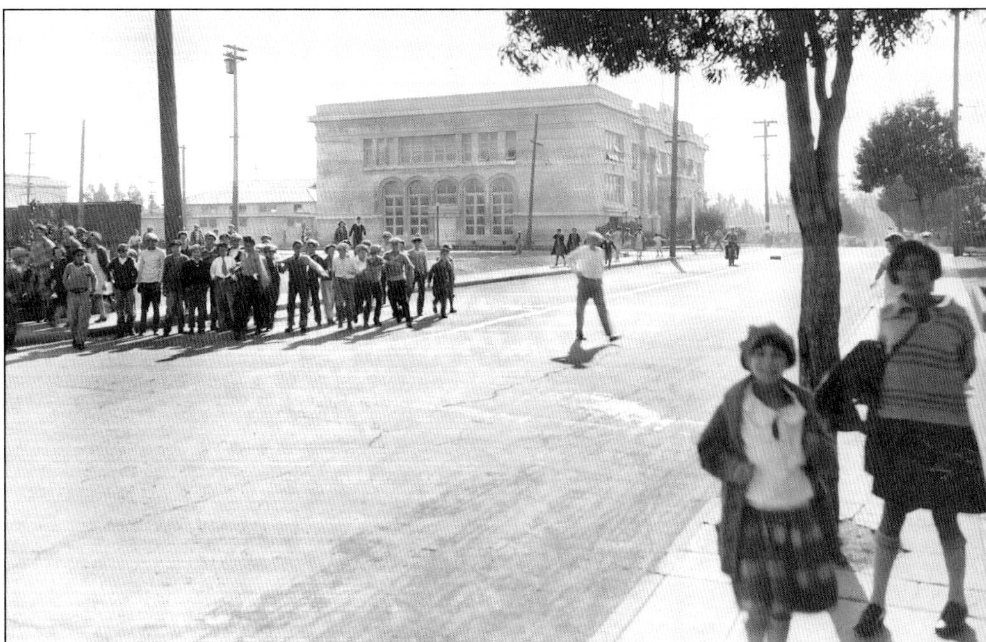

Pittsburg Elementary School, shown here in the 1930s, was located on Eighth and Black Diamond Streets. The first high school was located on the top floor. In 1928 Pittsburg High School was built on School Street.

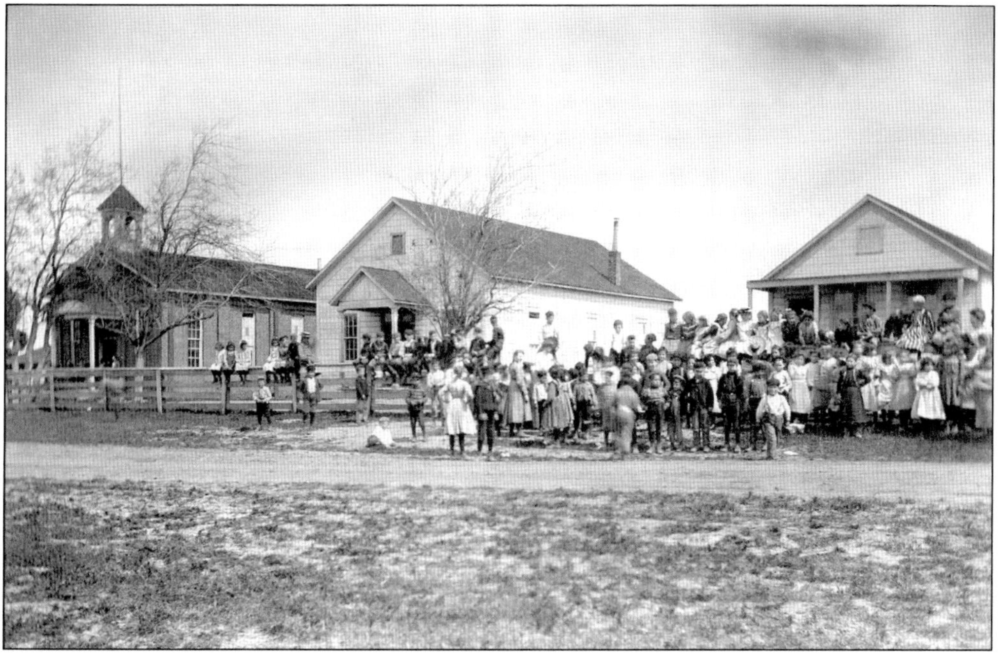

The brick schoolhouse to the left was the first school built in Pittsburg. When it became too small to hold the growing population of immigrants' children, the first elementary school, a two-story building, was erected on the same property.

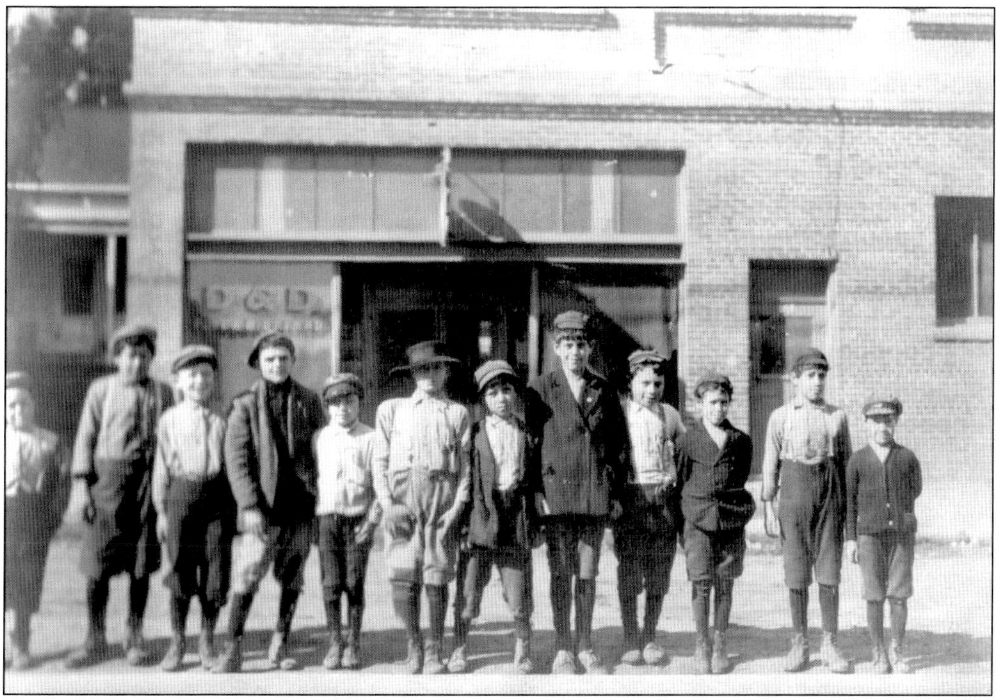

Many of the immigrant schoolchildren who attended the first school in Pittsburg did not understand English and had difficulty adjusting to the customs of their new home. This photograph was taken in the early 1900s.

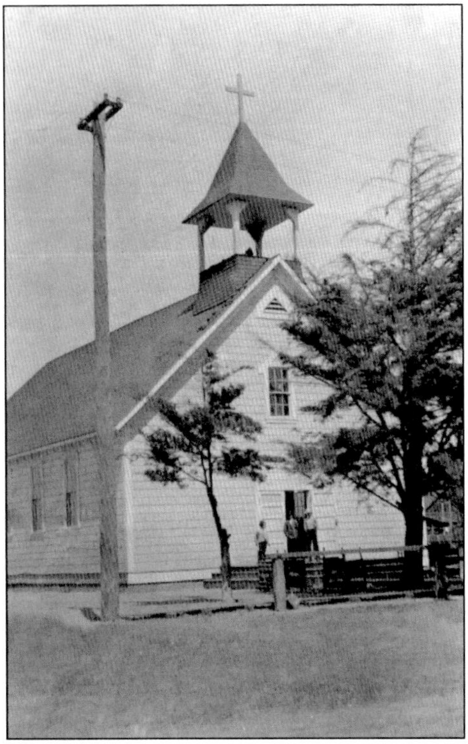

St. Peter Martyr church, located on Second Street, burned down in 1906. A second church was built on Eighth Street, and in 1930 another church was erected on Black Diamond Street for the growing Catholic population.

This photo shows a group in front of the Bay View Saloon in the early 1900s. Bars were a popular meeting place to discuss politics and a gathering place for fishermen and factory workers. The Bay View Saloon was owned by Dave and Louis Gatto.

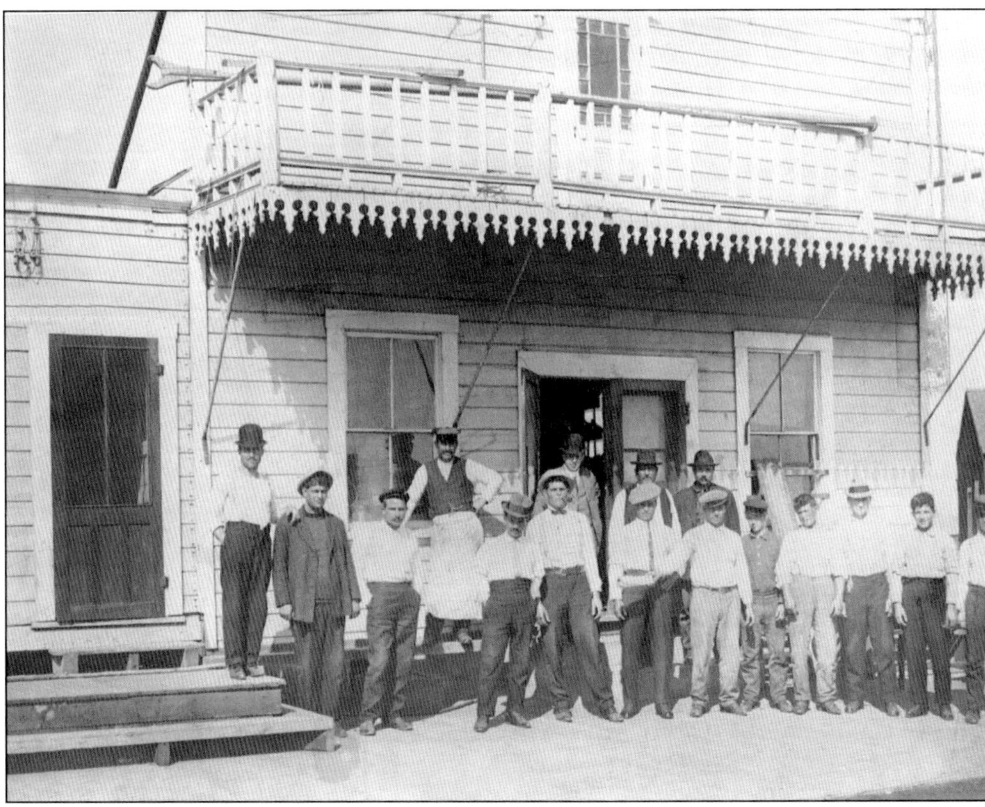

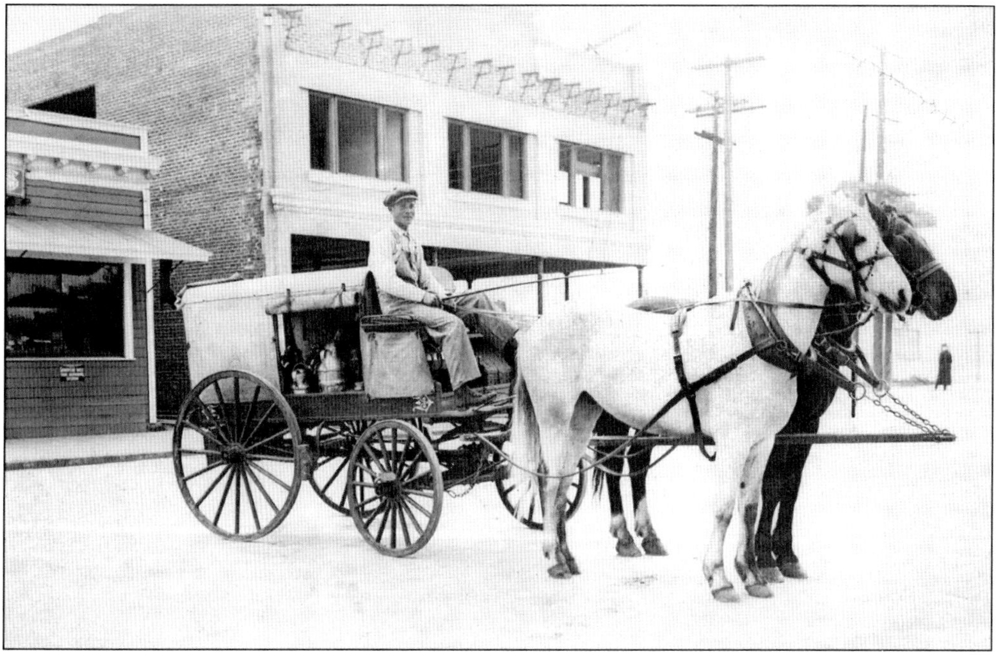

Diamond Dairy milk wagons, like this one c. 1916 carried jugs of milk to fill the containers provided by housewives on the drivers' routes. Wagons filled with vegetables, bread, or fresh meat and fish also made deliveries to homes.

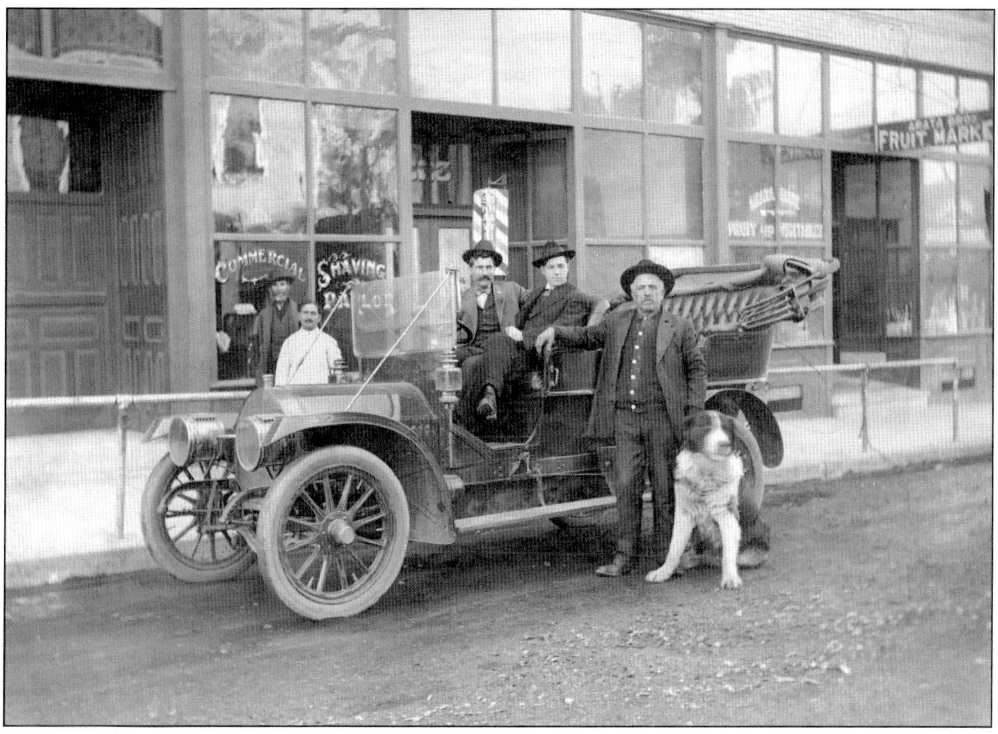

Three unidentified men stop by the barbershop for a shave and haircut. Note the man in front and the customer inside on the right of the photo.

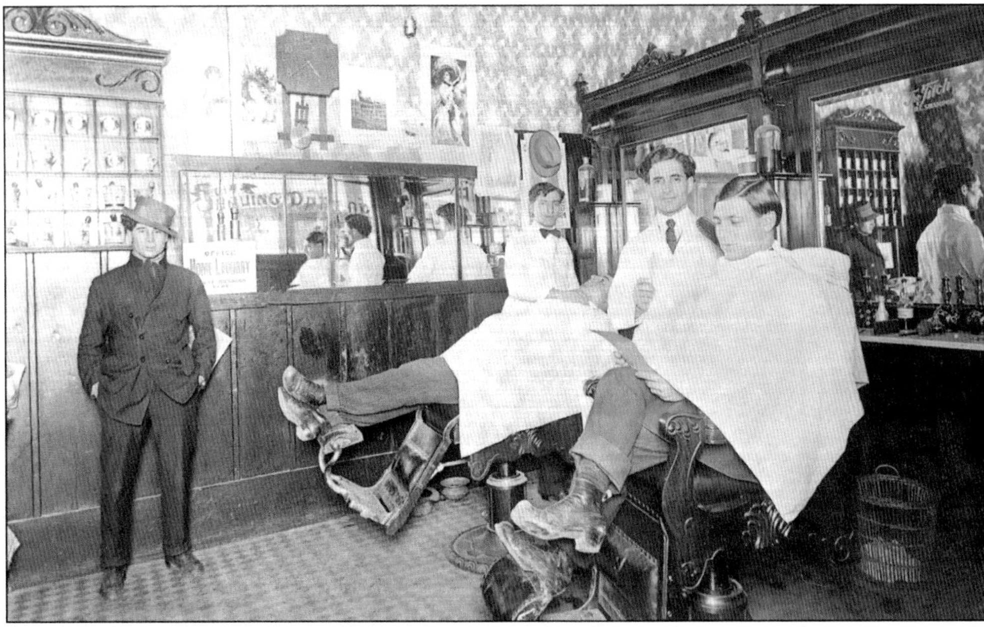

The Eagle Shaving Parlor & Barbershop was owned by Charles Valvo, shown here in the back preparing a customer for a shave. Camillo Lanzafame is the other employee, and Sam Belleci stands to the left. The clock on the wall says 4:39 and the calendar over the mirror indicates that the year was 1912. Lanzafame would go on to open a furniture store that is still in business today.

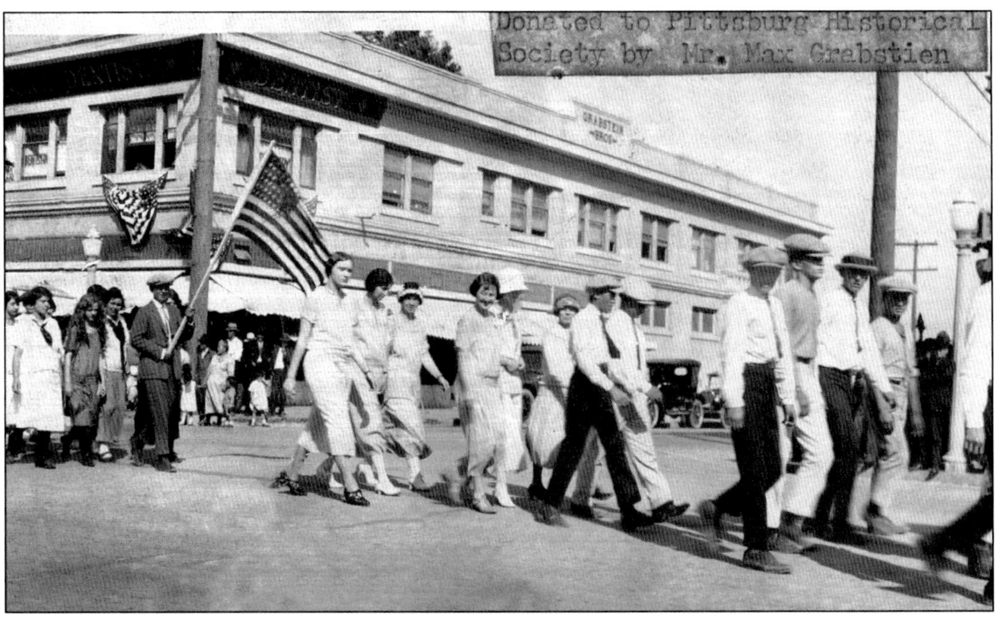

The 1930 Fourth of July parade passes through Pittsburg with the Max Grabstein Building in the background. Grabstein had a clothing store on the corner of Second Street and Railroad Avenue.

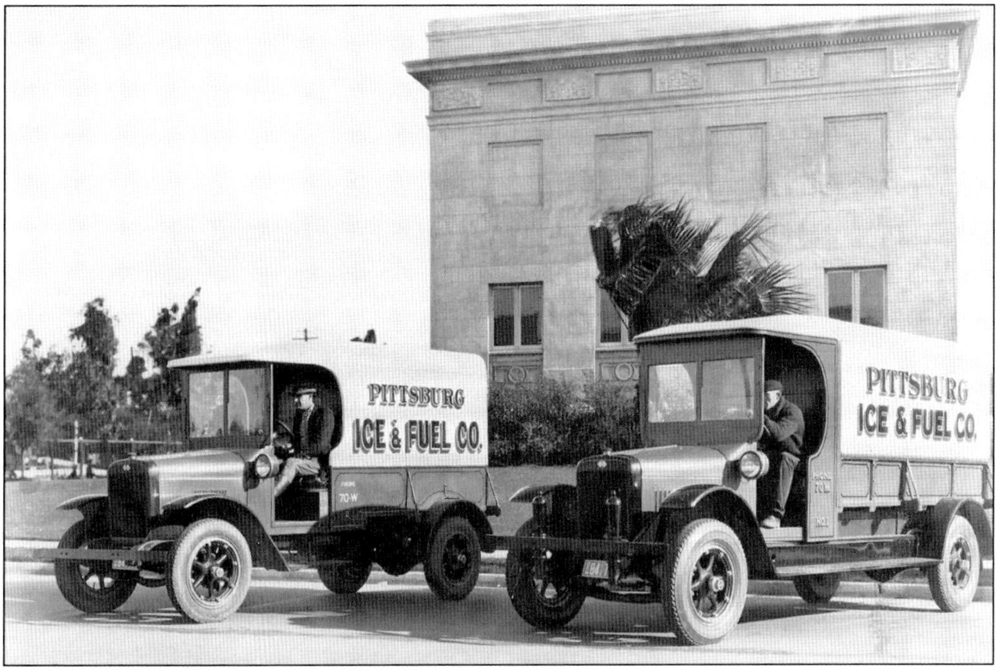

Pittsburg Ice and Fuel Company, owned by the Caruso brothers, was located on Black Diamond Street. Popular businessmen, Steve, Frank, Joe, and Vincent Caruso owned other businesses, including the Drayage Express, which delivered ice and coal; a livery stable; a bus service; and a hotel.

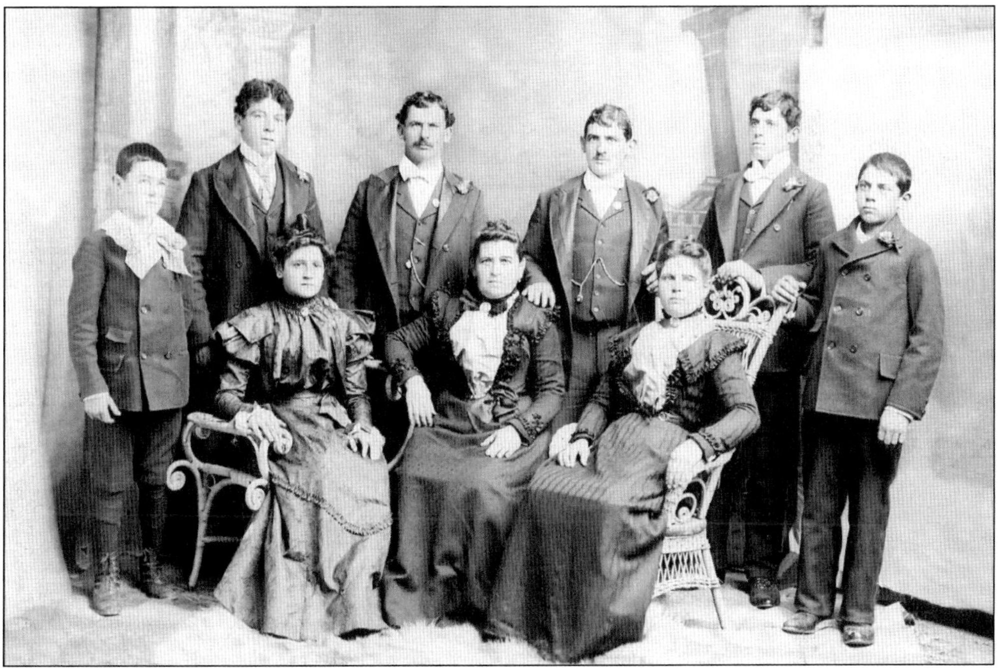

Concetta Carusa, widowed early in life with eight children to care for, sold her husband's fishing boat and bought a sewing machine so that she could work as a seamstress to support them. The family worked together in the business and became very successful entrepreneurs.

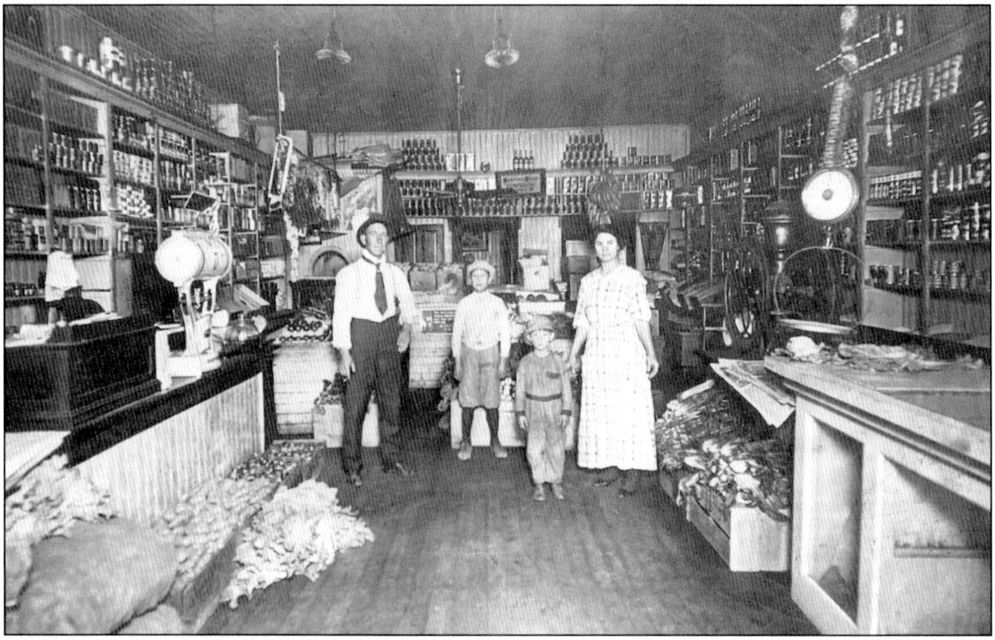

Pittsburg Free Market Store, located at 139 Black Diamond, was owned by Leonard and Carmella Canciamilla. The couple had three sons, Joe, Nicholas, and Monte, who became a mortician and opened the Pittsburg Funeral Home. Monte's son Joseph was the youngest to be elected to the city council and then went on to become a county supervisor and assemblyman from this district.

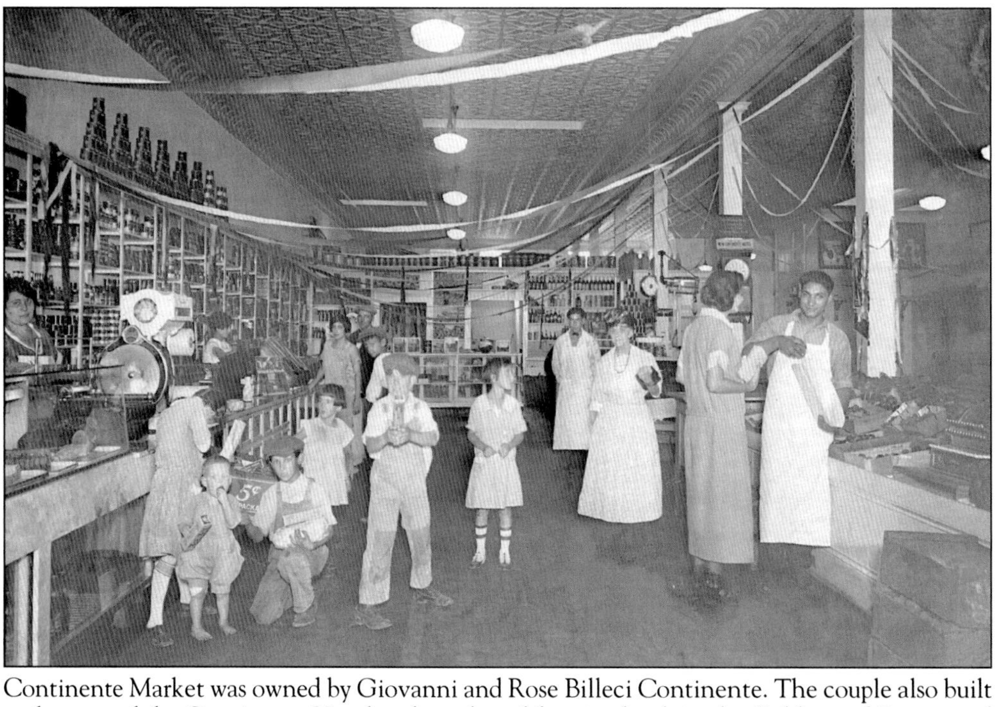

Continente Market was owned by Giovanni and Rose Billeci Continente. The couple also built and managed the Continente Hotel and purchased farming lands in the Oakley and Brentwood areas. Giovanni planted vineyards and sold the grapes for winemaking.

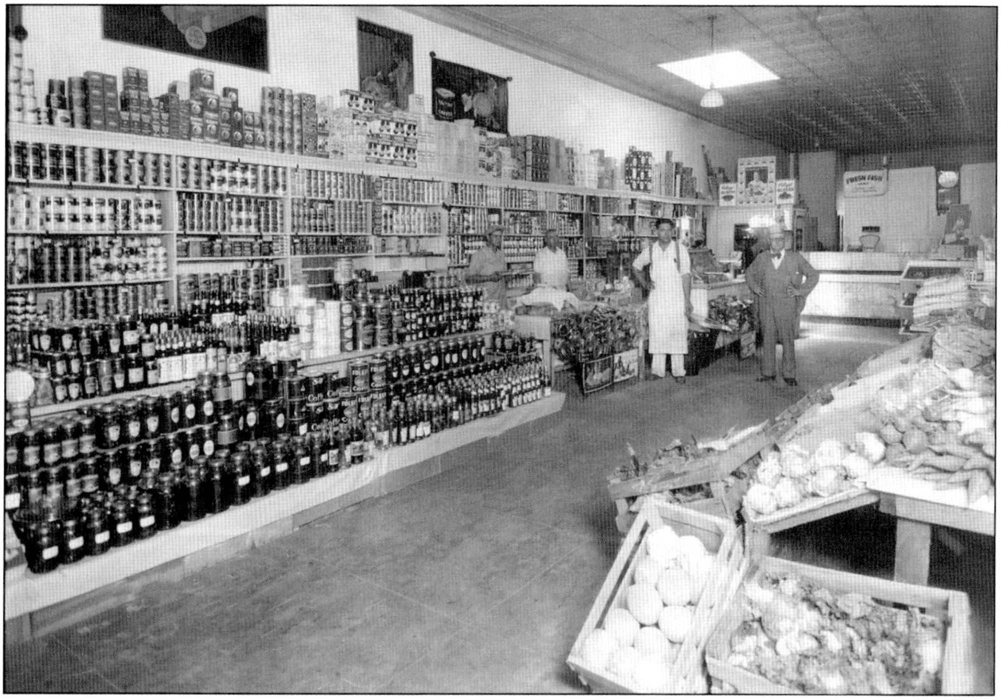

This *c.* 1932 photo shows the Noziglia meat market and Mauro Patane Grocery. The man in the white apron is Sal Nicolosi. The others are Valuto Cari and V. Compari.

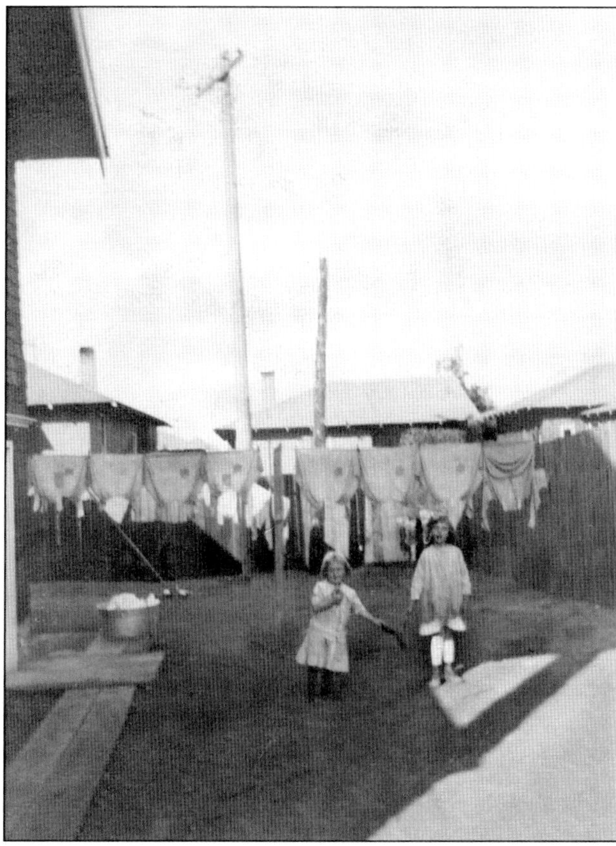

Monday was typically wash day, when mama would wash the clothes on a corrugated washboard, rinse them in a tub of water, then hang the clothes to dry on a rope line strung across the yard.

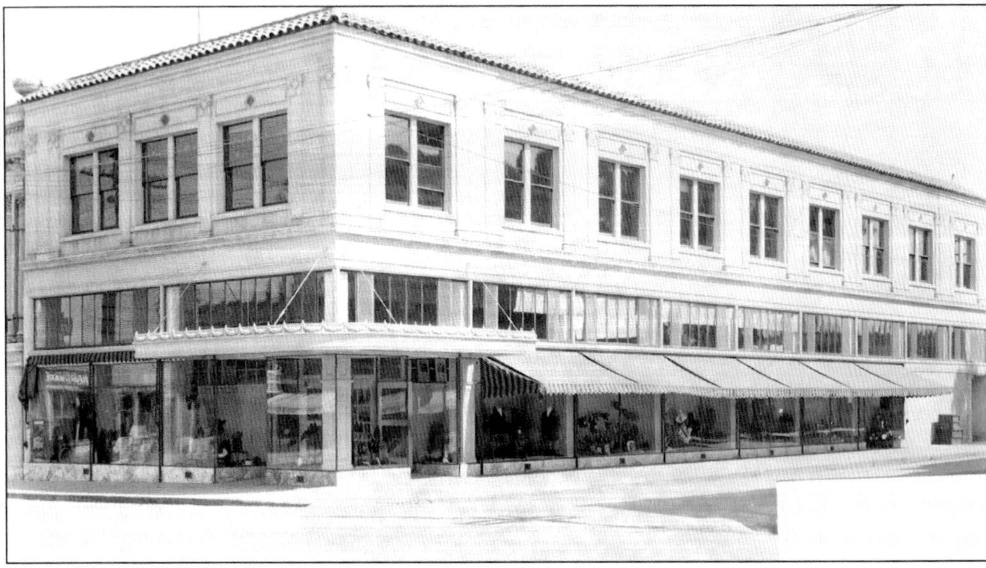

Senderman General Store was originally located on Black Diamond Street in 1878. In the 1920s another, larger store was built on Railroad Avenue, where it remained a lucrative business. After Senderman left the business, other companies like Karl's Shoe Store occupied the space during the wartime boom. The building was later sold to Sol Berg, who operated a business there well into the 1980s, then moved to another location.

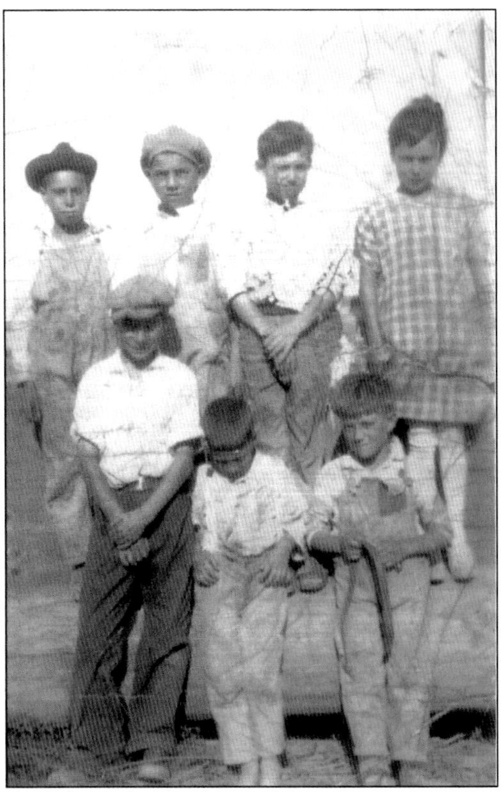

These Eastside kids, from left to right, are (front row) Tony "Sticks" DiMercurio, Joe DiMercurio, and Tonno DiMercurio; (back row) Neno Riso, Faro Scola, Vince "Caretta" Aiello, and Rose Ciaramitaro.

Vincent DiMaggio was one of the first members of the city government's board of trustees. Other members included Warren Croxen, William Buchanan, Jack Junta, and Dave Gatto.

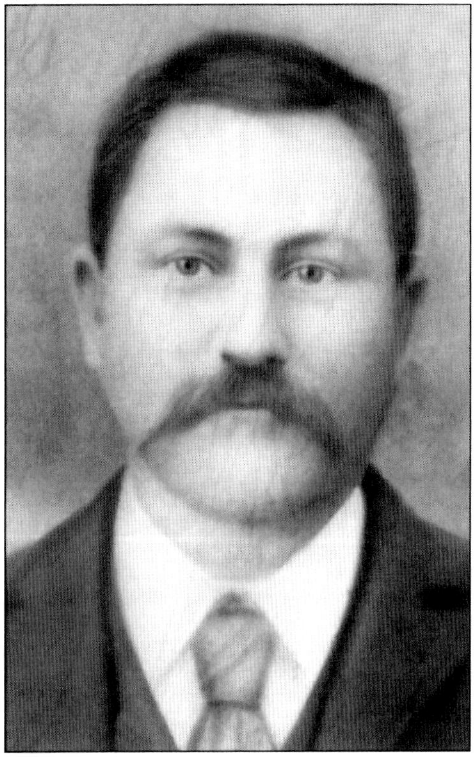

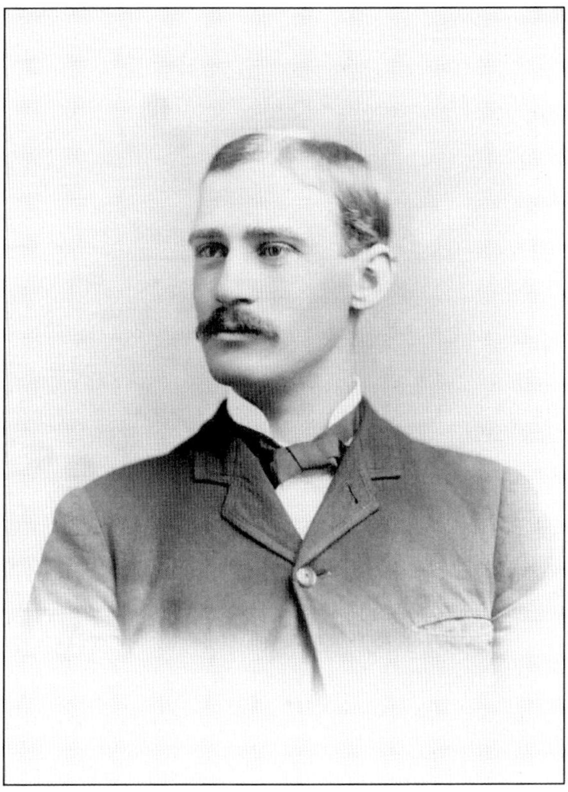

Warren Croxen was the son-in-law of F.E. Booth and superintendent over the Booth Canning Company in Pittsburg. Booth also had a cannery in Monterey, the heart of the sardine canning industry.

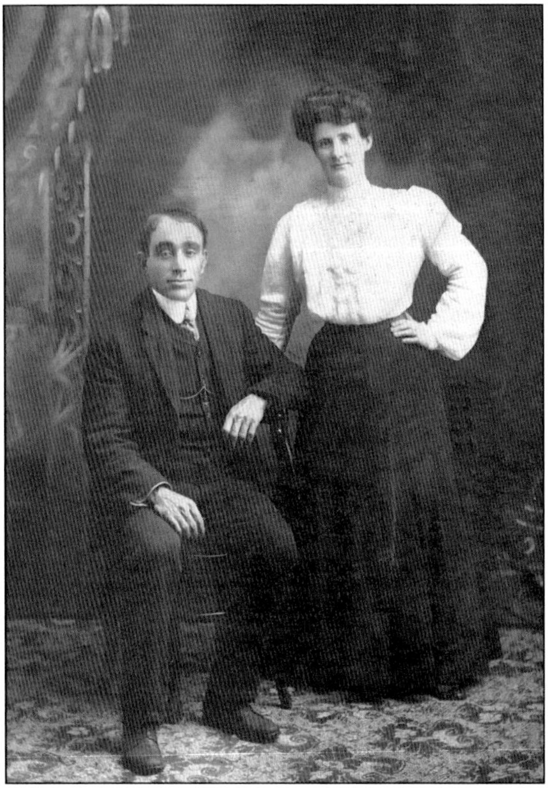

Jack Junta was born in Leghorn, Italy, and came to the United States as a child. In 1900 he opened a hardware store on Front and Black Diamond Streets. He was also affiliated with the American Fish and Oyster Company and sold fishing supplies in the store.

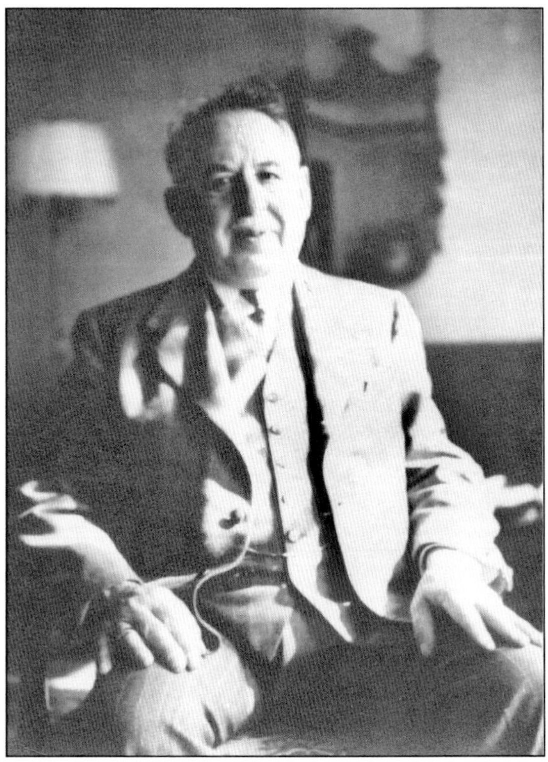

Dave Israel and his partner Ben Senderman owned a general store across the street from Junta's Hardware on Black Diamond Street. An important businessman in town, Israel was an asset to the city as a board member.

William Buchanan first served on the board of trustees, then moved on to become county board supervisor for 46 consecutive years, 30 of them as chairman. A native of New York Landing, born in 1867, "Billy" Buchanan opened his first store in 1884. Buchanan General Store finally closed its doors in 1949.

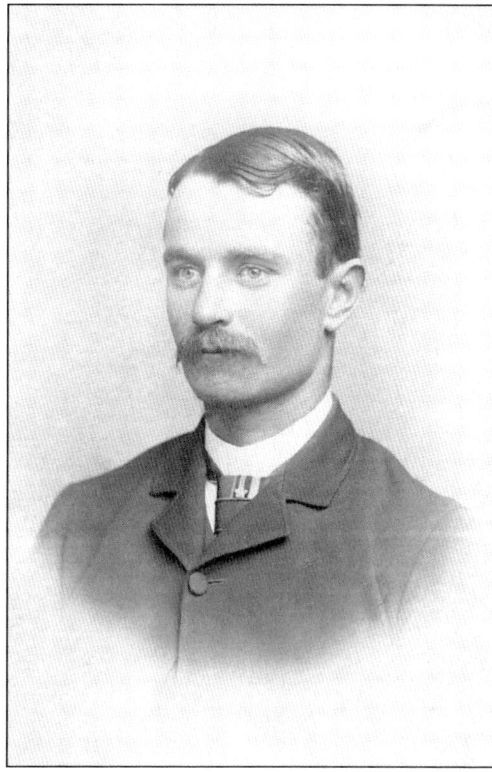

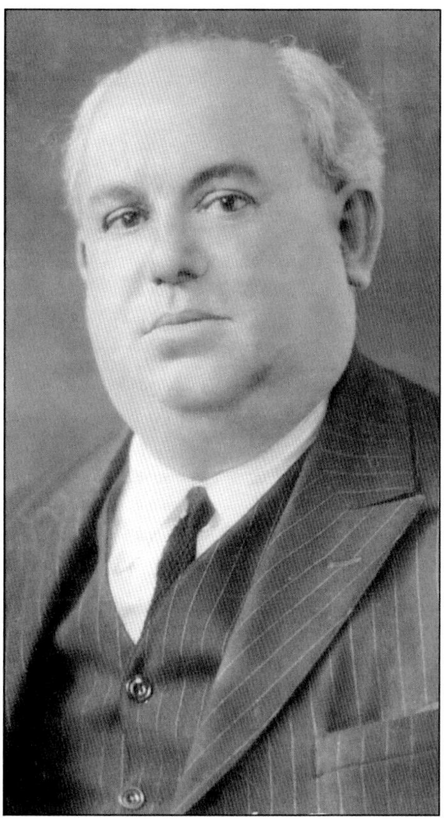

Dave Gatto was appointed city treasurer of Black Diamond and was reelected to the office for many years. He also served as deputy sheriff under Contra Costa County sheriff R.R. Veale. Gatto's son Michael became a lawyer, then a judge in Martinez.

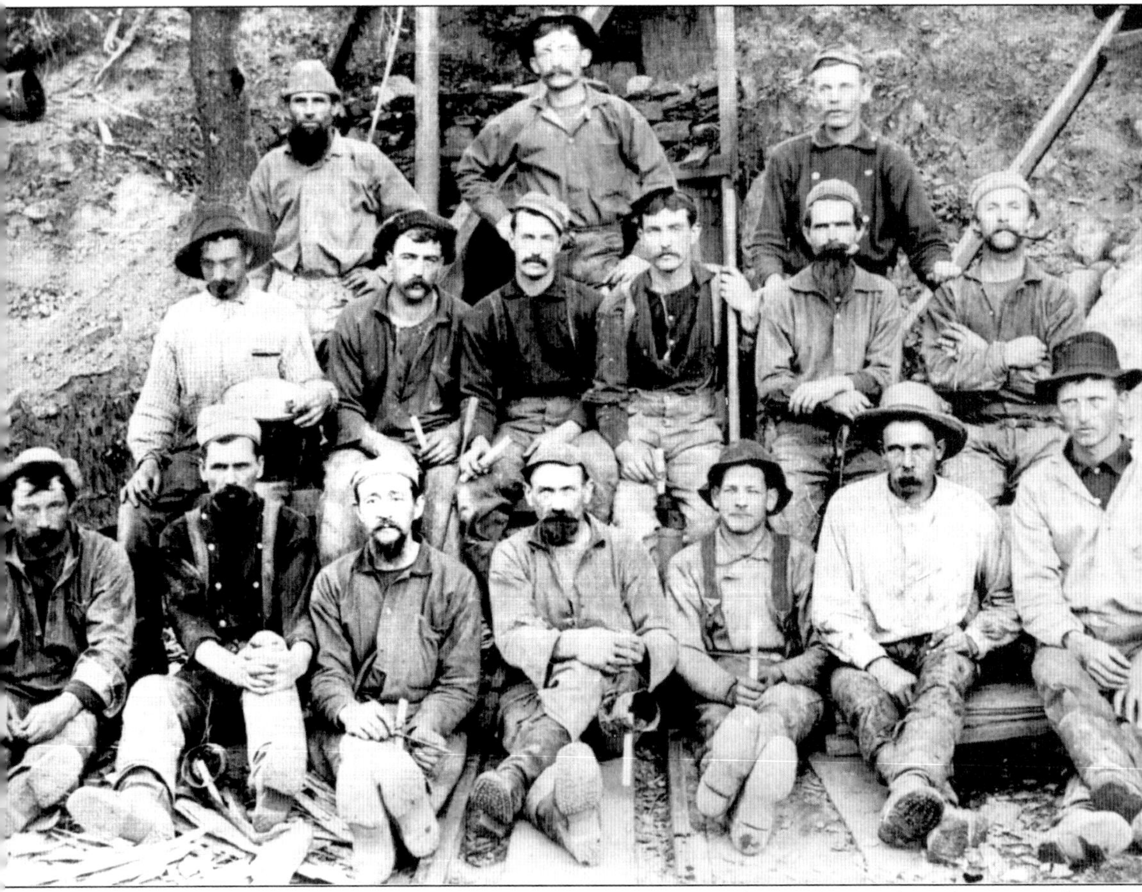

Welsh coalminers immigrated to the United States in the 1850s and took up similar mining work in Pennsylvania, West Virginia, and California. Locally, these families settled in Nortonville, Somersville, Judsonville, and Stewartsville.

Immigrants: 1850–1950

Since its founding, Pittsburg has experienced waves of immigrants lured by the natural resources of the city. The first people who came to work in the coalmines were the Welsh. Working at a trade they knew very well from the old country, these miners and their families stayed until the coal petered out toward the end of the 19th century. Chinese men came to California to work on the railroads and later in the canning and farming industries.

The San Joaquin and Sacramento Rivers, teeming with fish, attracted an earlier wave of immigrant fishermen from Italy to ply the trade they knew best. Boys and women took on jobs canning the fish and the produce from farms in the eastern part of the county. Many Italians continued to arrive at the turn of the century and well into the 1920s as families were sent for and relatives heard of the opportunities for success here. The 1900 census reports showed that 87 percent of the total population was Italian, 6 percent was Scots-Irish, 3 percent Jewish, and 1 percent Chinese.

Mexicans came to Pittsburg seeking work in the factories, although other work was also available to them. In the past 30 years, the Hispanic population has grown to comprise a majority of the total, and is due to increase in the future.

The Filipino population also has grown, with large numbers beginning to arrive in Pittsburg at the end of World War II. The presence of Camp Stoneman and the many industries during the war also contributed to the number of new residents from foreign countries

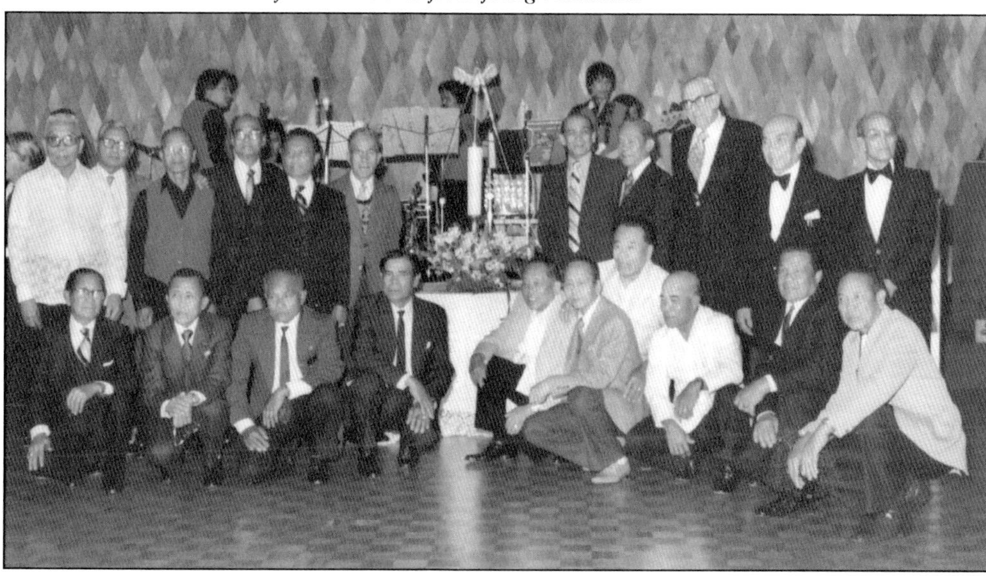

The Filipino Club was established by members of Pittsburg's Filipino population. Many Filipinos came in the early 1900s to work on the railroads and later in the canneries. Some also worked in the asparagus fields along the delta.

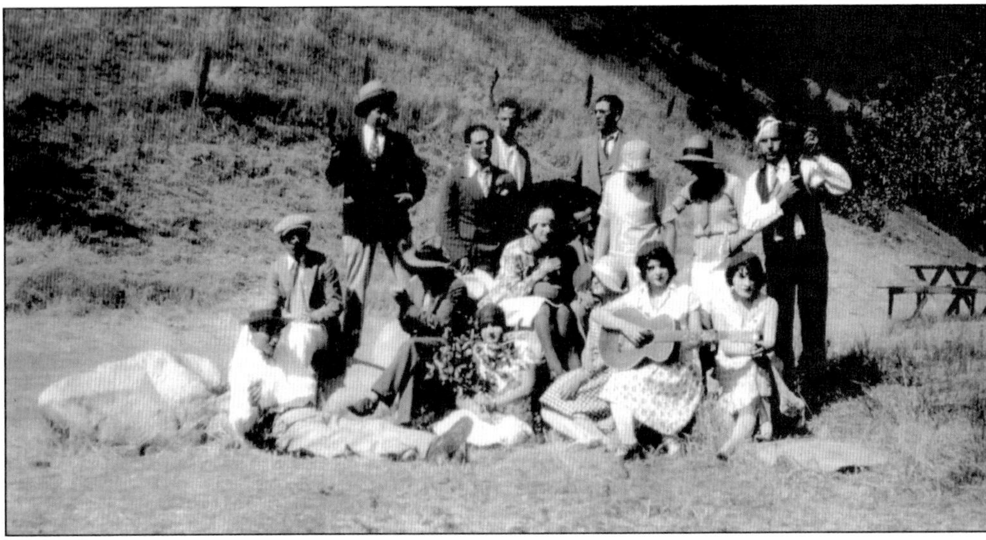

Newly arrived Mexicans, Greeks, and Italians began to enjoy local events, such as picnics in the hills of Nortonville. This group photo was taken in the early 1930s. Many Mexican immigrants came to Pittsburg on the encouragement of factory owners in the area.

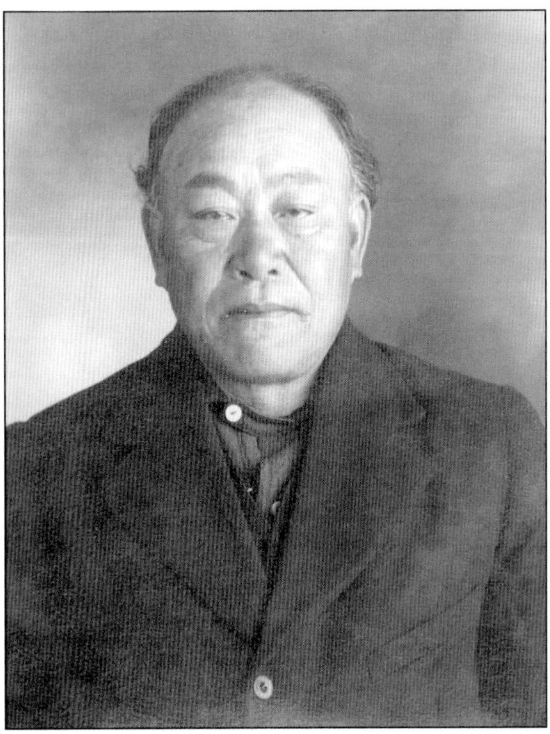

Ong Hung immigrated to the United States in 1898 and the Ong family is one of the oldest still living in the area. The family owned a grocery store.

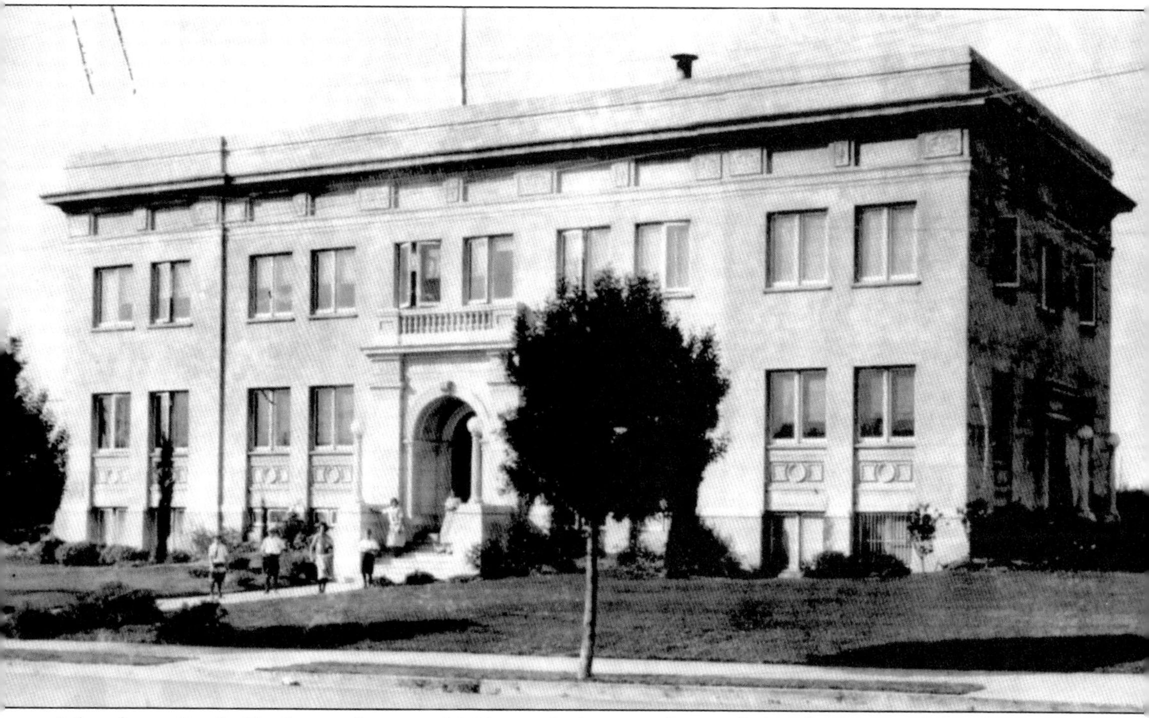

The first city hall, shown here *c.* 1904, used the top floor of this building while the fire department was headquartered on the bottom. The city owned one fire truck at the time.

CAPTAIN MAUPIN AND THE *DIAMOND*

A man whose family had a zest for life found himself heading westward from Kentucky, and in 1894 he arrived in Central California. Lan B. Maupin was 14 years old and delighted to find that the Sacramento River had river traffic similar to his beloved Ohio River. It wasn't long before he was serving an apprenticeship aboard a river dredge. In 1905 he assumed command of his own barge and acquired the title of captain. While traveling the San Joaquin and Sacramento Rivers, he met up with Barney Lanteri, a shipbuilder from Black Diamond, California.

Both men were true craftsmen—Lanteri with the artistic ability to design sailing ships and Maupin with the unique talent of being able to fashion almost anything with or without the proper materials. The two became great friends and traveled together to see the new flying machines being demonstrated at the Tanforan Race Track in San Francisco in 1909. After studying a Curtiss biplane pusher, they decided that they, too, could build one.

Lanteri assumed the task of constructing the plane of wood, while Maupin forged the metal parts and Mrs. Lanteri cut and sewed the fabric covering for the body of the plane. These talented young people built the aeroplane, named the Diamond, *in one year's time, including the test hop made on November 9, 1910. The shipyard became their workplace and the field behind (now the site of USS–POSCO Steel Company) became the runway from which the plane first went airborne.*

A trial run in 1911 was first executed by Capt. Thomas Baldwin, but the association ended over differences regarding Baldwin's insistence on using the aircraft for a parachute jump. Dick Williamson, a mechanic, taught a young chap named Weldon B. Cooke the rudiments of flying, and after a few exhibitions around Walnut Creek, Antioch, and Stockton, offers from Santa Rosa and Oakland brought in $100. The crew was off and running. An offer of $350 to fly over the 5,600-foot summit of Mount Tamalpais, successfully completed, brought in another offer of $300 to qualify for the 1912 Dominguez Air Meet. This endurance contest included the ability to remain airborne for a total of 17 hours and 15 minutes. The award for first prize was a fabulous $7,000.

After the Diamond's *moment of glory, the plane was eventually stored in the Oakland Airport where it met an inglorious end when the blast from a warming-up DC-6 rolled it into a ball. The remains were boxed and sent back to the Smithsonian Institute in Washington, D.C., until the Hiller Air Museum in San Carlos expressed an interest in restoring it. Due to the efforts of Newton Cravens, the* Diamond *was neatly restored to its original state and is now on display.*

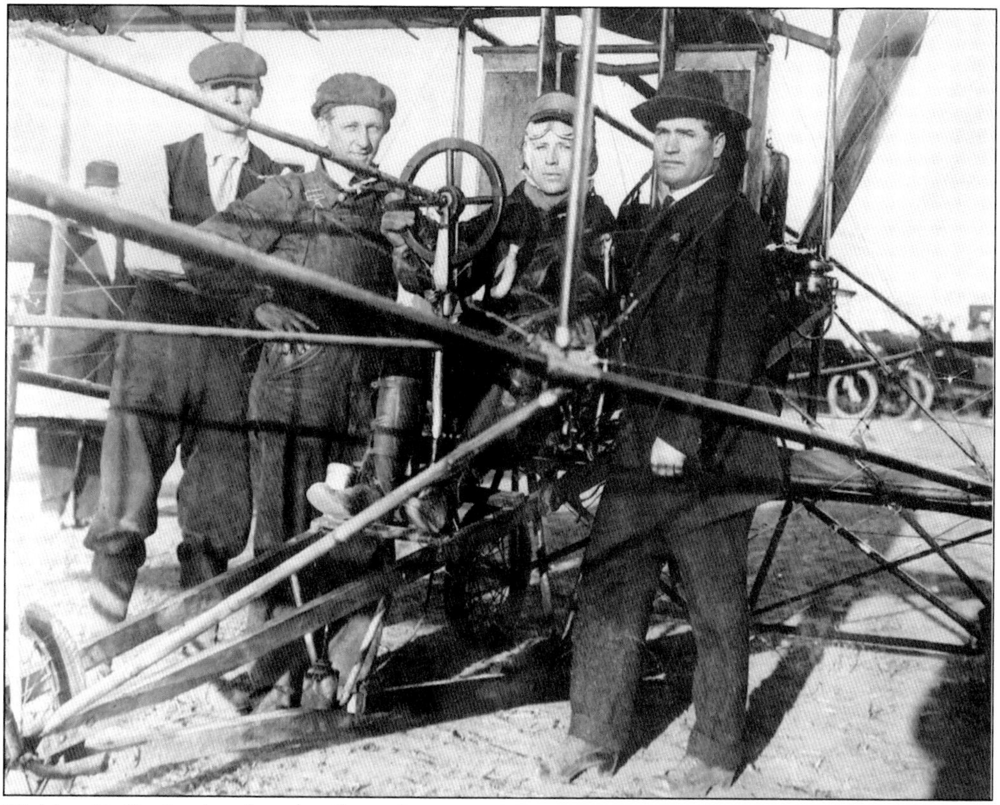

Weldon B. Cooke (at the wheel) was born in Oakland and became the daring pilot who flew the *Diamond* biplane in 1910 in Pittsburg, California. Capt. Lan Maupin is on the right. His partner was Barney Lanteri, a shipbuilder. This plane went on to win the Los Angeles Aviation Meet in 1912.

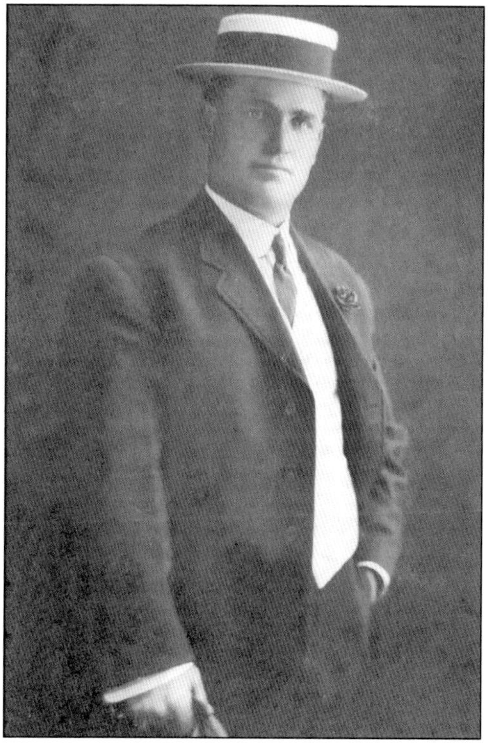

The *Diamond* was built by dredge captain Lan Maupin (right) and shipbuilder Barry Lanteri. After seeing a biplane on display at Tanforan Race Track in 1910, the two men copied the design of the plane, went back home, and built the *Diamond*.

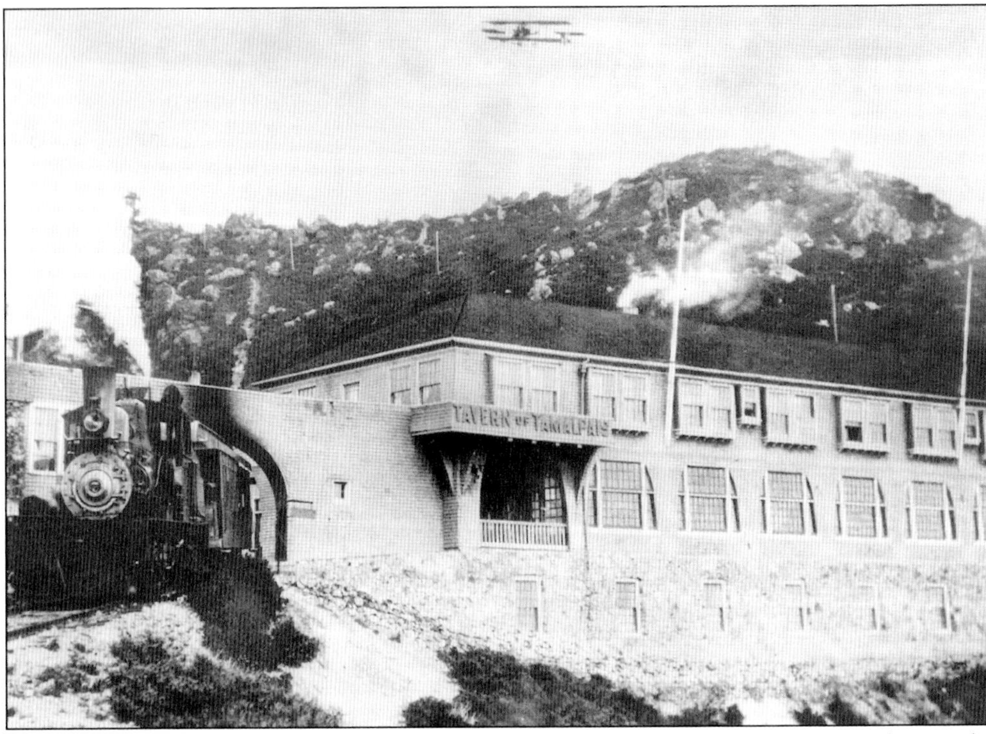

A 1911 flight over Mount Tamalpais by pilot Weldon B. Cooke gave the Diamond team the incentive to enter into the Los Angeles Meet in 1912. Note the train on the left with the airplane overhead.

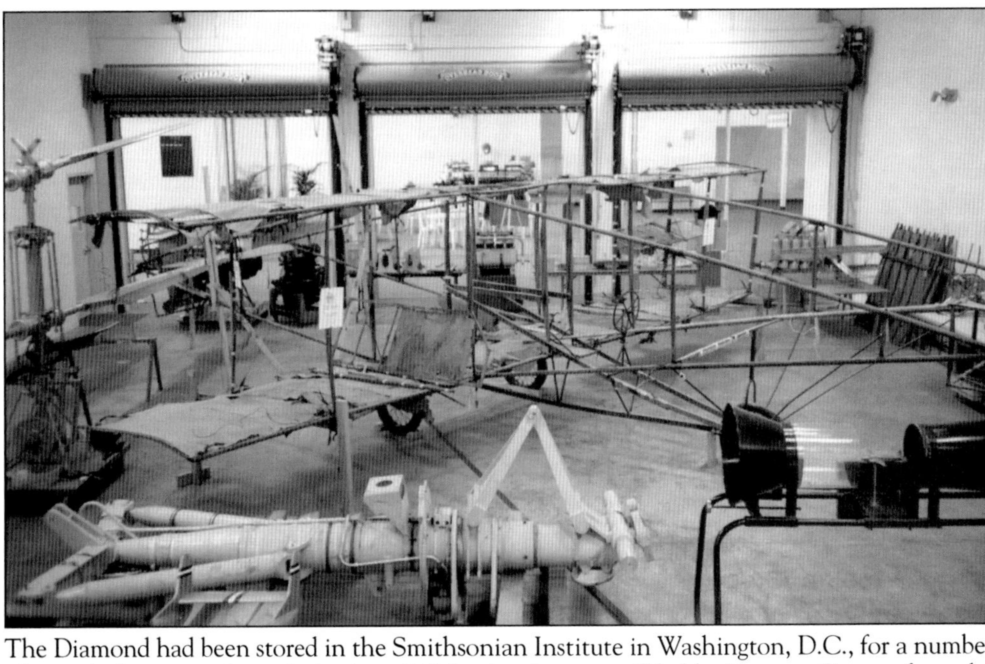

The Diamond had been stored in the Smithsonian Institute in Washington, D.C., for a number of years before it was brought back to California where a staff led by Newton Craven from the Hiller Aviation Institute restored it.

PITTSBURG'S FIRE DEPARTMENT

Most of the developing townsites in early California began with a volunteer crew of men who worked together to save neighbors' lives and property from natural disasters. One of the first was Charles Scudero. Born on November 30, 1872, he began his career at 12 years old in 1884. Pittsburg's fire department was organized in 1903 and, according to records, one of the most dramatic fires the department fought was in 1906, when the first Catholic church on Second Street was consumed. The bucket brigade was the first to act and was assisted by a horse-drawn wagon with a hose-mounted wheel. Unfortunately the church and every house on the block were destroyed.

In the 1930s Charlie Scudero served as chief of both the fire and police departments. His brother Carmello Lark Scudero, a son Charles, and V.J. Scudero also served as firefighters. In 1939, after 53 years of service, Chief Charlie Scudero died. His last request was that his body be taken to its final resting place in the big fire truck. His request was granted and hundreds mourned his passing. Charles Selleck followed as chief, and Lark Scudero, though a volunteer, acted as assistant to the chief.

In the following decades, Horace Shad Enea, who began his career in 1944, would become chief. Retired in 1975, Shad recalls riding the old 1920s museum piece, the Seagrave fire truck, which was donated to the Pittsburg Historical Society in 1976. Bob Berg remembers taking the Seagrave from the Leland and Railroad substation on a fire call. Before leaving the scene, the driver would move the vehicle back so that its nuts and bolts could be picked up and replaced on the old vehicle.

Like many departments, Pittsburg's also had a mascot. "Smoky," a dalmatian, rode with Shad Enea on many runs, and both the dog and the old Seagrave had starring roles in Columbus Day parades.

After World War II, as men returned from military service, many former football players who had graduated from Pitt High joined the fire department, among them Denny Papas (captain), Pete Aiello, Vince Aiello (who later became chief), Claude Battaglia (captain), Sandy Rosetti, Joe "Diddy" DiMercurio (captain), Lester Bartolemei, Walt Laederich, Richard Enea, Frank Aiello (captain), Vince Culcasi, Tony Davi (captain), Art Wendt (assistant chief), Joe Grillo, and Bill Silveira (assistant chief). Volunteer firefighters included Red Cappucini, Monte Canciamilla, Horace Lombardo, Ramey Seeno, Art Bernstein, John DeVito, Phil Balogna, Dom San Filipo, Pete Galli, and Vince Belleci. Volunteers were paid $1 per call.

The fire department was called on to assist in such disastrous events as the explosion at Port Chicago on July 17, 1944, which caused great devastation to the town. Two ships loaded with ammunition blew up, killing 325 sailors, while injuries to civilians occurred when the glass windows in surrounding homes imploded. The firefighters of the City of Pittsburg were also enlisted to assist the U.S. Army at times. During the World War II, soldiers without passes would sometimes try to cross the canal for a night on the town. Some were not so fortunate as to successfully make the leap to freedom, having had too much to drink, and fell into the water. The fire department was hired to drag for the victims of these drownings. The river also took many other lives and the firemen were called on to recover those bodies as well.

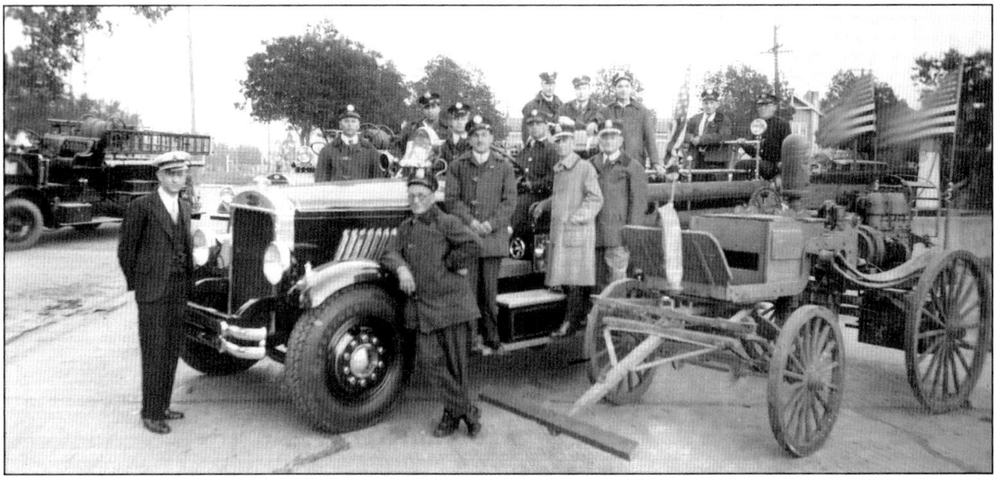

The Pittsburg Fire Department in 1930 included Charles Scudero (at the wheel), Charles Ferreri (on the running board), along with Assistant Chief Charles "Lark" Scudero and A. Spurgion. Acting Chief Charles Selleck is in the foreground. In the background, from left to right, are George Bentinella, Frank Aiello, Ben Rough, Tom Anderson, and Lester Bartolomi. The first fire buggy is to left.

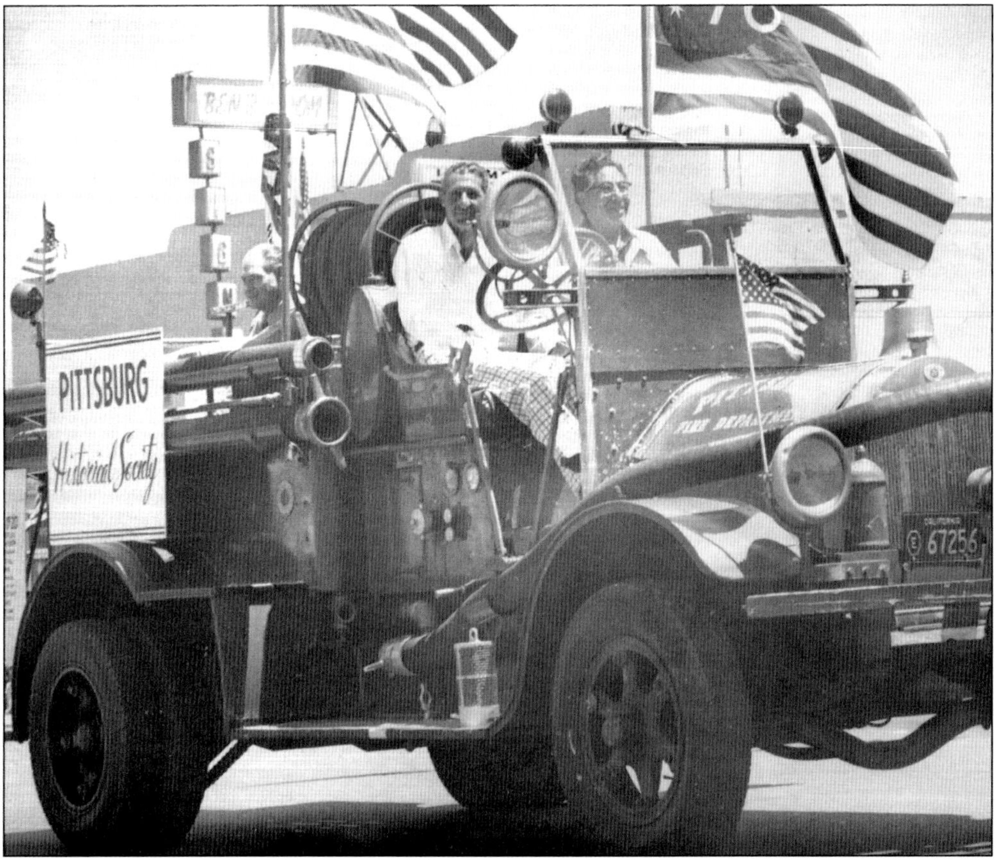

Shad Enea and Jack Aiello parade the old 1920 Seagrave fire truck now owned by the Pittsburg Historical Society.

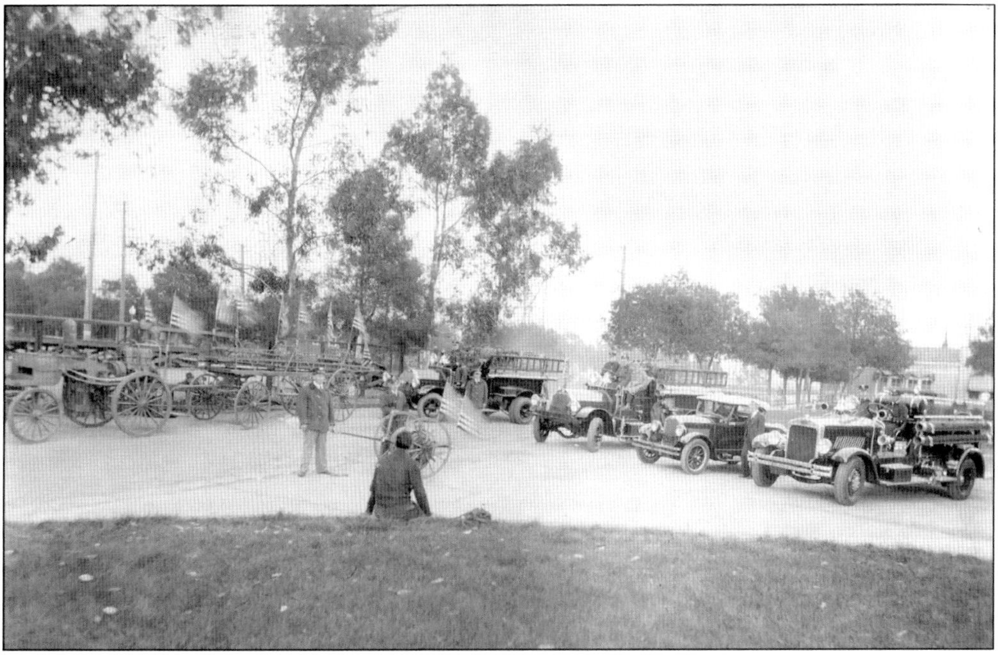

This collection of old fire trucks from different eras includes the first fire wagon, which was pulled by a horse and carried a large drum of water. Buckets were used before the department added hose connections to carry the water.

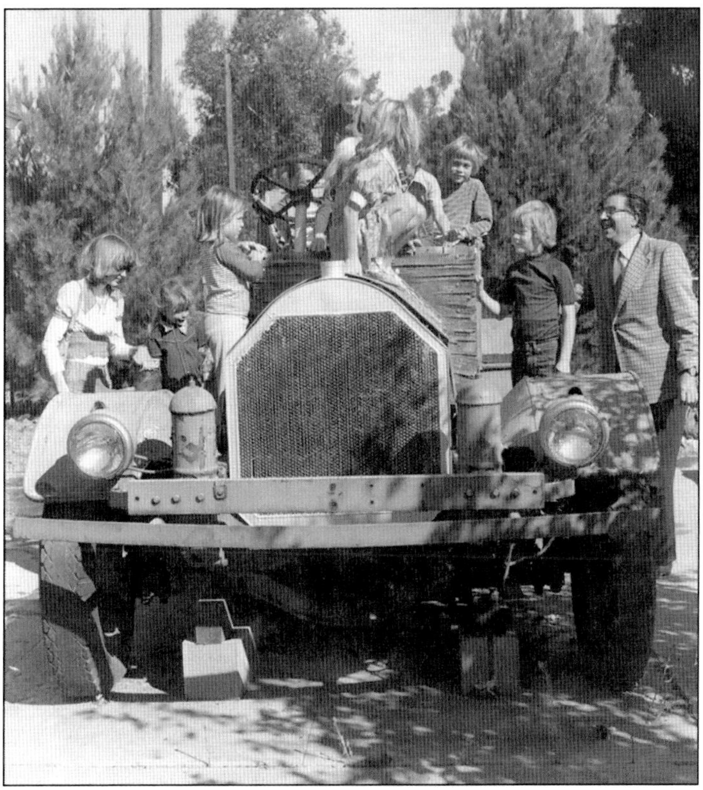

This 1920 Seagrave fire truck was donated to the historical society in 1973. Jack Aiello, curator of the museum, shows a group of schoolchildren the truck. The Seagrave has been restored and is now on display at the Pittsburg Museum.

Crime Busters of Pittsburg

New York Landing's first law enforcement officer came from Nortonville, the coal mining town just to the south. Back in 1880 when only a handful of hardworking fishermen comprised the population of the village, a fearless official named Frank Swears was sworn in as a local constable.

Swears saw to it that law and order were maintained, a job that kept him busy considering the steady stream of questionable transients flowing in and out of the town.

Charles Scudero assumed the role of fire chief in 1904 and held it until his death in 1936. Well known for his devotion to duty, he acted as both the fire and police chief, and few major crimes occurred until his last years as chief.

The newspaper headline of December 13, 1935 read: "1 Officer Killed, 3 Shot in Gun Duel with Merchant." Officer John Buckley was only 39 years old when he was gunned down by a 28-year-old Pittsburg grocery store proprietor. Grief-stricken over a soured relationship and half-crazed with liquor, Luciano Garcia Sanchez came out of the Paloma Café on Black Diamond Street with his gun drawn. Officer Buckley was shot through the heart and Sanchez ran from the scene only to be cornered when he took shelter inside the closet of a house on York Street. Police officers in pursuit caught up with him. Shots were exchanged with Deputy Chief Sal Jimno, Patrolman Chris Maze, and Capt. Daniel McNeil. Jimno sustained a shot to the arm during the gun battle, but after a lengthy convalescence in the hospital, recovered completely.

The late 1930s and 1940s saw an upswing in crimes and misdemeanors. Gambling and vice reigned as the country recovered from the Great Depression, and both illegal prostitution and gambling halls presented a big problem to the police department. The Pittsburg Independent News *recorded an incident that happened during the purging of gambling joints in Pittsburg.*

The sheriff's department had sent out men to raid about l2 taverns, or card rooms, where gambling was evident. Twenty-two slot machines were confiscated. But sometimes the urge to play cop just can't be resisted and average citizens decide to pitch in and help lawmen clean up the city. Such was the case with Joe, a local resident to the rescue. Joe entered a local establishment, looked over the slot machines with a critical eye, and warned the attendant, "These machines are under arrest. Keep away from them machines." "I am deputized by the police, and these machines are under arrest," he reiterated. the final reply was a hard right to the jaw, which knocked the unfortunate fellow to the floor and removed forever any desire he had to be a law enforcement officer.

Even though the incidents reported in the newspapers of the 1930s and 1940s reflect a simpler time in our history, the reader must keep in mind that this small unsophisticated California town was typical for this era. The story is in no way meant to impugn the integrity of some of the local citizenry but, rather, to paint a verbal picture of the somewhat colorful happenings of that time in our history that made it into the papers of the day.

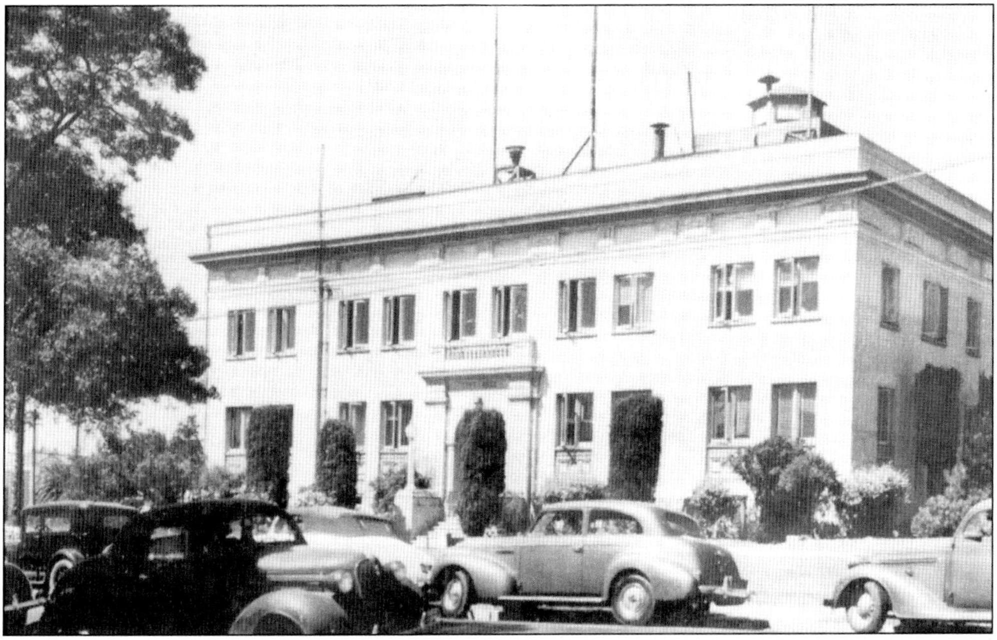

Pittsburg City Hall was built in 1922 for $75,000 on Ninth Street at Railroad Avenue and Cumberland Street. The building housed both the police department and the fire department. The main entrance was a large archway flanked by massive columns made of simulated marble.

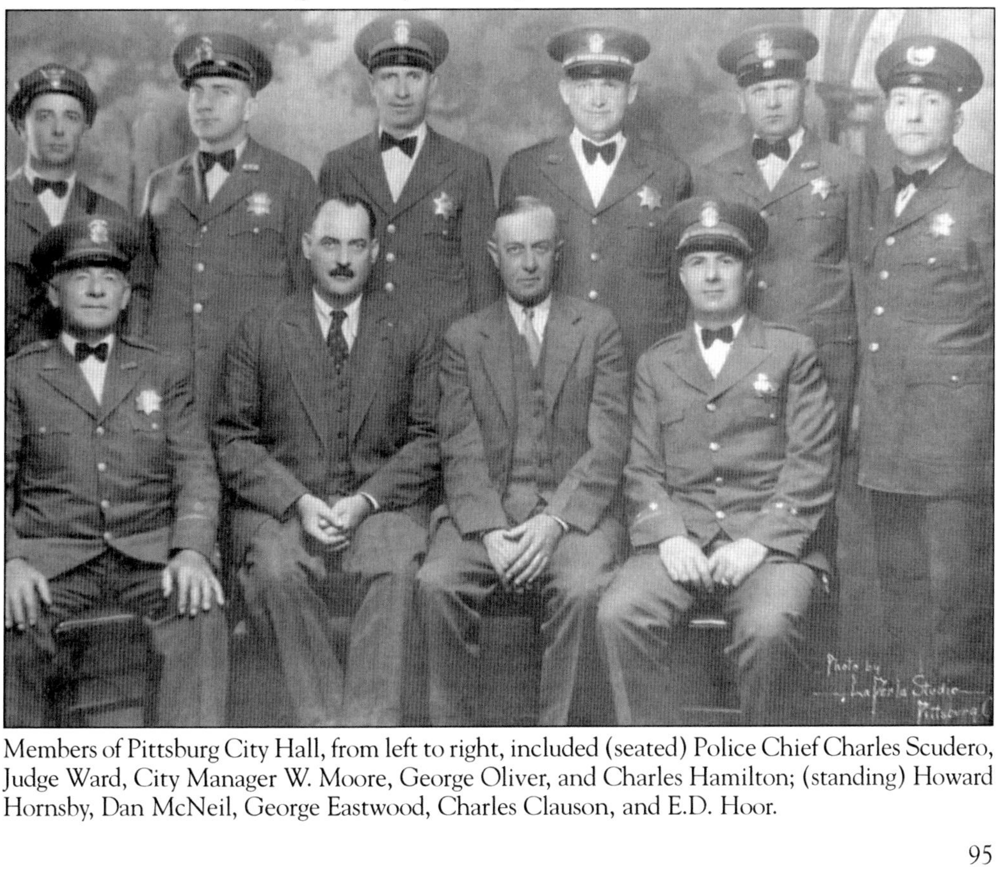

Members of Pittsburg City Hall, from left to right, included (seated) Police Chief Charles Scudero, Judge Ward, City Manager W. Moore, George Oliver, and Charles Hamilton; (standing) Howard Hornsby, Dan McNeil, George Eastwood, Charles Clauson, and E.D. Hoor.

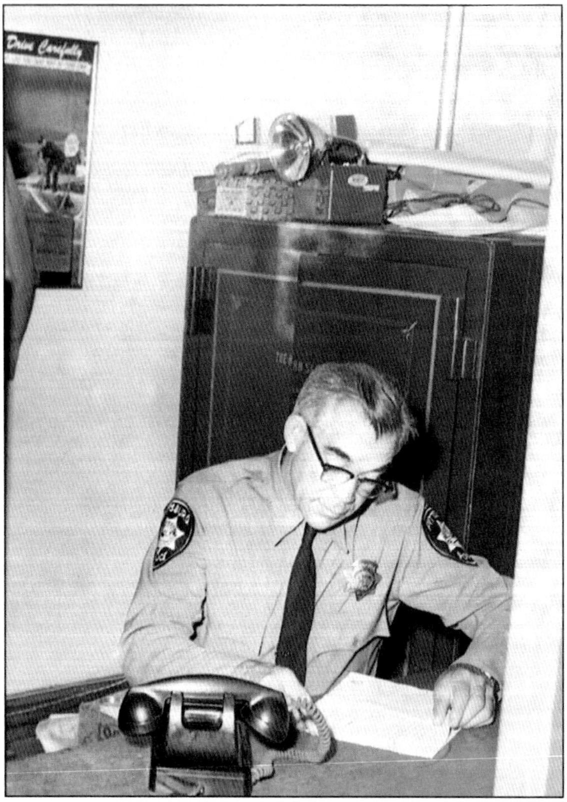

Sgt. Neno DiMaggio was known in his youth as a fighter who went under the name of Shannan DiMaggio.

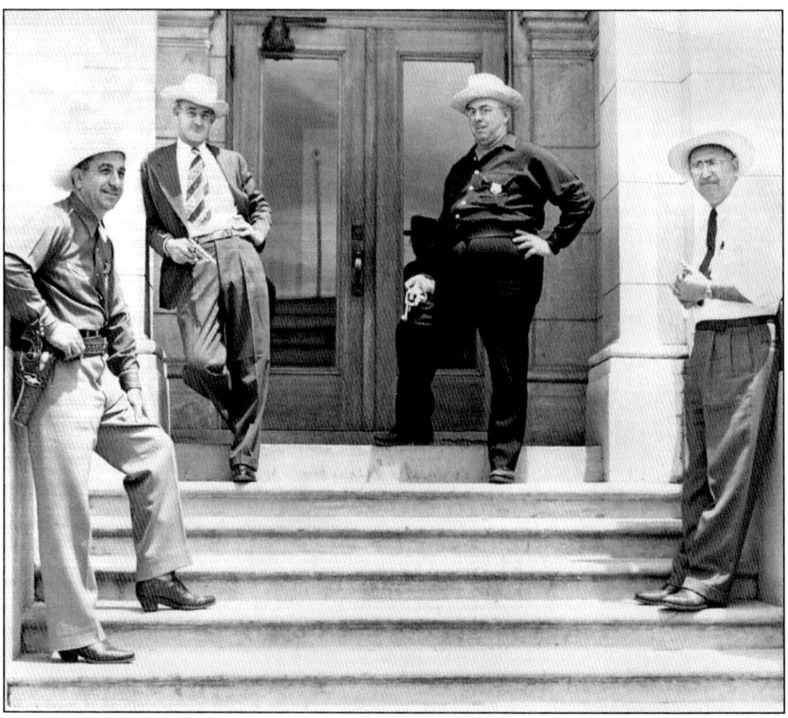

Shown here, from left to right, are Police Chief Sal Jimno, city attorney Walter Lynch, and city clerk Frank Taormina.

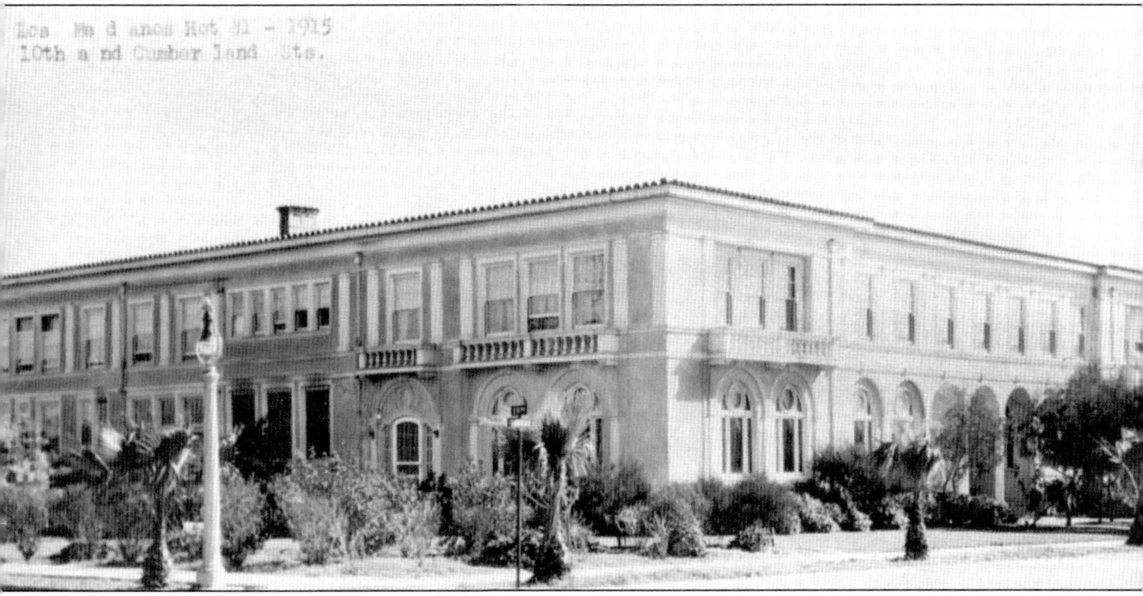

Los Medanos Hotel was built by C.A. Hooper Company in 1917 for a mere $60,000 and was one of the most elegant hostelries in the East Bay. Headliners performing at the California Theater lodged in the hotel when they came to town. On September 28, 1980, the landmark structure was destroyed by fire. Virtually nothing remained and it is vacant as of this writing.

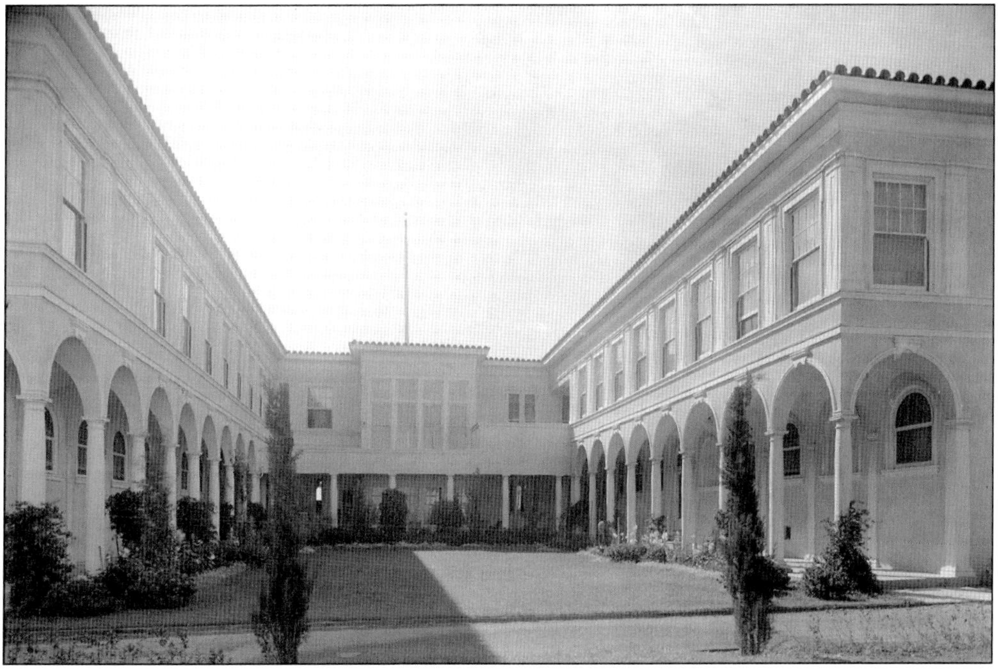

Beautiful courtyards with arched pillars led from the walkway of the hotel. Expansive lawns where cricket was played separated the two wings. The Los Medanos burnt down in September 1980 and a truly elegant building was lost.

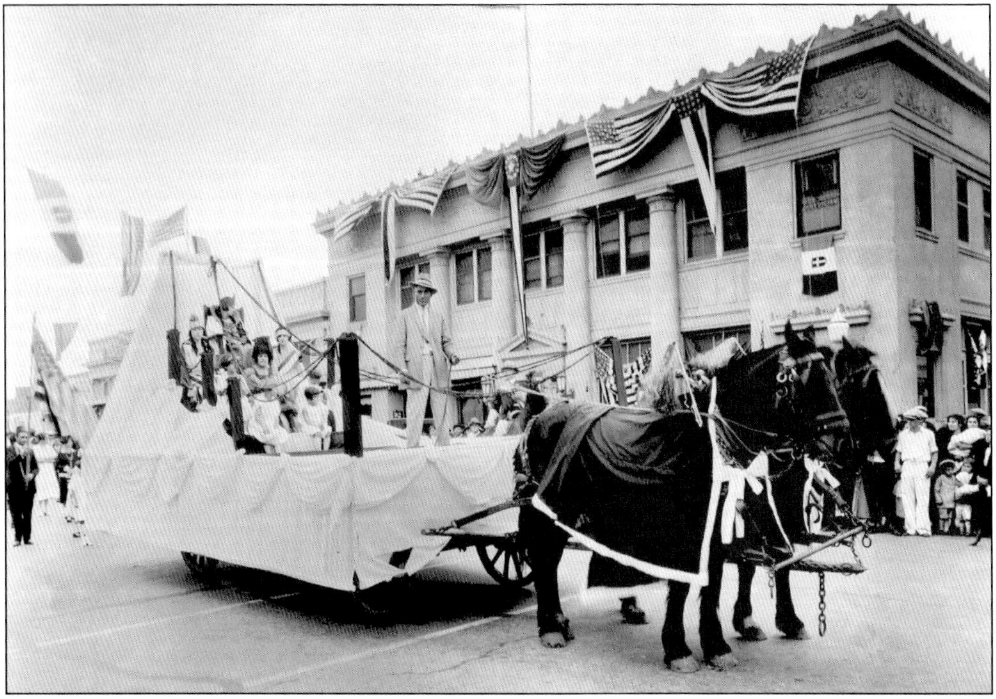

Frances Ascanio DeRosa was one of the early Columbus Day queens in 1925. In the background is the stately American Trust Bank, which still stands today.

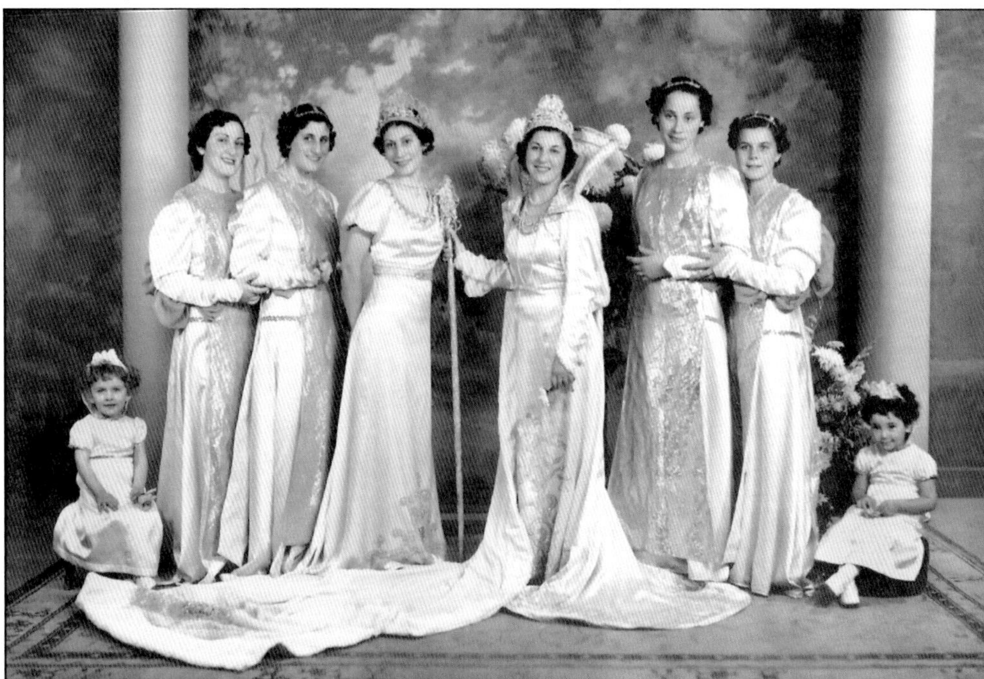

Shown here, from left to right, are Ida Flossi Carlson, Rose Pizzimente, Katie Seeno, Celia Viscuso Doppie, Queen Connie Guiliano, Angeline Guistina, Rose Ferrera Hernandes, and Kathy Russo.

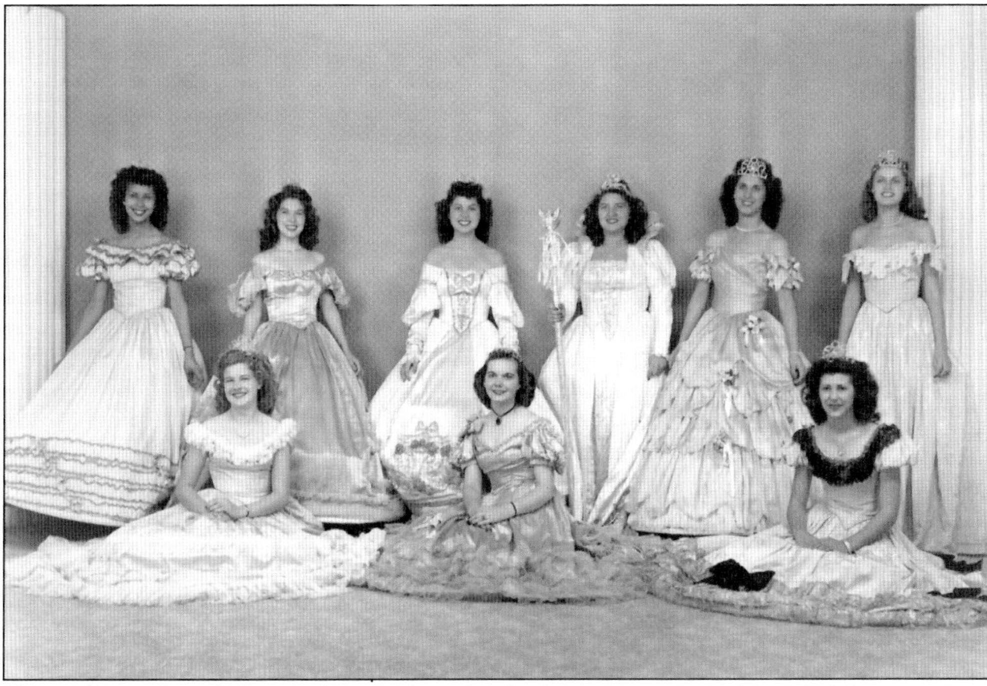

Shown here, from left to right, are (standing) Virgie Matamoroz, Nina DiMercurio, Lucy Drybol, Queen Rose Continente, Rose Scudero, and Geogene Dein; (seated) Doris Puckett, Leona Howery, and Mary Lopez.

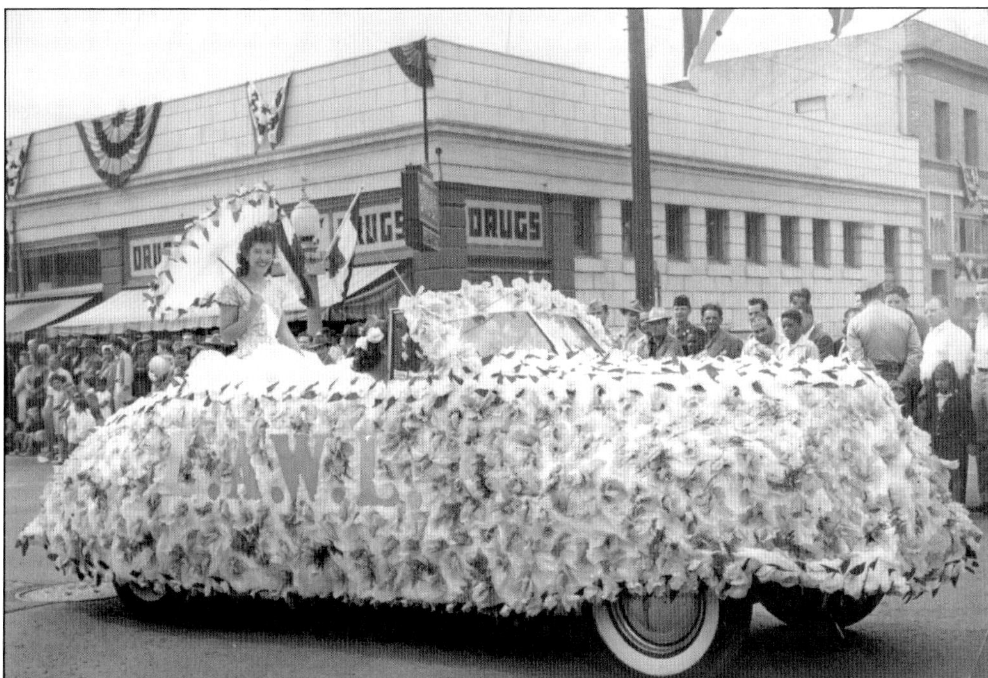

Many of the floats in the Columbus Day parades of the 1950s were elaborately decorated. A member of the queen's court rides aboard this one.

COLUMBUS DAY PARADES

In 1911, a group of patriotic Italian Americans decided to celebrate the landing of Columbus in the new world by electing a king and queen of the Columbus Day celebration. Salvatore Pizzimenti was selected to be the first king and Dolly Canevaro the queen. As the parades grew, the celebrations attracted thousands of people from near and far. In 1914 the event turned into a two-day affair and a grand ball was held in the evening, presided over by elected queen Jennie Flores DeVincia with her consort, Salvatore Davi, as Columbus.

During World War I the parades were discontinued because of the war and the influenza epidemic that followed. In 1925 the festivities resumed with Frances DeRosa reigning as queen and Susky Enea as Columbus. Over the years the festival continued to grow. By 1947 the event included the Columbus Day Bass Derby with Columbus arriving by seaplane. A pet parade was held on Saturday before the four-hour parade. Hailed as the greatest Columbus Day ever, there was also a spectacular air show, and a boxing show held outdoors at Pittsburg City Park.

The last big parade was held in 1957 and not until 1972 would another celebration be planned. Italian festivals have taken the place of the parades, featuring Italian folk dancing and various booths displaying the cultural heritage of Italy as well as ethnic food.

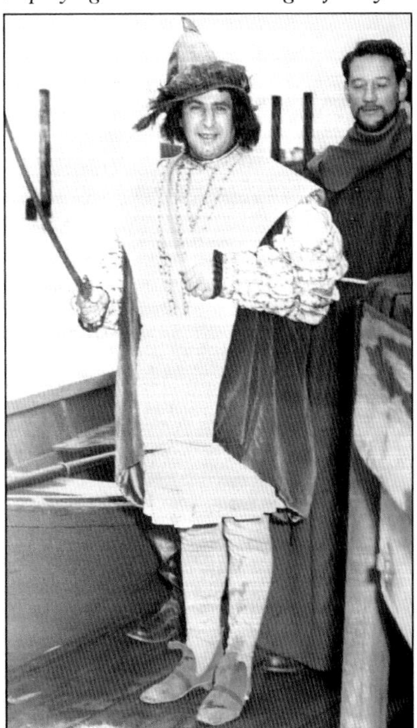

The 1957 Columbus Day "king" was Sal Aiello. It would be 1972 before another celebration like this came to Pittsburg because, in the interim, several major events took place that deeply affected the community. The river was closed to commercial fishing, Camp Stoneman was shut down, and the city went into an economic freefall.

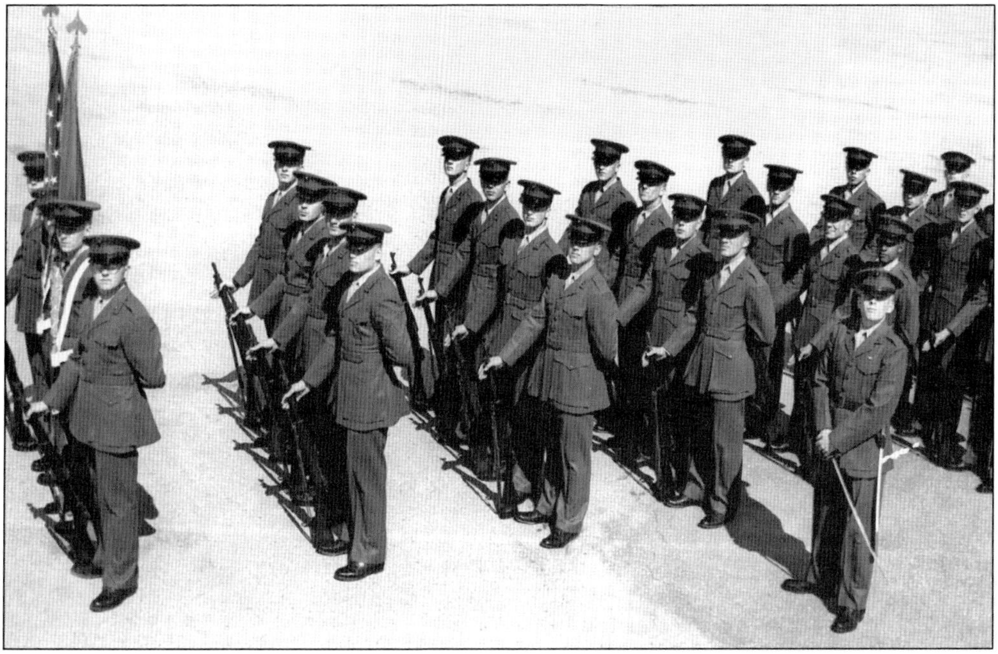

Soldiers from Camp Stoneman and sailors from Port Chicago march and perform drills for the crowds attending the parade.

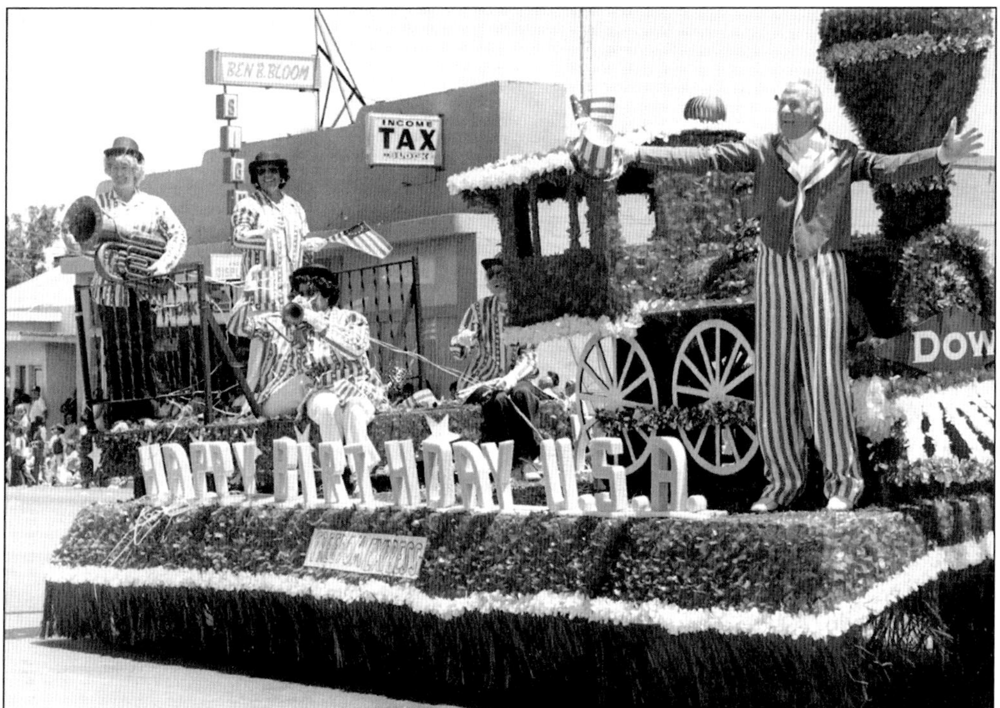

Benny Bruno plays Uncle Sam on a float from Dow Chemical Company. The best-decorated floats were awarded prizes.

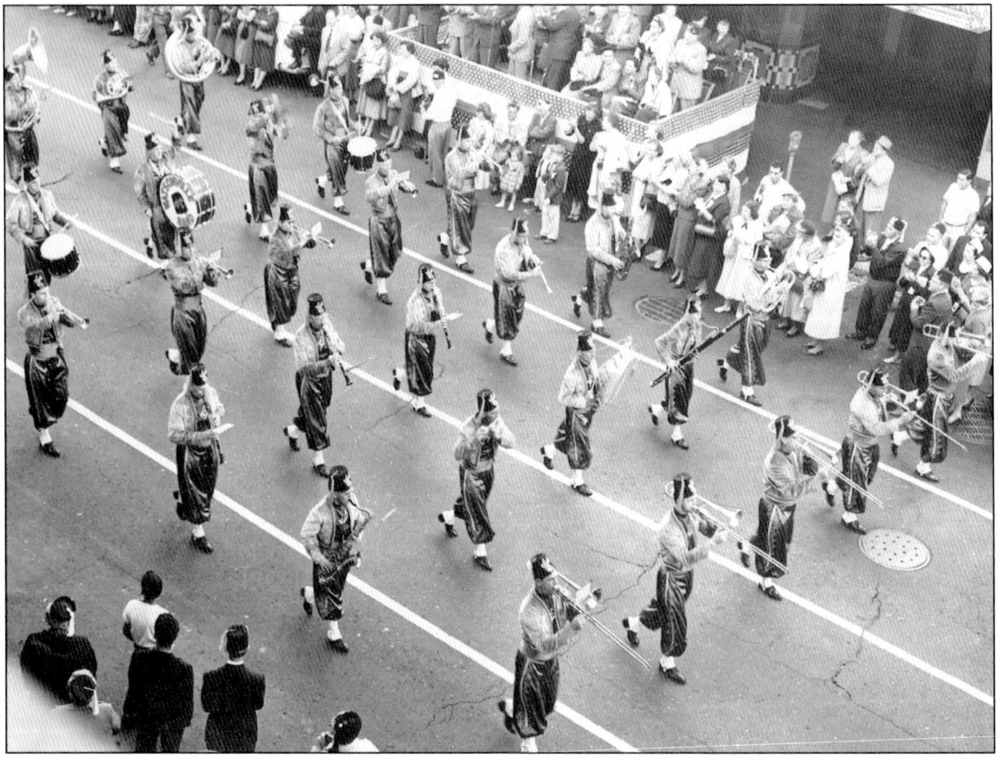

Clubs and organizations from all over the the state sent drill teams and marching bands to perform in the city's Columbus Day parades. Over the years, the parades drew crowds of close to 100,000 people.

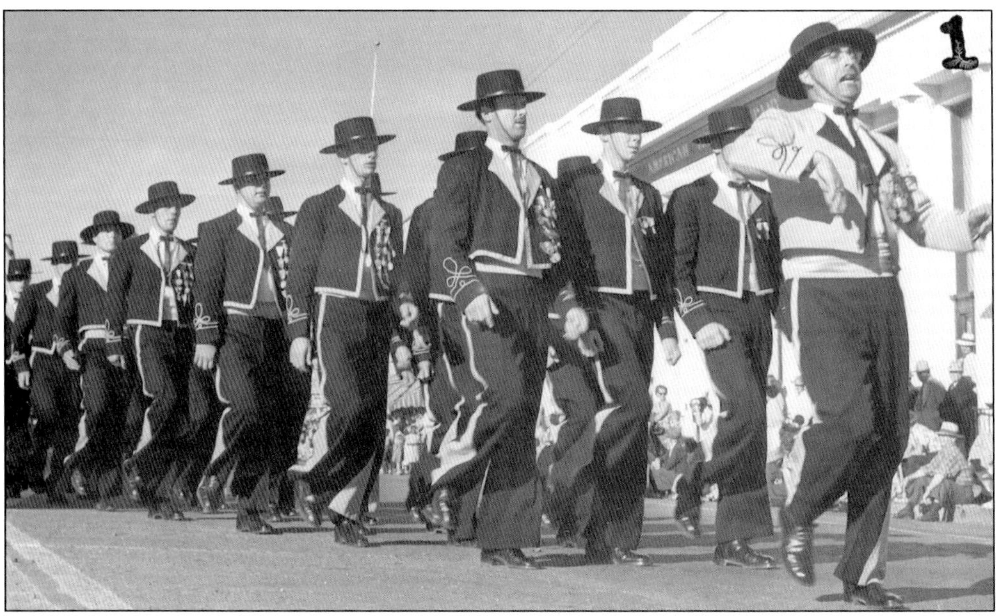

The endless variety of drill teams, like the one shown here dressed in a Mexican-themed costumes, delighted the crowds attending the Columbus Day festivities.

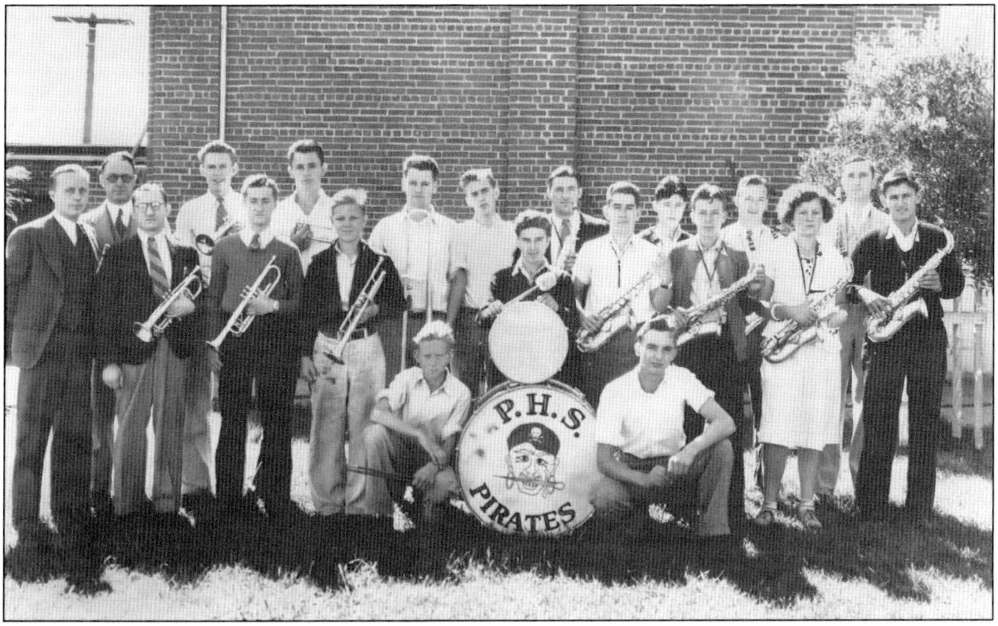

Music was a very important part of the education of children in Pittsburg. In 1931 Clarence Fornwall formed the Pittsburg High School marching band. Fornwall (left) taught music for 52 years. Joey Lucido (next to Fornwall) played trumpet, sax, and drums. Both were career bandleaders and performed in city functions for many years.

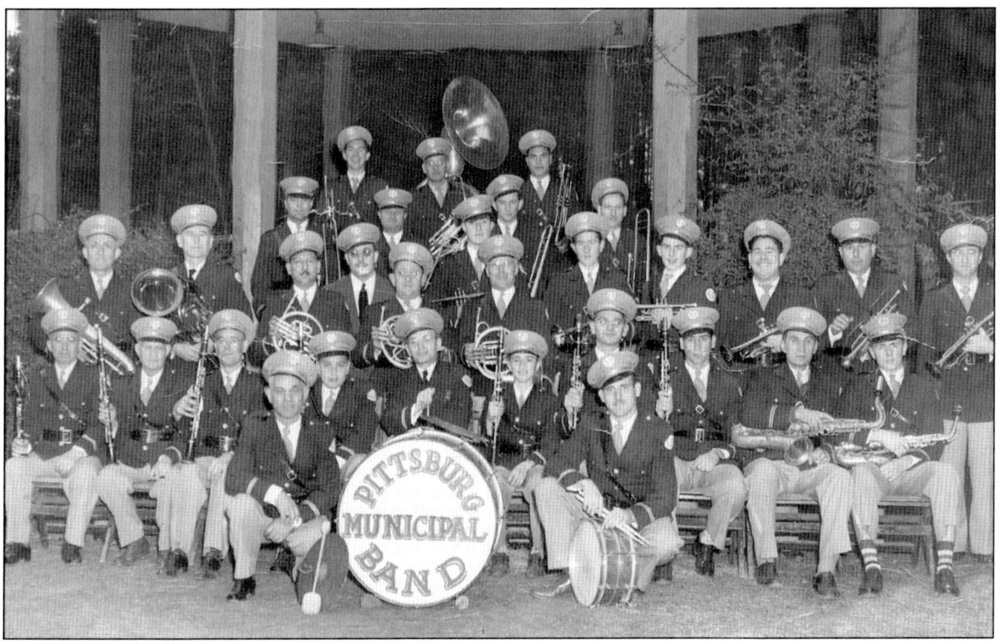

Members of the Pittsburg Municipal Band were dedicated men who played at all city functions and parades. Some of the members have been in the band for all of their musical careers. Longtime musicians include Joey Lucido, Tony and Joe Enea, Johnny Buffo, Joe Anello, Charles Verduzco, Eddie Barraco, Delta Lanzafame, and the youngest player in this picture, Matthew DiMercurio.

The Music Man

John Philip Sousa, the greatest bandmaster that America ever knew, made an impression on all Americans of the last century. Small towns and large cities alike never missed a beat when it came to a parade (patriotic or otherwise) with marching bands strutting their stuff.

Professor Pietro Sarafine, who came to California from Verona, Italy, was the first of a long line of directors of the various bands that were formed in the second and third decades of the 1900s. Sarafine worked with the man and boys for a year before the first public performance was held. A march composed by the professor was taught and band uniforms were purchased for the first public tryout. The novice band marched in cadence into the tree-shaded City Park, as half the town followed along with the snappy martial composition. Seated, the band waited expectantly as the professor raised his baton. Silence fell over the crowd and the band played on and on until the cheering audience stopped its clamor for more.

The concert had stirred the hearts of both the performers and the appreciative audience alike. During the early years, band members would gather as a unit in front of the stores that lined the streets of Black Diamond. Merchants contributed much-needed funds to the growing band. By 1916, the well-liked professor moved on, leaving a void that was filled by Professor Emilio Civita. He also came to Pittsburg from Italy in answer to an advertisement in a New York newspaper. Coming directly from the colder climes of New York, he wore a long black overcoat, scarf, and shoulder-length hair. Waiting at the Southern Pacific station, band members greeted with pleasure this odd-looking man with a slight frame.

Civita was a graduate of the Conservatory of Naples and, in time, proved to be a dedicated musician. Under Civita's tutelage, the band gained in knowledge and showmanship, and Civita also gave private lessons to supplement the subsidy he received from the city. With headquarters at Savoy Hall on Black Diamond and Third Street, the band was in demand at all sorts of city functions, as well as traditional parades and religious celebrations. The Columbia Broadcasting System executives heard the band when it performed at the Monterey Peninsula centennial celebration and asked the musicians to record their music. CBS recorded their tunes at the band's headquarters, and the recordings made the band even more popular.

After a long period as director, Professor Civita died in Pittsburg on May 26, 1966. He is remembered to this day by older band members. Some of the early music makers were Tony Enea, John Buffo, Joe Molino, Tony Davi, Camillo Lanzafame, Sal and Eddy Barraco, Frank Lucido, Joey Lucido (who became band manager and director after Civita's death), Neno Dimaggio, Frank Lombardo, and Joe Anello.

The Mexican Band under the leadership of Professor Arnulfo Molino was formed in the early 1920s. Louis Tiscareno of the Pittsburg Historical Society played the saxophone. In the 1930s a Filipino orchestra was performing for its citizens. The Camp Stoneman military bands marched in the Columbus Day parades. Various schools and organizations also formed marching bands, with the Pittsburg Marching Band and the Jazz Band from Pittsburg High School under the leadership of Orin Cross. Many awards were given to this group. Pittsburg continues its illustrious history in music excellence today.

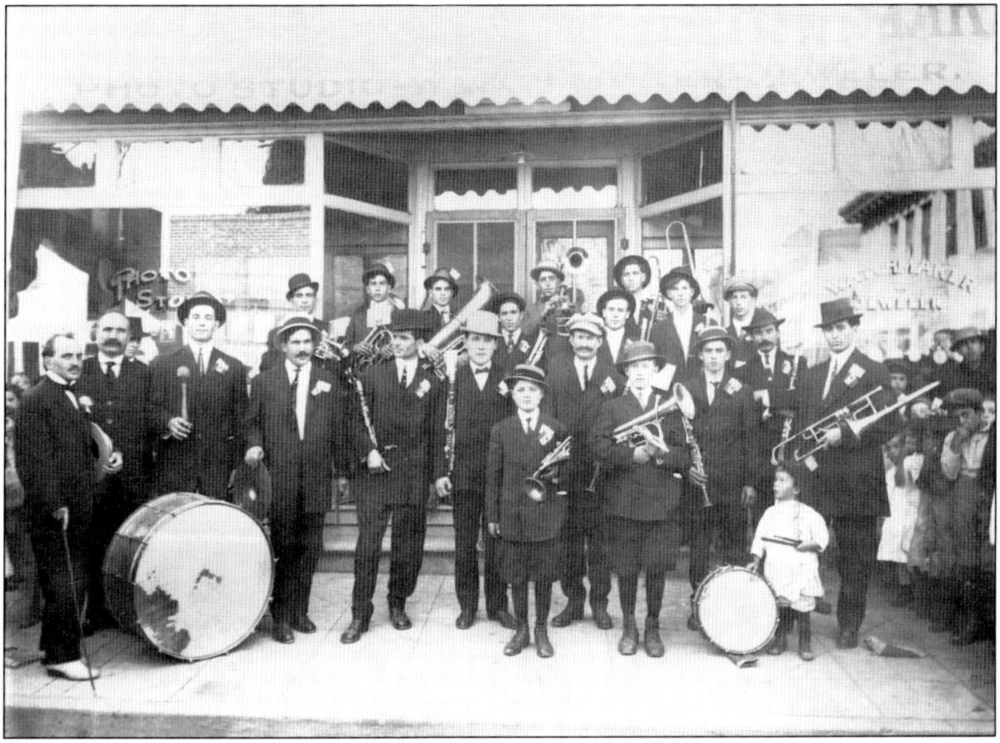

Professor Civita is shown on the left of this 1914 photo. Tony Enea, the boy in the center with the horn, was a musician who played organ in silent movies at the California Theater and continued to play piano and other instruments until his death at 93.

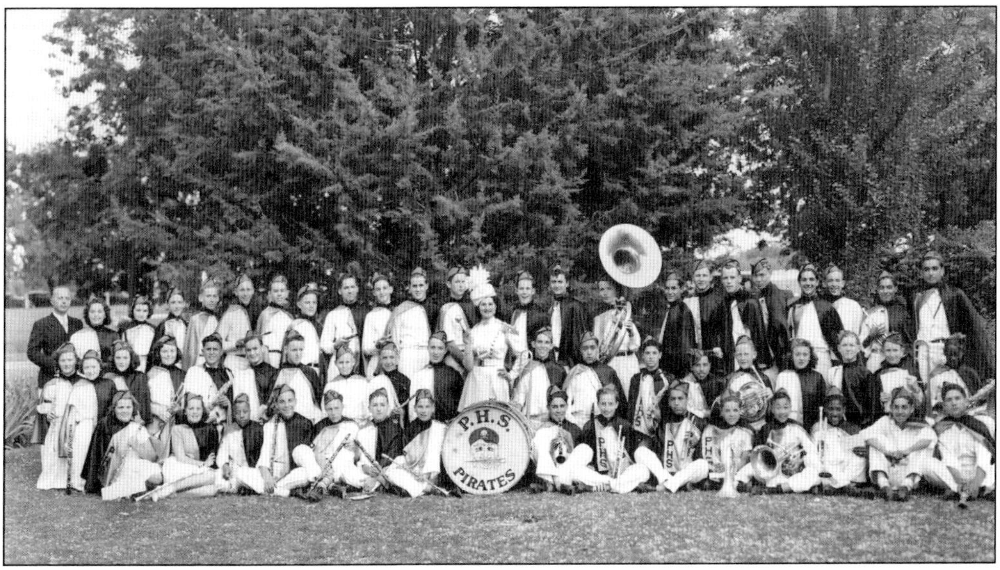

In April 1939 Clarence Fornwall (left) lead a large band at Pittsburg High School during a picnic in the park. The drum majorette was Bess Ferrera Affinito.

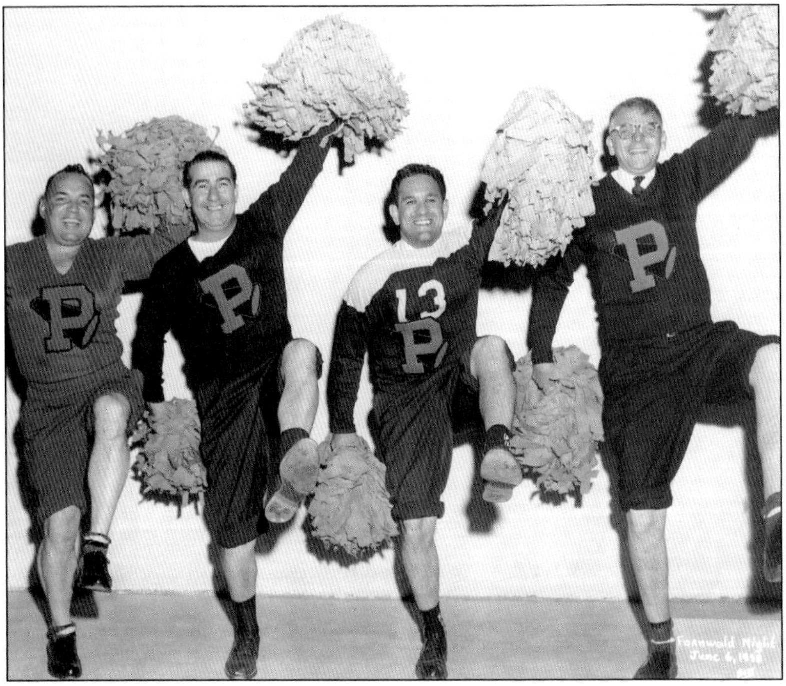

The alumnae cheerleading team hams it up for the Clarence Fornwall reunion. Fornwall's career lasted 46 years and was as phenomenal as his musical engagements, which sent him around the world and to the "big little city of Reno" and Lake Tahoe, where he entertained and made friends with entertainers from Hollywood.

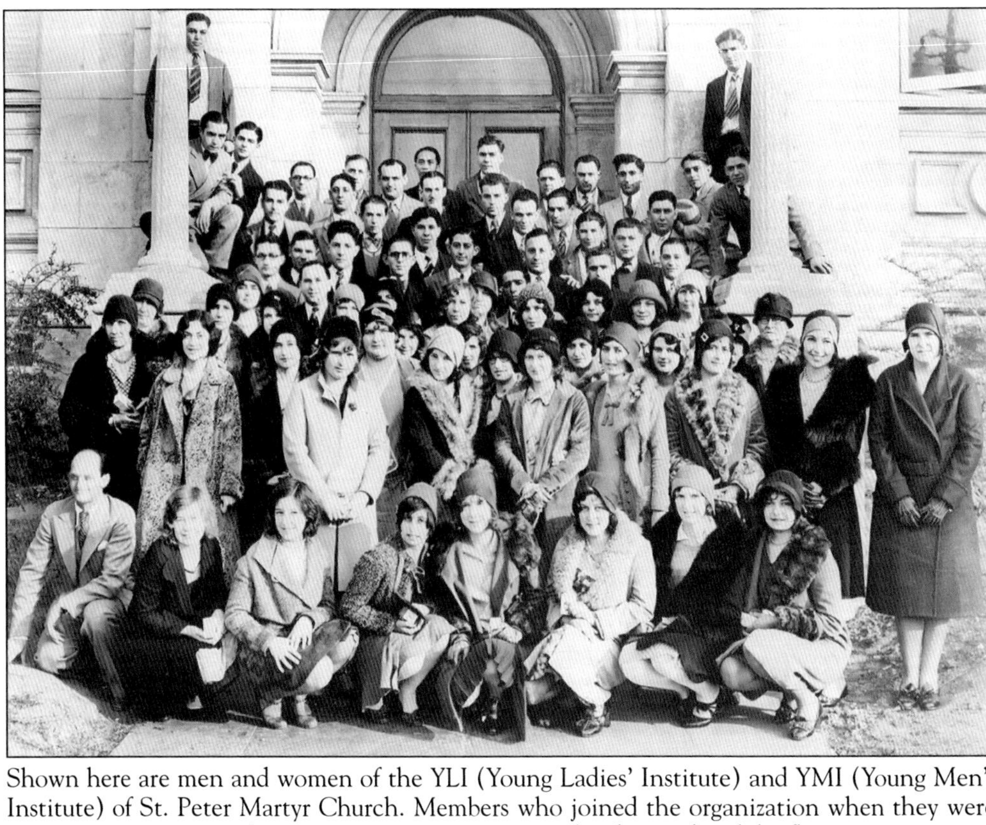

Shown here are men and women of the YLI (Young Ladies' Institute) and YMI (Young Men's Institute) of St. Peter Martyr Church. Members who joined the organization when they were very young went on to become a senior citizen group that keeps the club afloat.

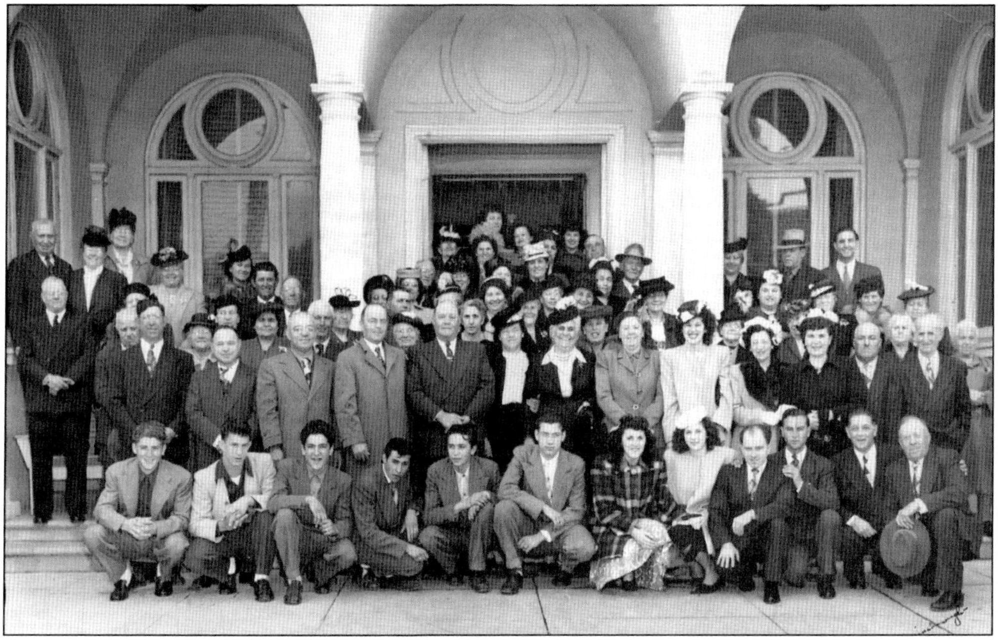

Members of the International Catholic Federation, pictured here, included Red Harris, Paul Costa, Nick Borelli, Sal Magna, Sam Belleci, John Magna, and John De Vito. Mrs. Julianna (near the center in the hat) was known as the best raffle-ticket seller at St. Peter Martyr.

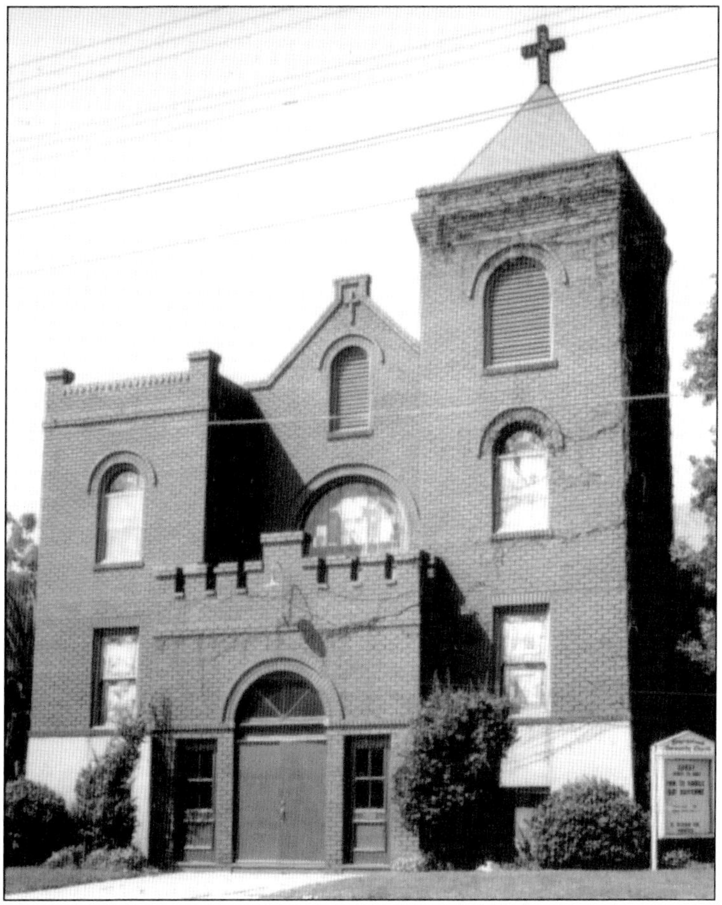

This landmark church, located on Ninth and Los Medanos Streets, was founded in 1882 as the New York Congregational Community Church. A red brick structure, the architectural design appears to be Gothic and includes colorful stained-glass windows. The seating was originally composed of 50 solid oak pews arranged in a half circle.

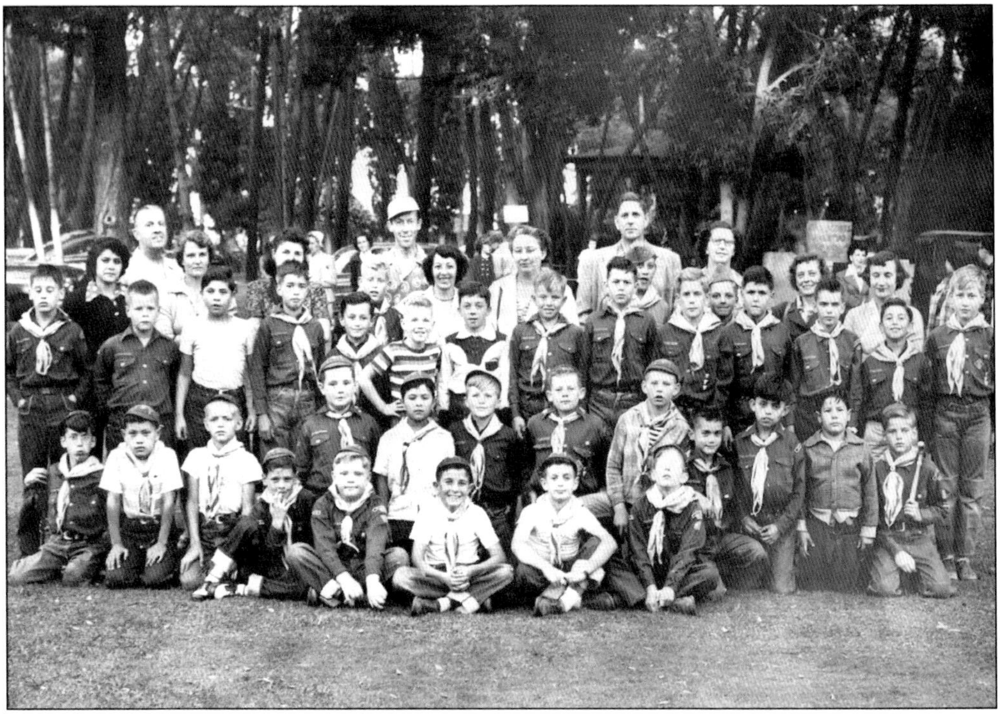

This Cub Scout Jamboree took place on June 22, 1950. Organizations like the Girl and Boy Scouts, Girls' League, and various clubs and sports kept the young busy and involved in civic affairs.

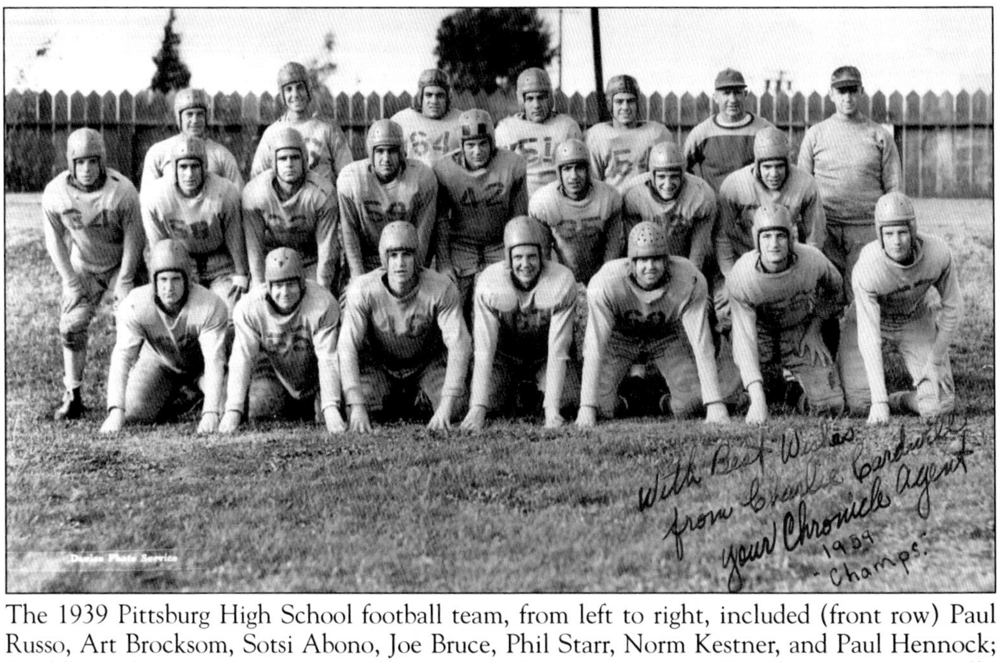

The 1939 Pittsburg High School football team, from left to right, included (front row) Paul Russo, Art Brocksom, Sotsi Abono, Joe Bruce, Phil Starr, Norm Kestner, and Paul Hennock; (middle row) Jay Hacket, Vince Colone, Ken Cole, Jim Pappas, Fred Pardi, Mario Trentinelli, Frank Billeci, and Frank Lopez; (back row) Herk Pardi, Carl Colombo, Dante Viedoville, Bob Scudero, Mario Magaroli, Coach Bryan, and Coach Bankhead.

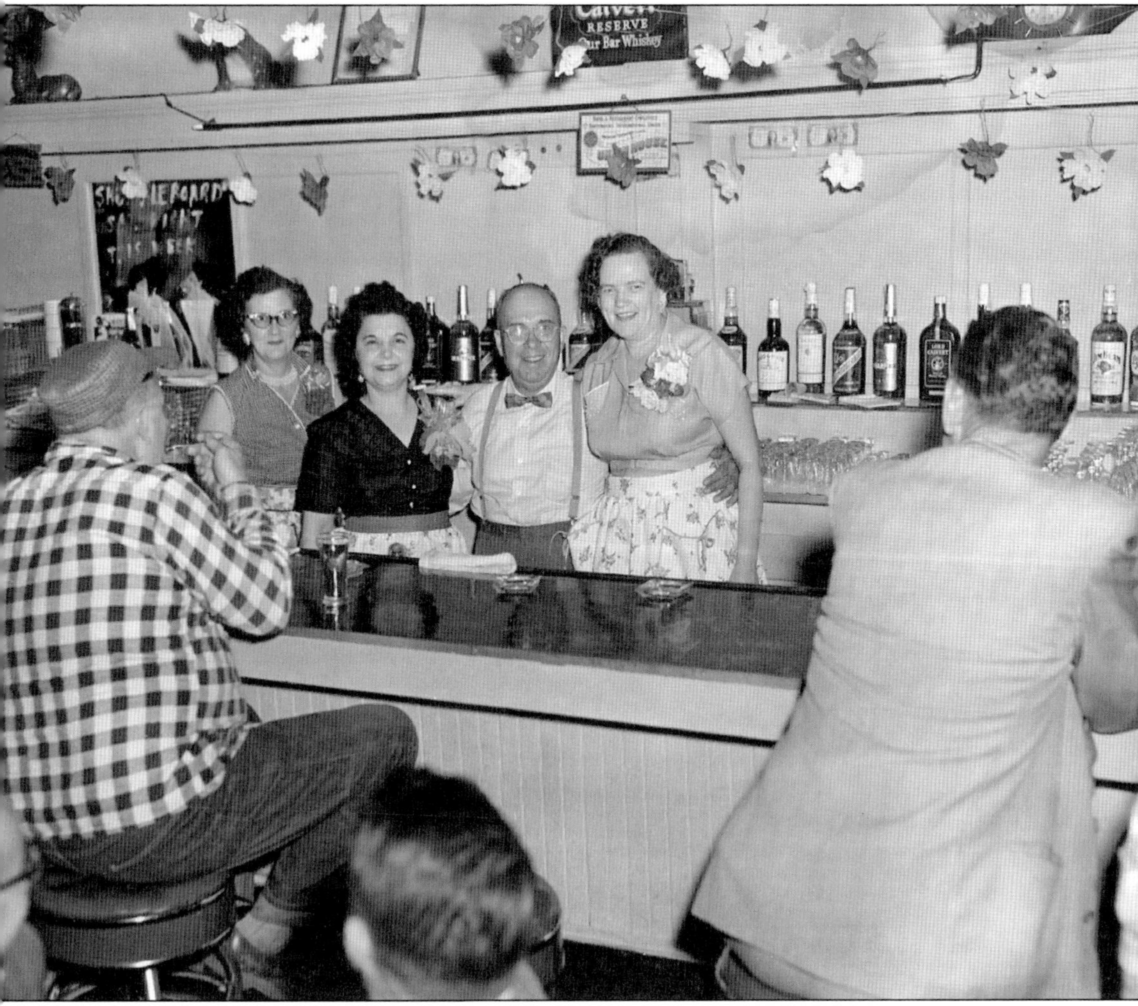

During the 1940s, bartenders were kept busy as their saloons became a meeting place for locals and the military from Camp Stoneman and Port Chicago.

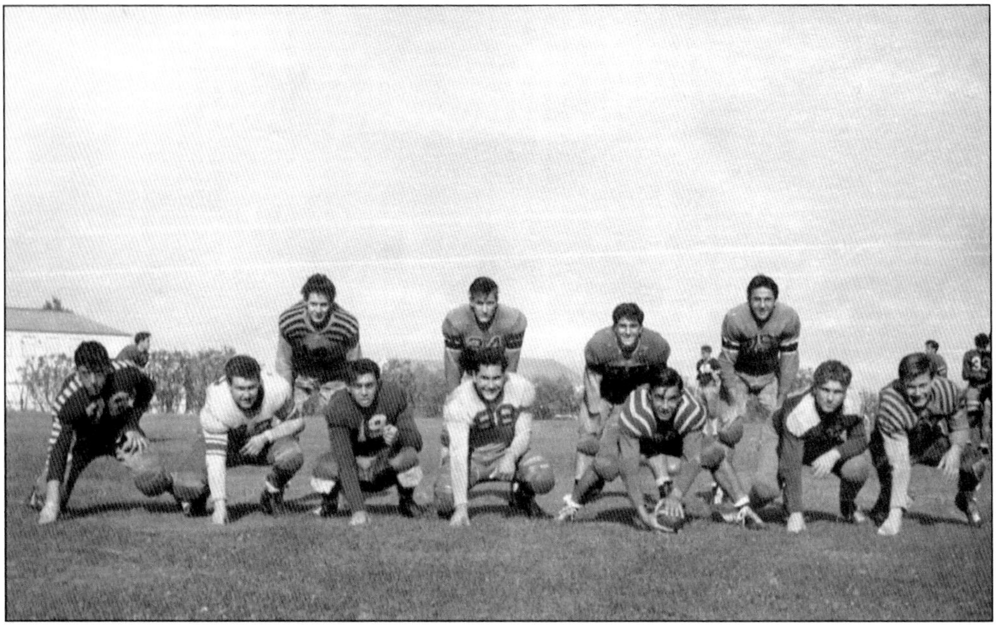

Pittsburg's first unbeaten football team came in 1944, under Coach Paul C. Heilman. Offensive line starters for the first "perfect" season, from left to right, were (front row) Pete Frumenti, Larry Patten, Pete Aiello, Vince (Truck) Evola, Joe Crespo, Charles Galli, and Neil Hennock; (back row) backfielders Tony Lopez, Bob Renzenbrink, Denny Pappas, and Don Baker.

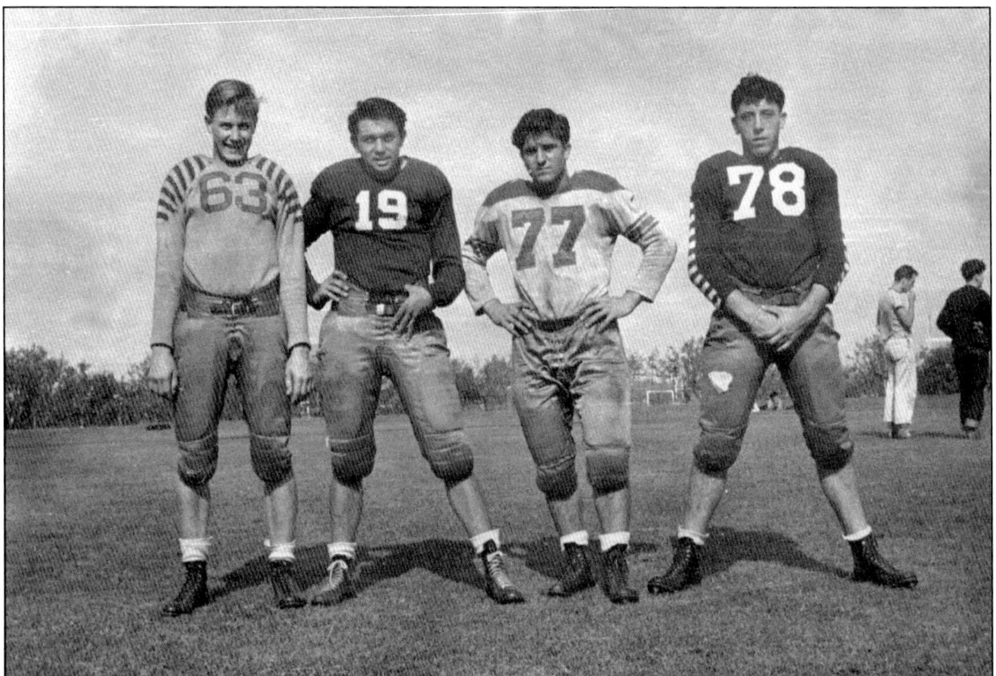

From left to right, Neil Hennock, Pete Aiello, Denny Pappas, and Pete Frumenti are shown here as one tough bunch of players. Some of the coaches for the Pittsburg Pirates that headed up winning teams were Pat Bryan, George Galli, and Tony Knapp.

Charlie Galli, the city's football historian for the last 60 years, has collected over 100 files of information, programs, and souvenirs from 1942 to the present. In that time, five teams have gone undefeated and untied, in the years 1944, 1951, 1954, 1956, and 1964.

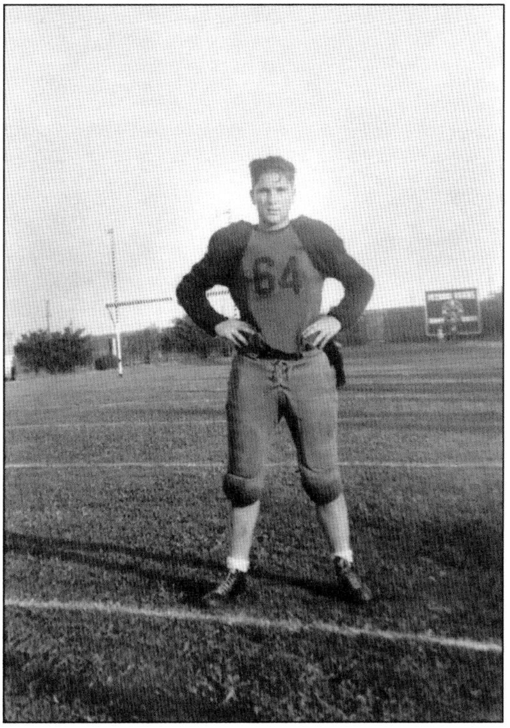

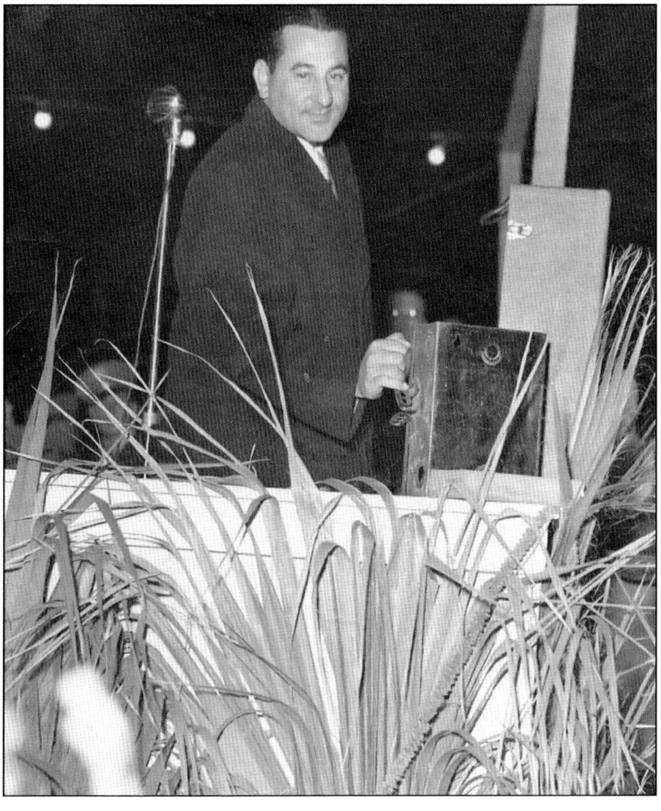

Mayor Vincent Davi's energy extended not only to his civic duties, but business interests as well. Shown here in 1940, Davi contributed heavily to numerous charities and good causes. He became director of the Canners' League of California and a chairman on the board of trustees of the Pittsburg Community Hospital District.

CAMP STONEMAN

At the confluence of the Sacramento and San Joaquin Rivers, where waterways form a "highway" into San Francisco Bay, and two rail lines—those of the Sante Fe and the Southern Pacific Railroads—provide links to the rest of the nation, is a location of unsurpassed excellence that became a strong influence in the selection of Pittsburg, California, as the building site of Camp Stoneman.

Soon after the Japanese attacked Pearl Harbor in December 1941, the U.S. Army found an urgent need for a large cantonment where the processing of vast numbers of troops could be staged. This staging area would allow men and material to be marched to overseas assignments; where records and issues could be completed, reviewed, and corrected; and where more than 80 percent of 40,000 soldiers would be transients. This small Contra Costa city proved ideal for the purpose and a site was selected on acreage in the south part of town that was being used for pasture at the time.

Plans for a camp near the San Francisco Bay had been in the blueprints of war prior to the Japanese attack on Pearl Harbor. The main requirement was the availability of all three types of transportation, namely water, rail, and road. Pittsburg filled the bill, and on January 1, 1942, the war department began negotiating for the purchase of the C.A. Hooper property and authorized the establishment of the post on January 3, 1942. Construction of the main camp began on February 11, 1942.

Contra Costa County responded with the patriotic fervor that accompanies a stepped-up wartime economy. Carpenters began building the foundation forms of the future barracks and warehouses and within the month 700 men from far and near had signed up to help. As soon as the barracks were built, the troops began to pour in. The influx of workers was housed in trailers and tents at the waterfront, an area appropriately called "Tent City."

After the war, the camp began mustering out returning soldiers. The wartime number of men who were processed through Camp Stoneman and discharged out of the army there was over 2 million.

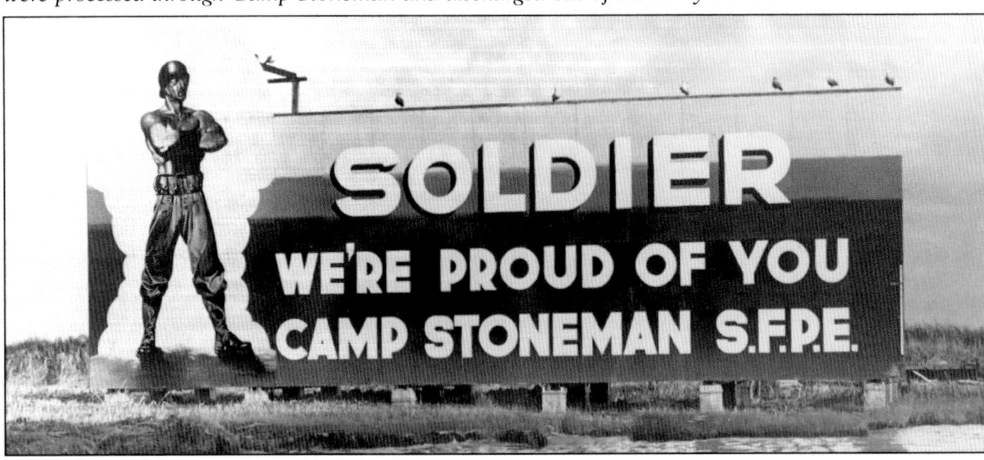

The billboard placed at the entrance to the river leading to the port at Pittsburg was indeed a welcome sign for the soldiers returning from the South Pacific in 1944.

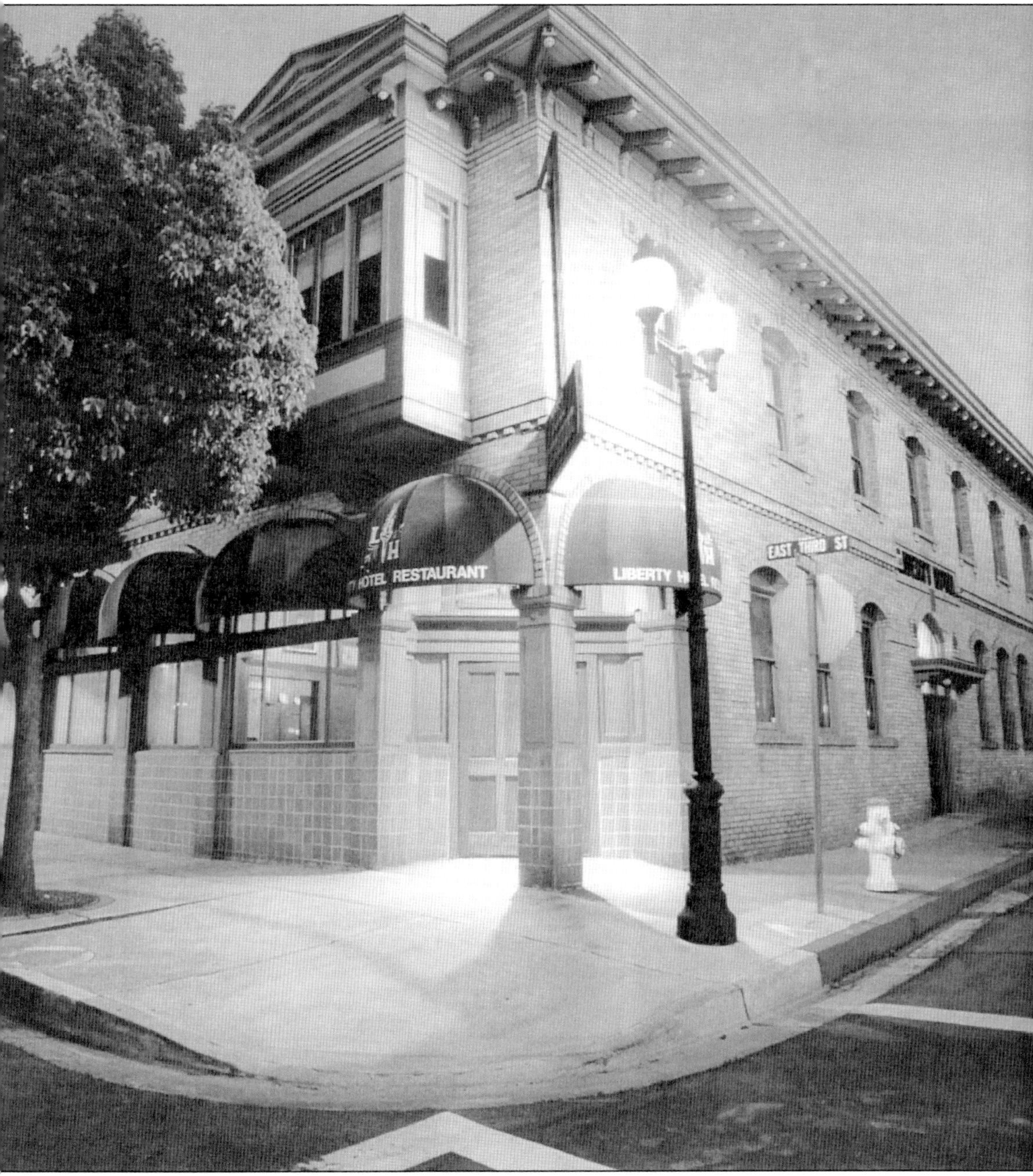

Guests staying at the Liberty Hotel could walk through the Grecian arched portals of its beautiful courtyard, which lead out onto the lawns, or enjoy the outdoors while sitting in lounge chairs.

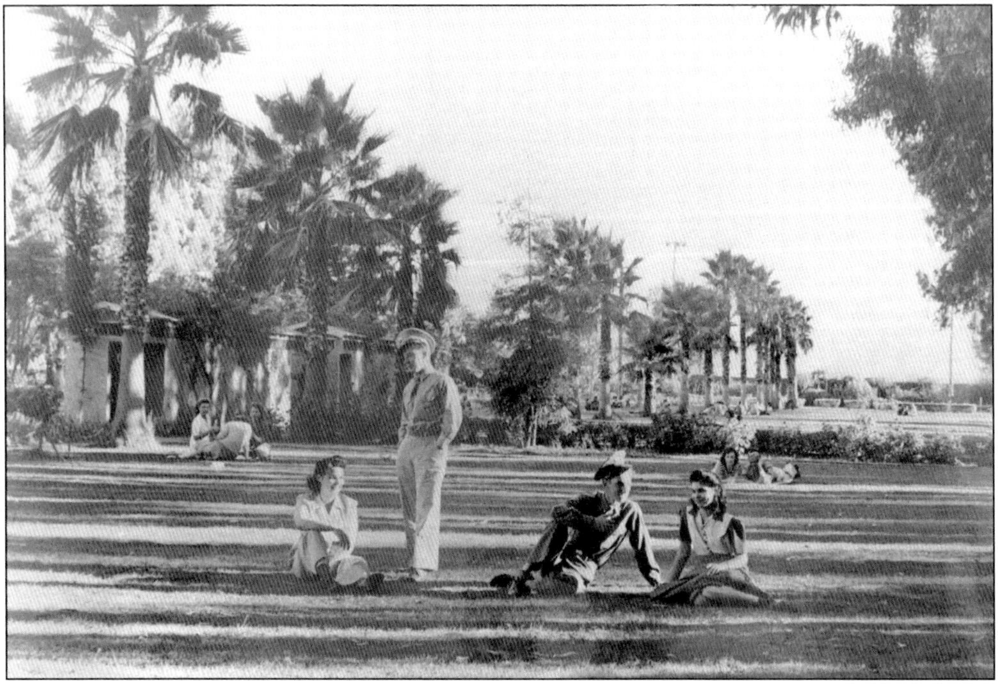

Pittsburg City Park has expansive lawns where peacocks roam freely, an aviary with exotic birds in fenced-in towers, and a gazebo where entertainment might consist of a local band concert or dance floor space for jitterbugging.

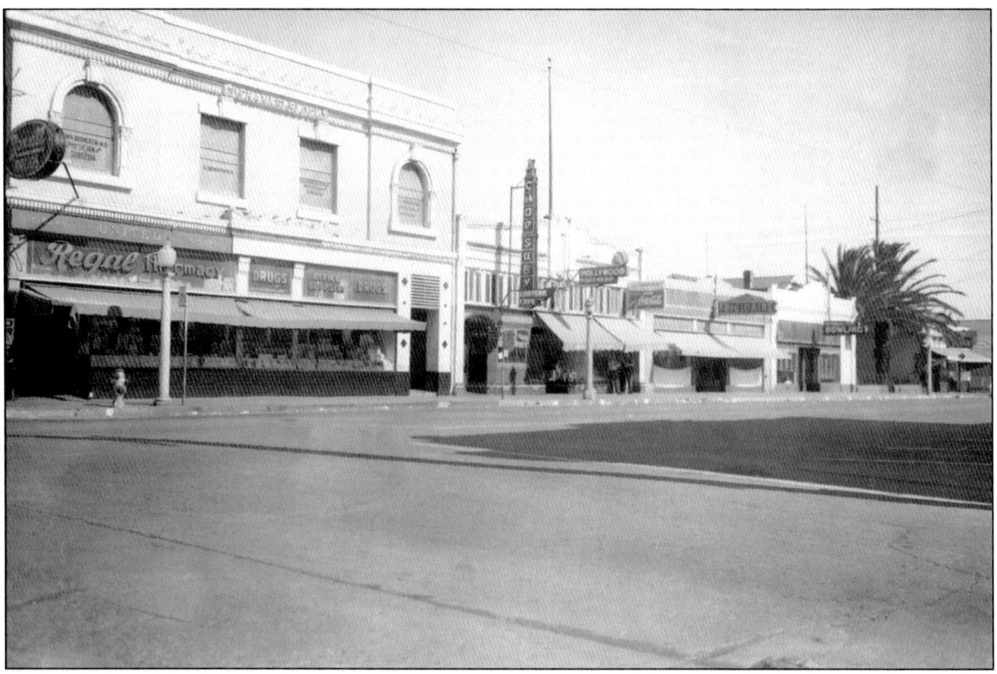

The old Regal Pharmacy (left) and other stores along the strip were part of the business district that extended from Railroad Avenue to Second Street.

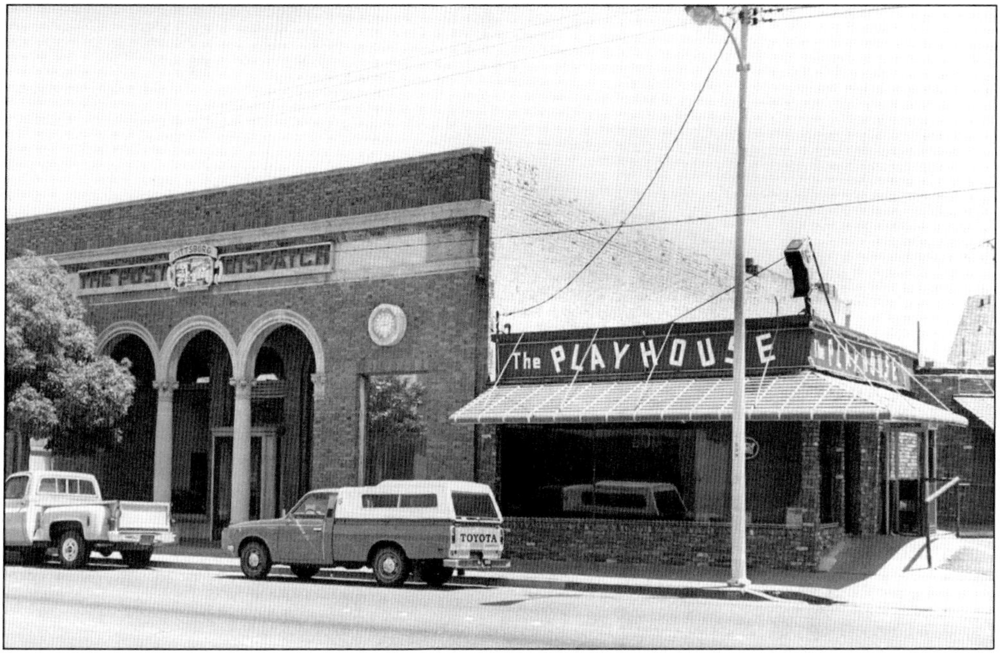

This picture shows the Post Dispatch Building, with the Play House next door. Newspapers were printed and distributed from the Cumberland Street side. Also home to Coast Counties Gas and Electric Company at one time, the building is now the Pittsburg Museum at 515 Railroad Avenue.

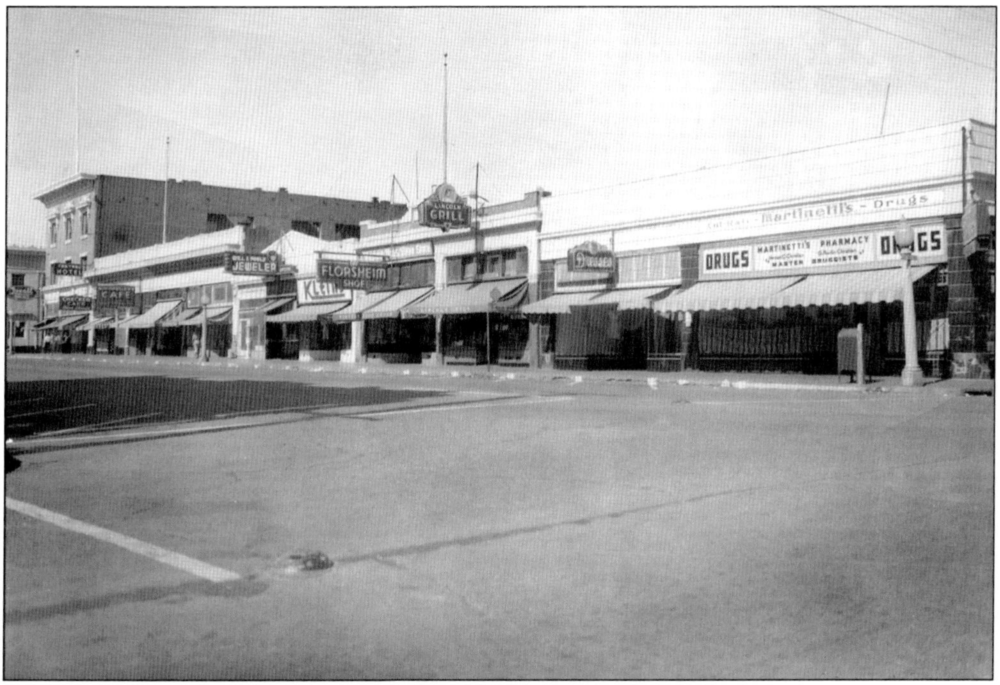

This view of Railroad Avenue and Third Street shows the Central Hotel at far left, along with Checkers Cafe, Pool Jewelry, Klein Dress Shop, Lincoln Grill, the Elite Dress Shop, and Martinetti Drug Store.

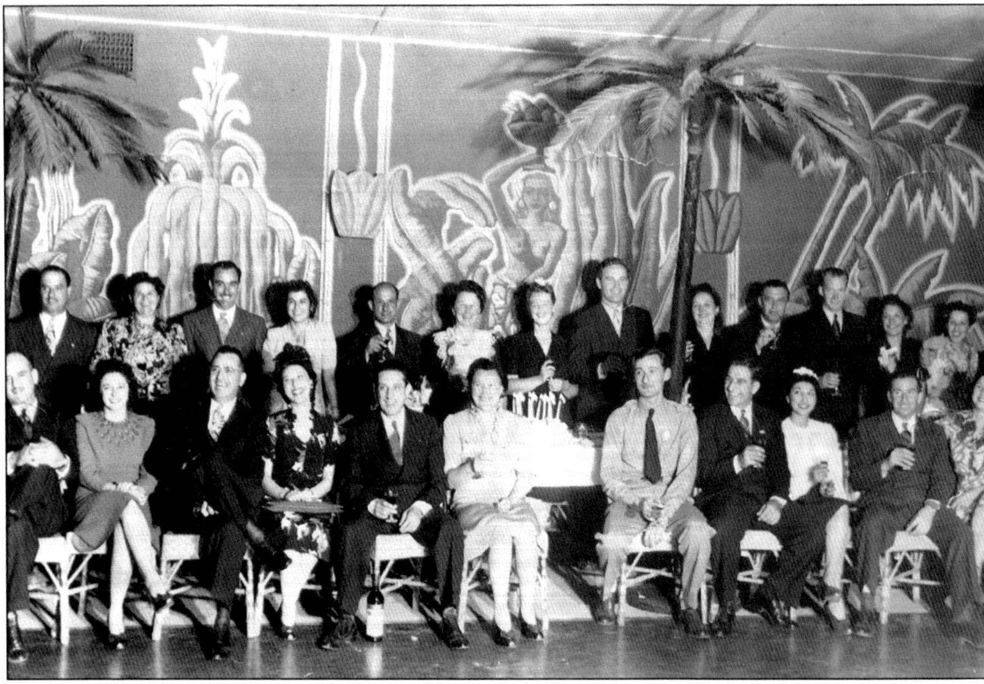

The Tahiti Club, located on Harbor and Tenth Streets, was a popular nightclub in the 1940s. Mr. and Mrs. John Parde, Mrs. and Mrs. Neno Enea, Rose and Russell Mutulo, Mrs. and Neno Davi, and Joe Ferrante were all members of a social organization called the "Rendezvous Club" founded by Horace Ascanio, which frequently met at the Tahiti.

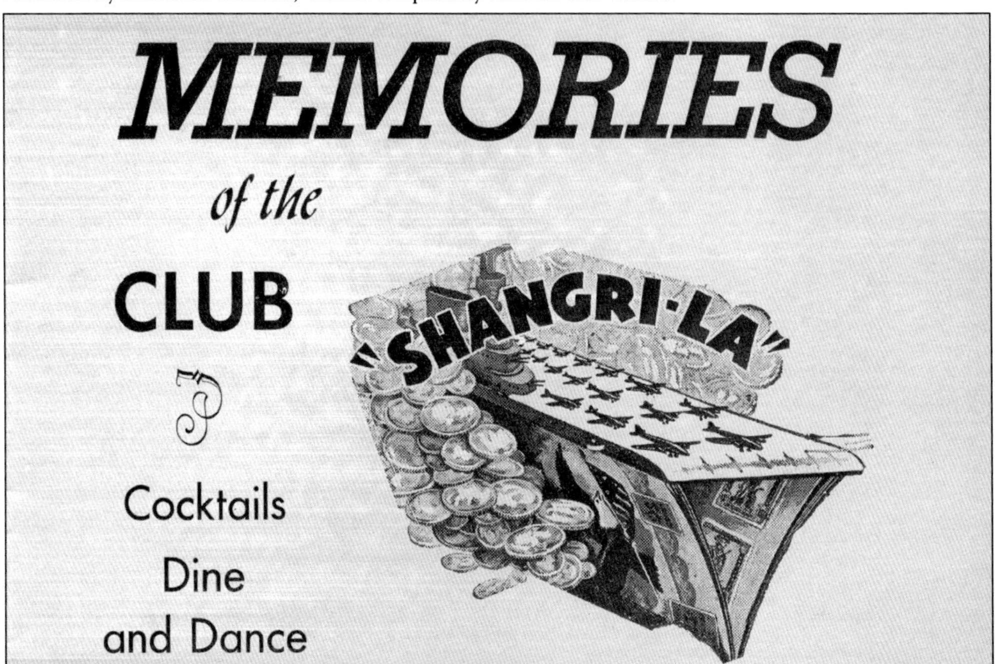

Memories of the Shangri-La Club on Tenth Street in Pittsburg still can invoke nostalgia for those old enough to recall a very distinct time in the city's history.

In the 1940s, Carlo's Pizza on Railroad Avenue next to the California Theater was a great (and cheap!) place for food. The restaurant moved to California and Railroad Avenue and continued to do business.

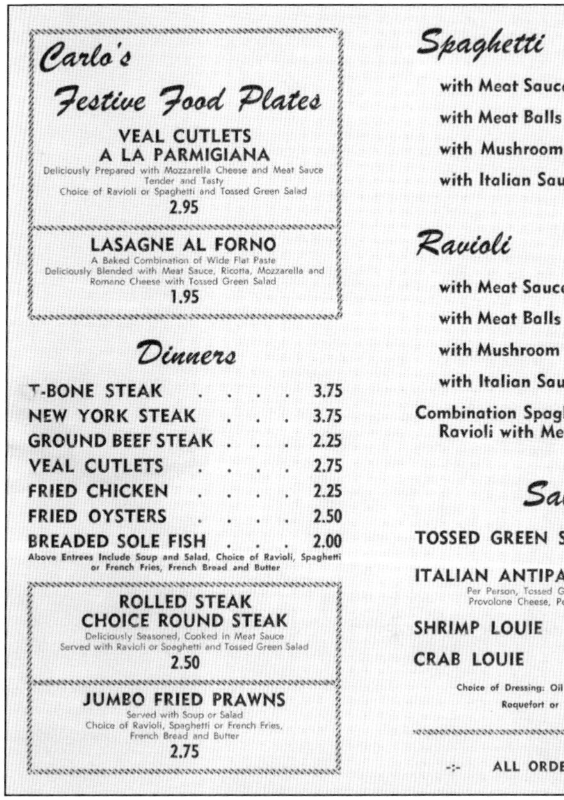

Carlo's

Festive Food Plates

VEAL CUTLETS
A LA PARMIGIANA
Deliciously Prepared with Mozzarella Cheese and Meat Sauce
Tender and Tasty
Choice of Ravioli or Spaghetti and Tossed Green Salad
2.95

LASAGNE AL FORNO
A Baked Combination of Wide Flat Paste
Deliciously Blended with Meat Sauce, Ricotta, Mozzarella and Romano Cheese with Tossed Green Salad
1.95

Dinners

T-BONE STEAK	3.75
NEW YORK STEAK	3.75
GROUND BEEF STEAK	2.25
VEAL CUTLETS	2.75
FRIED CHICKEN	2.25
FRIED OYSTERS	2.50
BREADED SOLE FISH	2.00

Above Entrees Include Soup and Salad, Choice of Ravioli, Spaghetti or French Fries, French Bread and Butter

ROLLED STEAK
CHOICE ROUND STEAK
Deliciously Seasoned, Cooked in Meat Sauce
Served with Ravioli or Spaghetti and Tossed Green Salad
2.50

JUMBO FRIED PRAWNS
Served with Soup or Salad
Choice of Ravioli, Spaghetti or French Fries,
French Bread and Butter
2.75

Spaghetti

with Meat Sauce
with Meat Balls
with Mushroom
with Italian Sau

Ravioli

with Meat Sauce
with Meat Balls
with Mushroom
with Italian Sau
Combination Spagh
Ravioli with Me

Sa

TOSSED GREEN S
ITALIAN ANTIPA
Per Person, Tossed G
Provolone Cheese, Pe
SHRIMP LOUIE
CRAB LOUIE
Choice of Dressing: Oil
Roquefort or
-:- ALL ORDE

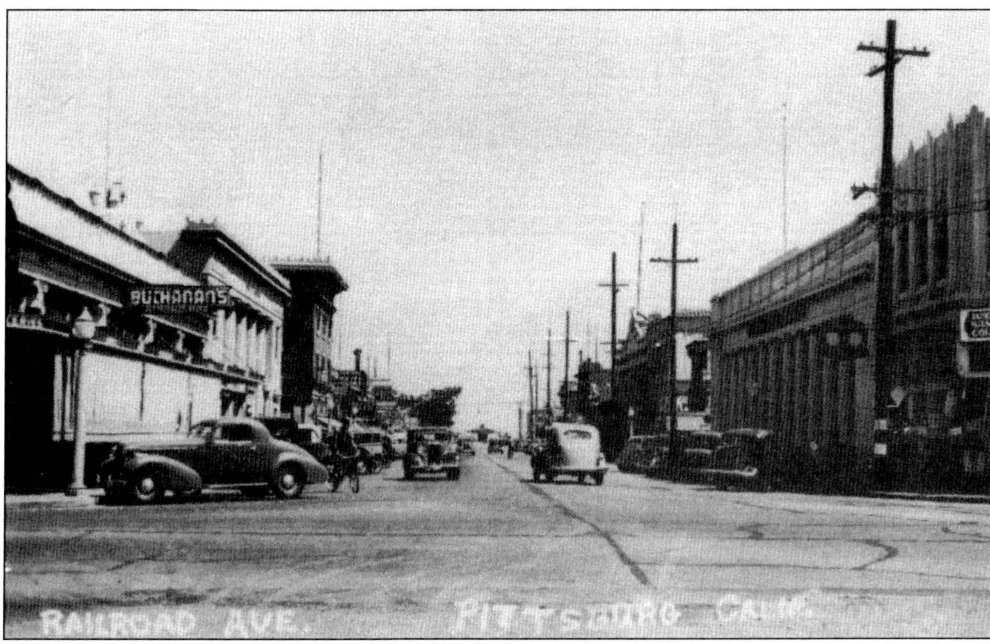

In this photo. the Buchanan Store, Bank of America building, and Central Hotel can be seen on the right. The Modern Drug on the right-hand side of Railroad Avenue also had a soda fountain. The building next to the drug store is the American Trust Building.

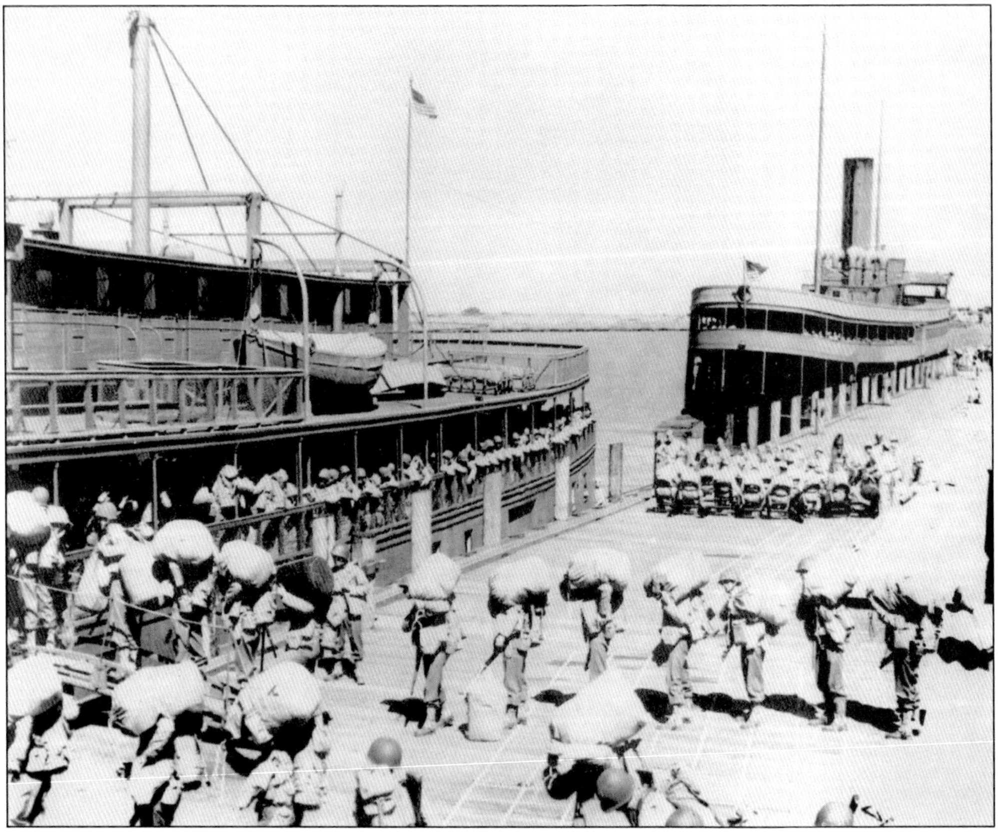

While the folks at home were living ordinary lives in a town where war loomed on the horizon, soldiers by the thousands were headed to the Far East war zone. Troops from Pittsburg's Camp Stoneman boarded ferries for the trip to San Francisco's ports.

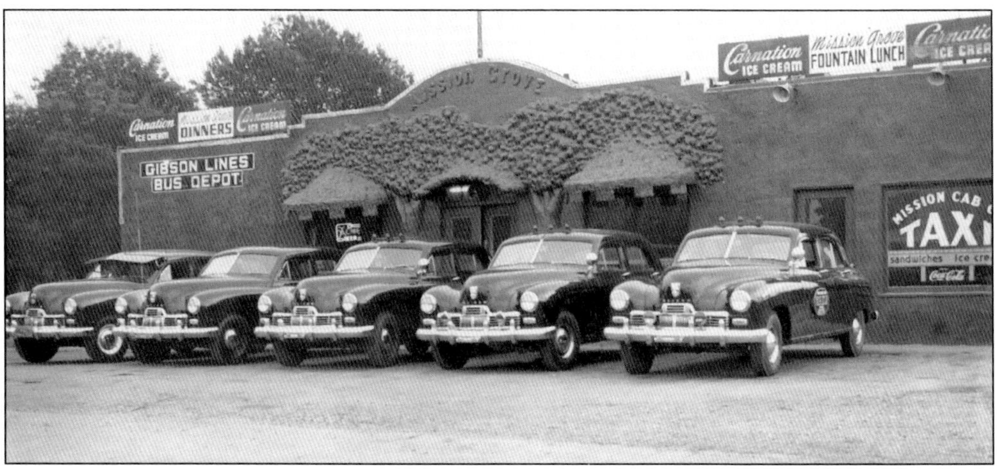

Mission Grove Orange House, a landmark in the city for years, also housed the Gibson bus lines and Mission Taxi Cab. When drive-in fountains became the rage, Pittsburg Pirate Drive Inn added one of the many fountains that were made for "hanging out" with the gang.

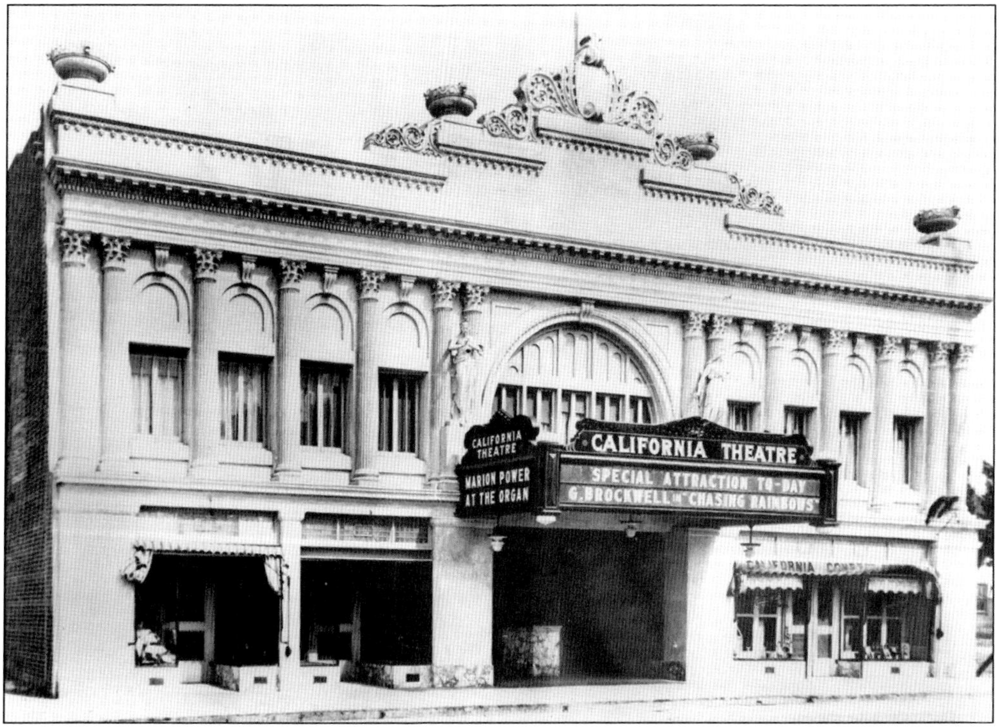

The California Theater has been entertaining the community with live entertainment and movies since the 1920s. Tony Enea was the organist at many early shows. A fine musician, Enea also played piano and other instruments for the Good Shepherd Church until he was 90 years old. He also entertained at nursing homes until his death.

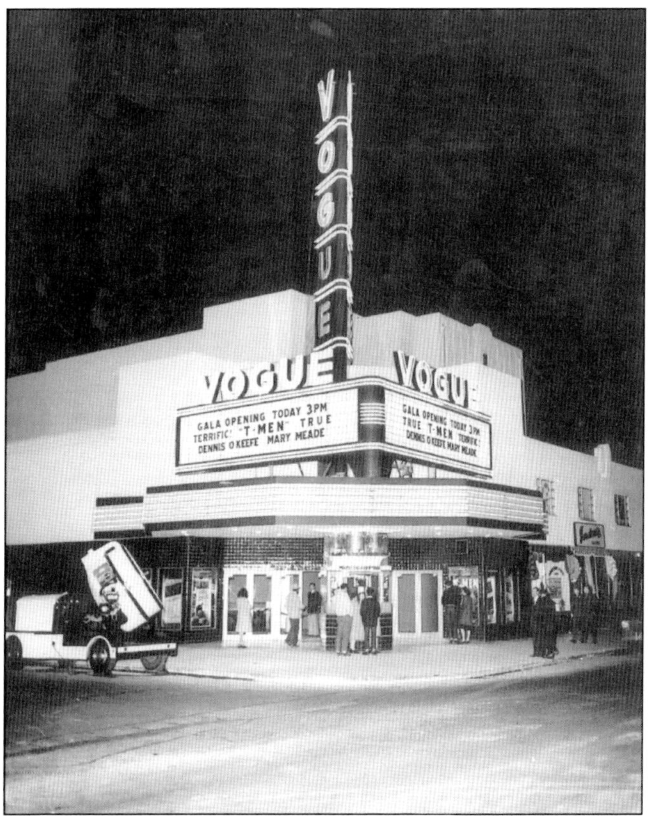

A popular entertainment was attending the Vogue Theater for a Saturday afternoon matinee or evening movie, starring the latest glamour girl of the hour.

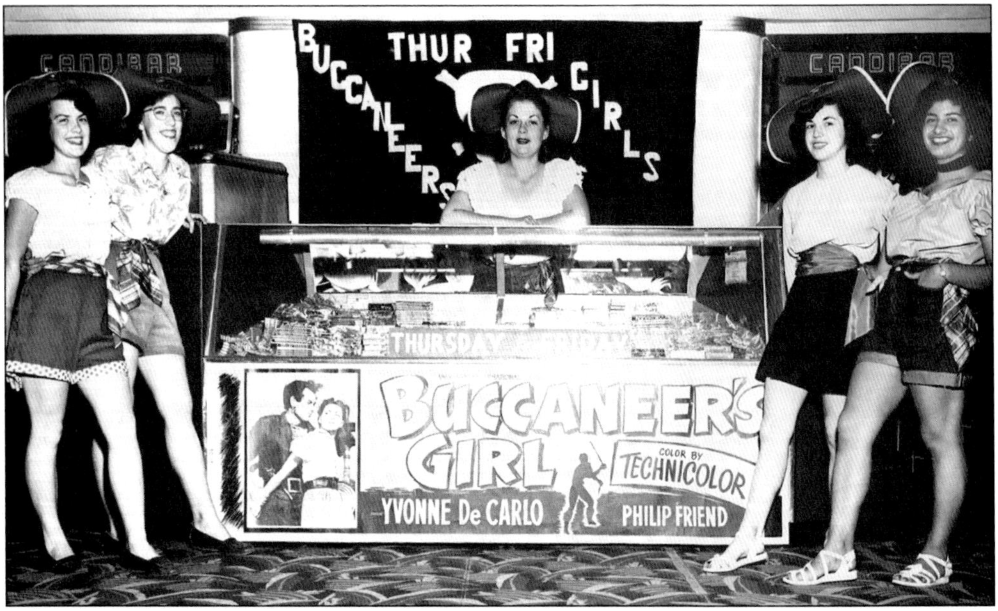

Enean Theater girls dress for the movie *Buccaneer's Girl.* Young people could always get jobs at the movie houses as ushers and usherettes who were employed to show patrons to their seats. Uniforms were tailored of serge wool in the above-the-knee style that was popular in those times.

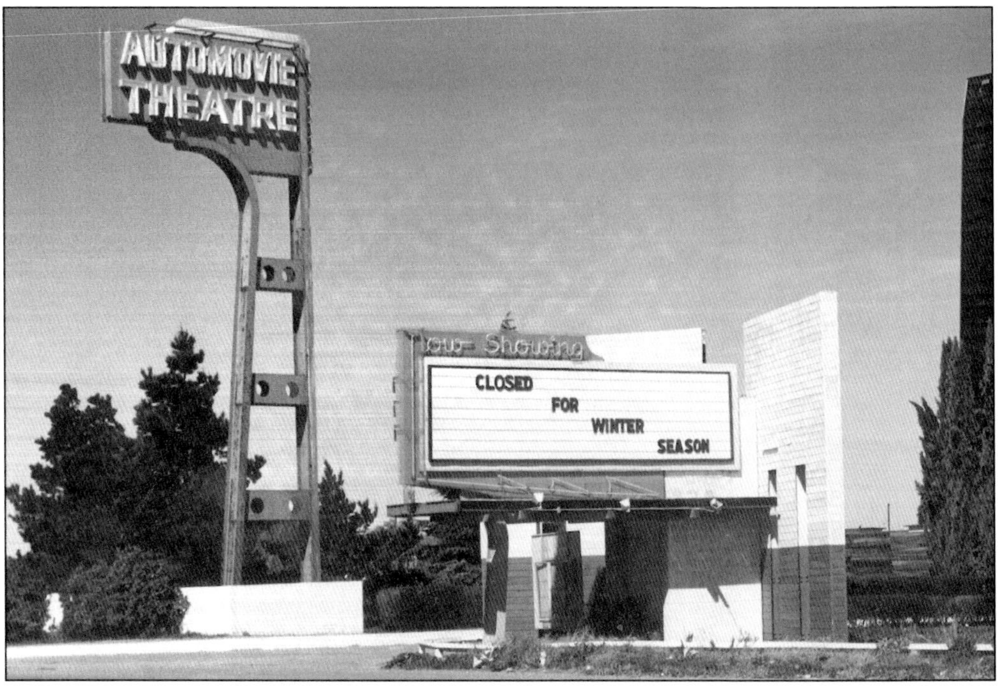

"Take your girlie to the movie" might have been a song for the 1950s. The Automovie Theatre was a special place for young people to enjoy a show and get to know each other. The sound system consisted of a speaker attached to the car door, and the outdoor popcorn and drink stand provided the treats. All this for a buck!

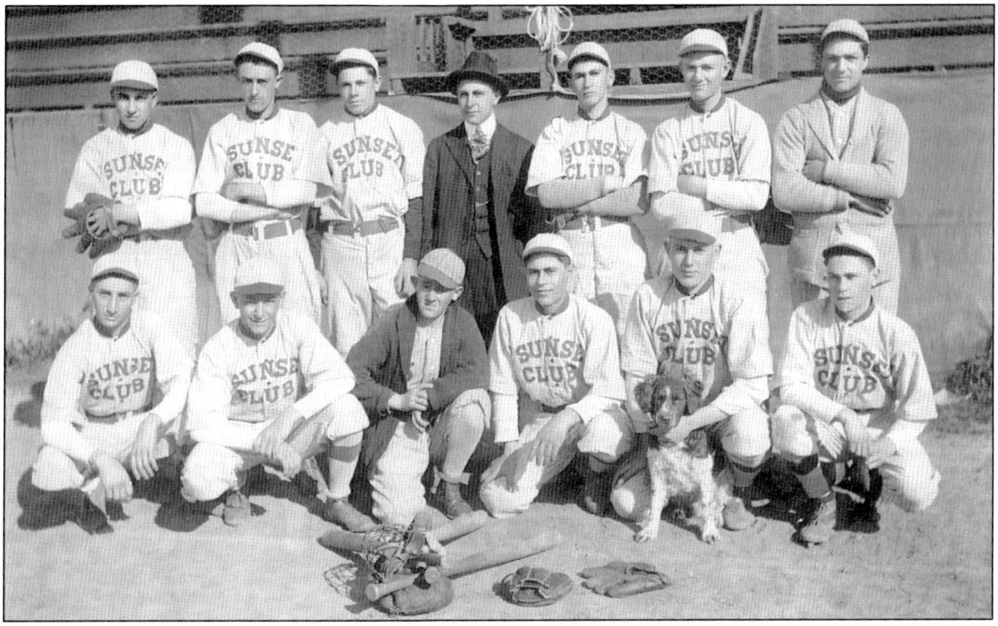

The Sunset baseball team was one of the many teams sponsored by the city's merchants or industries. This photograph appears to have been taken around the 1930s.

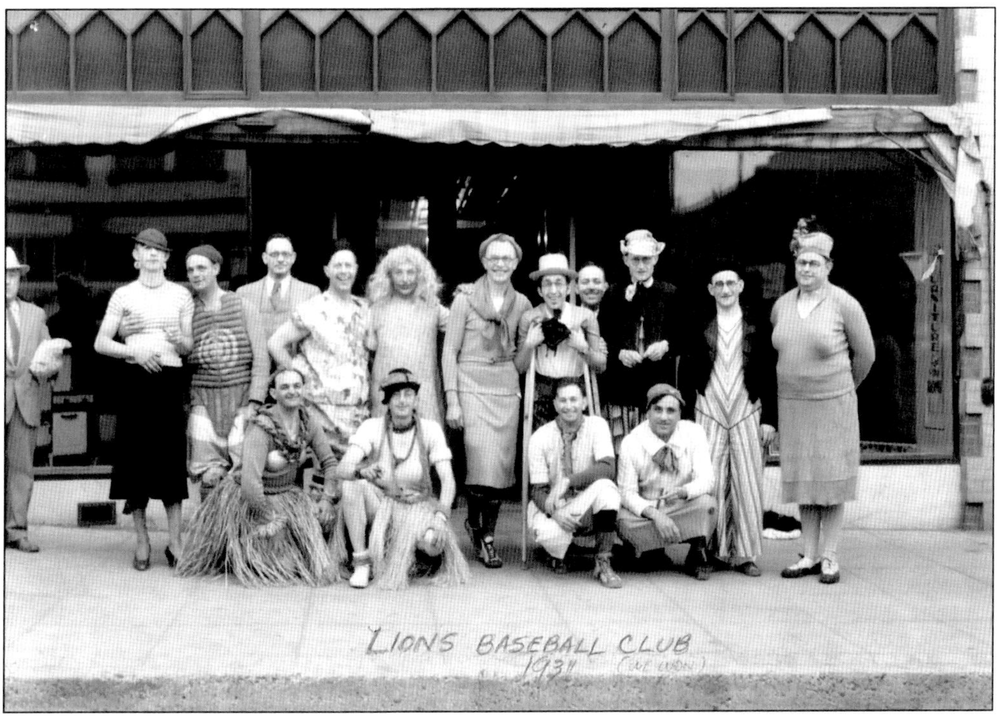

The "ladies" of the 1931 Lions Baseball Club team are Harry Freed (on crutches) and Bill Pacini. Shown kneeling, from left to right, are Nino Davi, Frank Billeci, Bert Davi, and Bert Melrose.

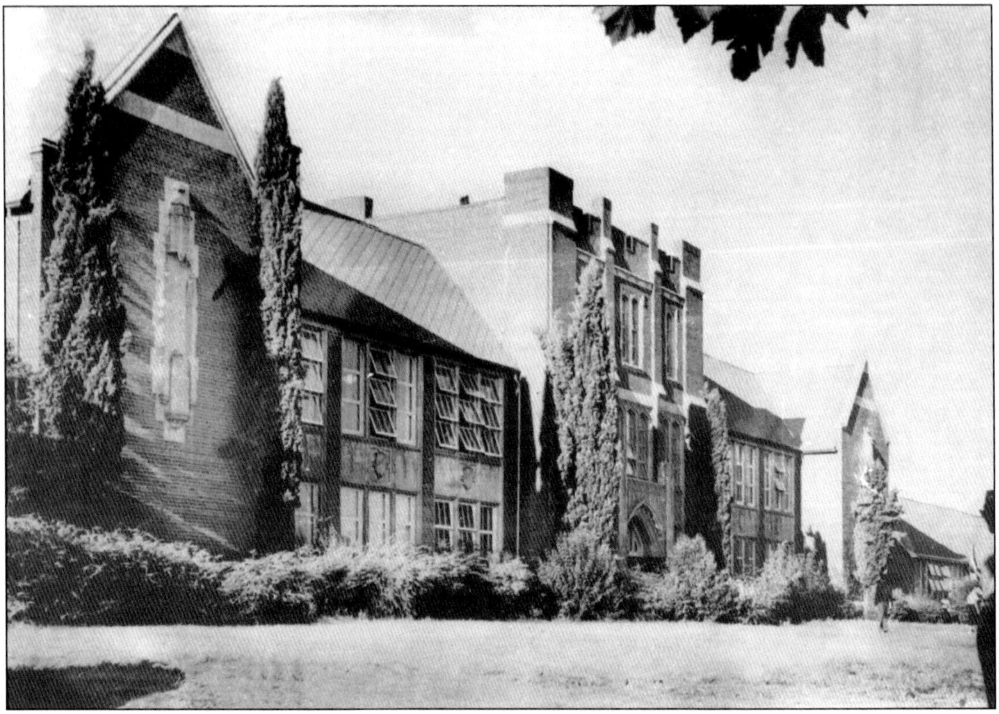

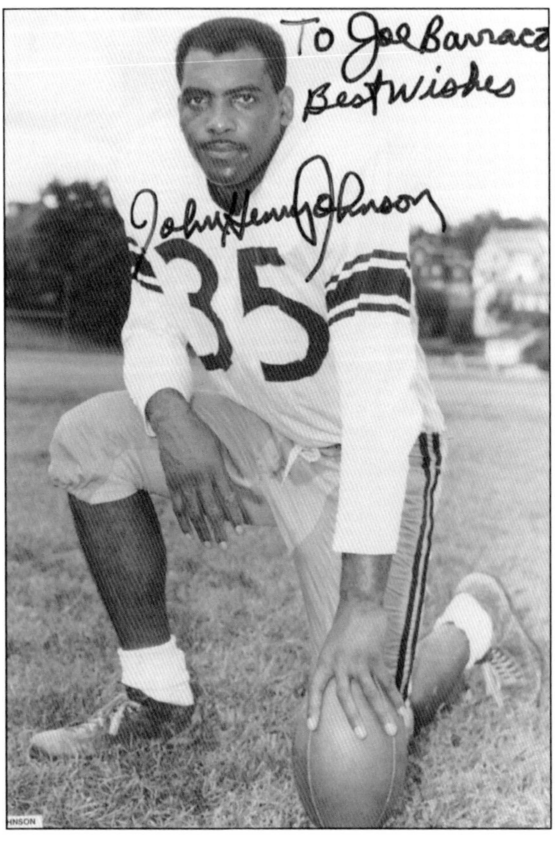

Pittsburg Junior High School, pictured above, was built in 1927 on School Street and had compulsory classes in English, math, history, and civics. Pittsburg High School was located across the street, and the schools' combined enrollment in 1930 was 359 students. In 1940 enrollment had reached 445. In 1954–1955, major reconstruction on this school resulted in the creative arts building with a large theater, swimming pool, and bleachers for sport events.

John Henry Johnson, a football great who went on to play for the San Francisco 49ers, Detroit Tigers, Pittsburgh Steelers, and Houston, was chosen by the *Oakland Tribune* in 1970 as the greatest East Bay athlete in 50 years. He was an all-around athlete, breaking records in track and baseball.

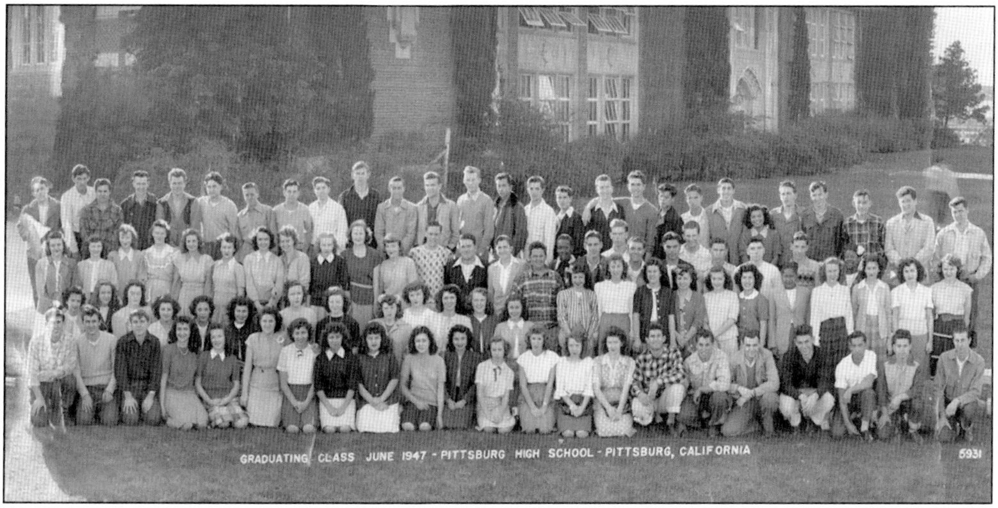

The class of 1947 is notable for the number of students who are now serving in city government, including Mayor Mary Erbez, city planner Jack Garcia, architect and former mayor Joe Barraco, successful businessman Irving Berg, theater owner Sylvester Enea, and Rose Scudero, who was recognized for her efforts to change the "enemy alien" status of Italians during World War II.

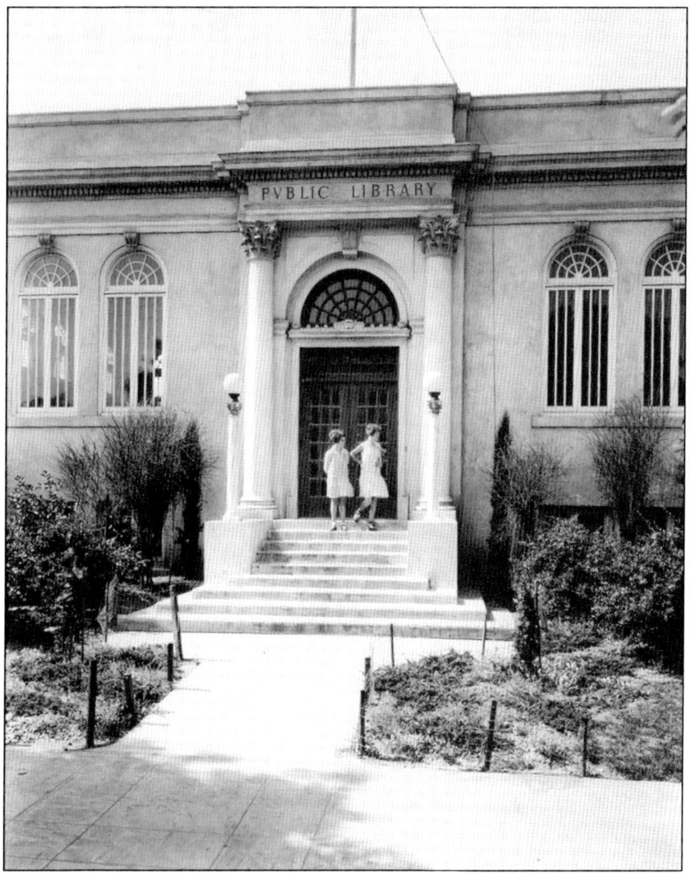

The Pittsburg Public Library was built in 1925 and designed by architect A.W. Cornelius, who designed several other buildings in town. The classic structure has curved window and door treatments and dual columns at the entrance.

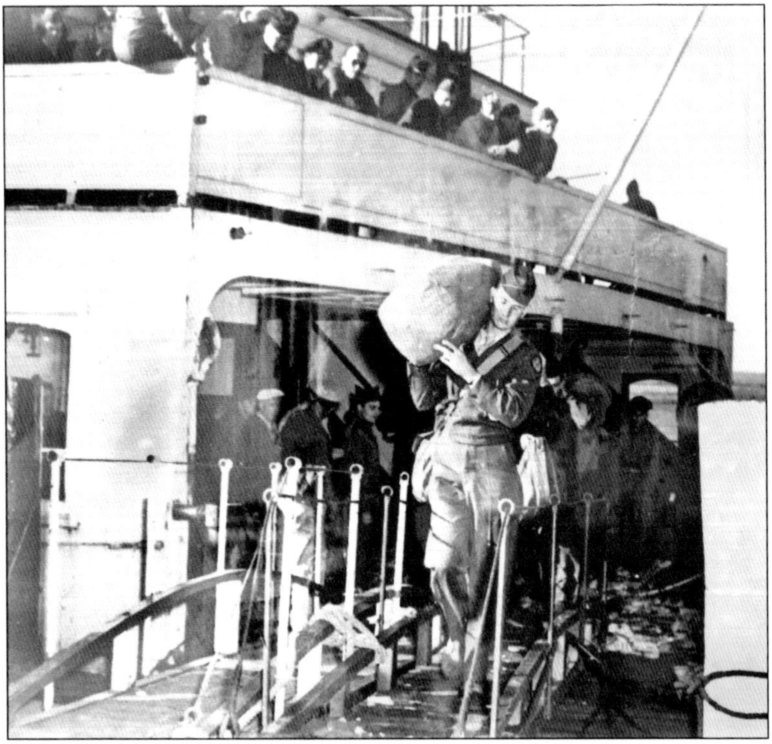

When the war ended in 1944 and the men came home, often the ferries that first took them to San Francisco and off to the war zone were the same ones that brought them home again.

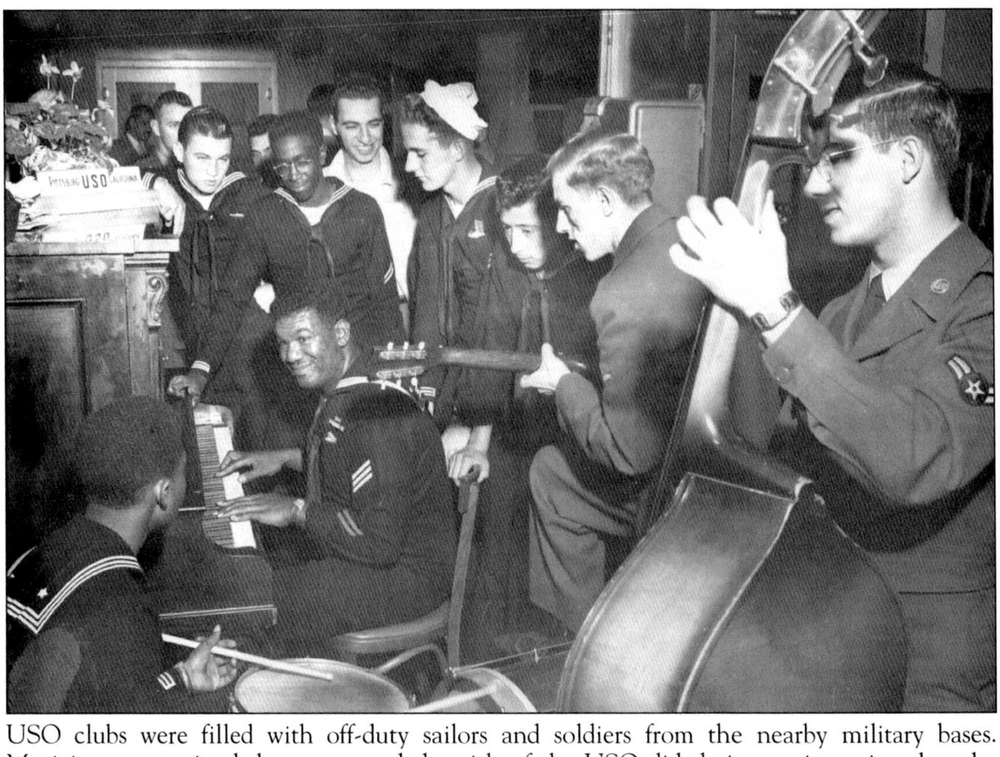

USO clubs were filled with off-duty sailors and soldiers from the nearby military bases. Musicians entertained the troops and the girls of the USO did their part in seeing that the lonely times were less painful for the men and women in service.

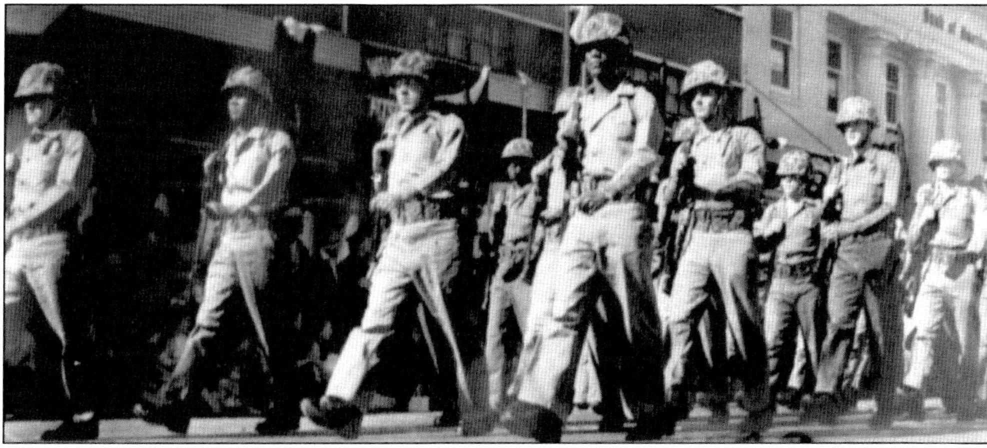

The 159th Division included eight boys from Pittsburg: Ben Ramirez, Anthony Belleci, Carlo De Vito, John Gava, John Garcia, Ben Bruno, Jack Garcia, and Richard Meza.

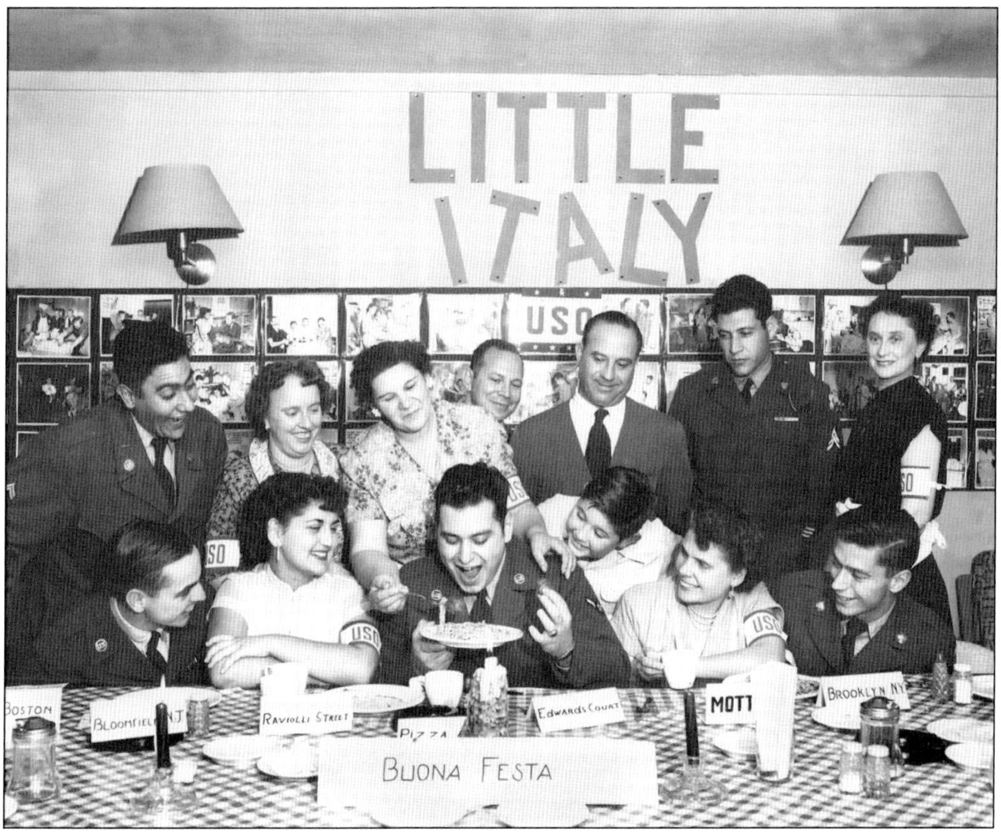

Soldiers from the New York, New Jersey, and Massachusetts enjoy a "good feast" cooked by the Italian Ladies of the USO. Many of the soldiers came back to Pittsburg after their discharge from the army to marry hometown girls.

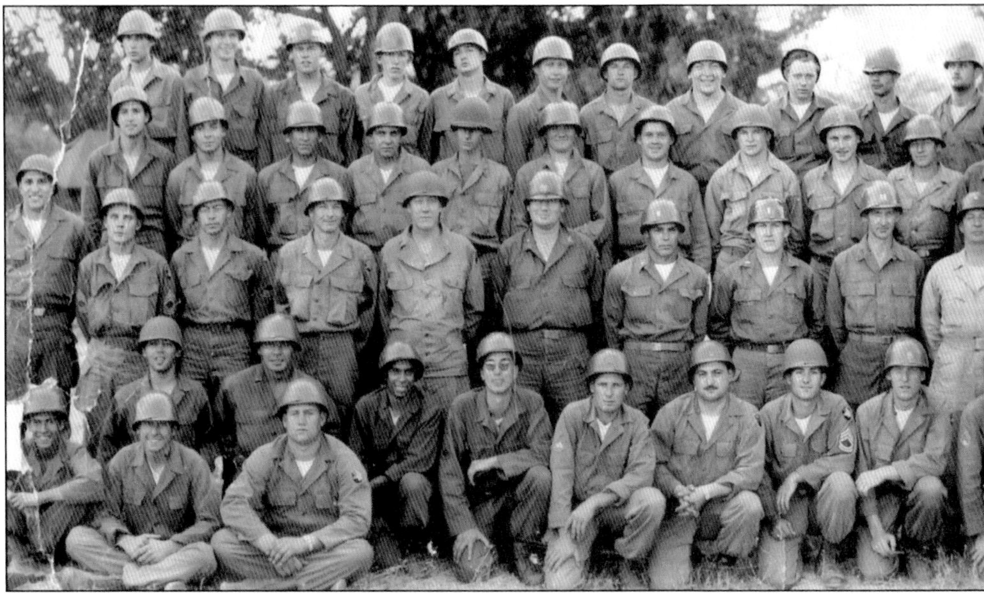

Camp Stoneman's permanent army personnel are shown here in 1947. Many of the soldiers remained in Pittsburg when they were mustered out of service. The camp's presence left an indelible impression on the townspeople and was an important phase of Pittsburg's history.

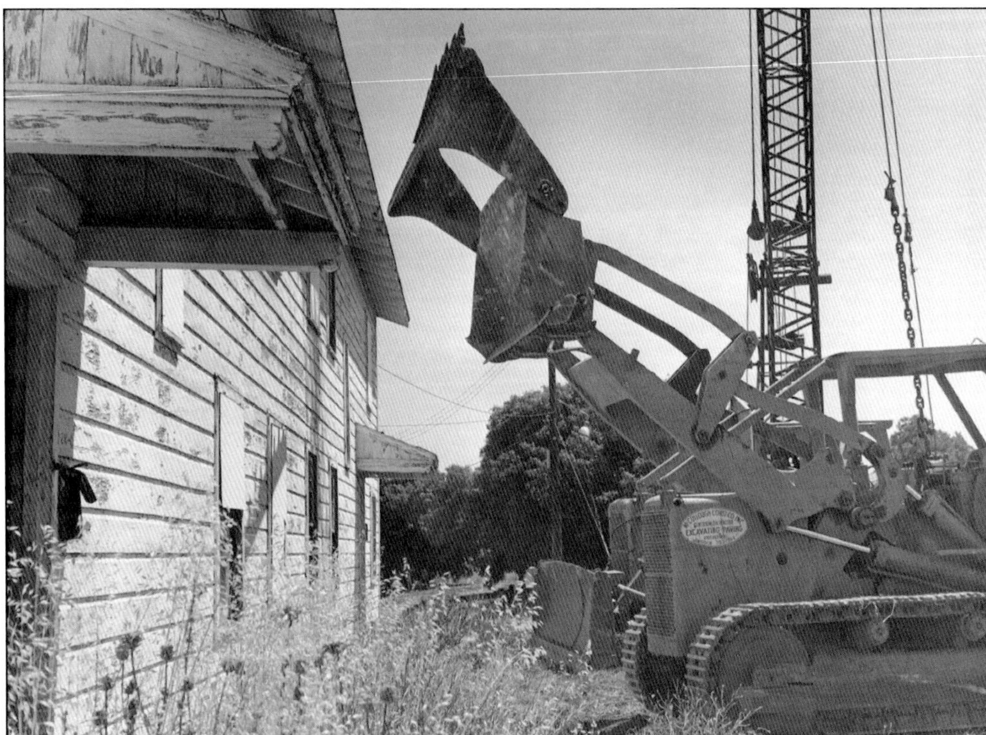

In the late 1950s, the barracks were torn down and the camp was sold back to the city, which dismantled all of the remaining buildings except for the storage sheds. The land has lain dormant, although the storage sheds have been used for various purposes.

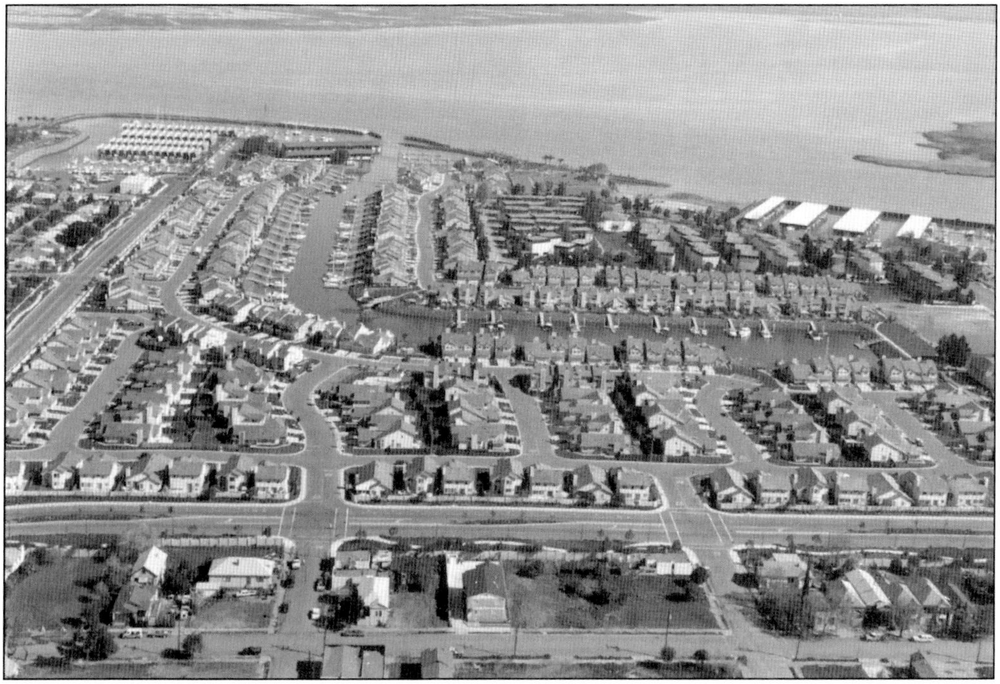

This overhead view shows the waterfront, boat harbor, and access to the river. This was the vision of the city fathers after the older homes had been demolished. The homes were just the start of a building boom that extended housing eight blocks on both the east and west sides of Railroad Avenue.

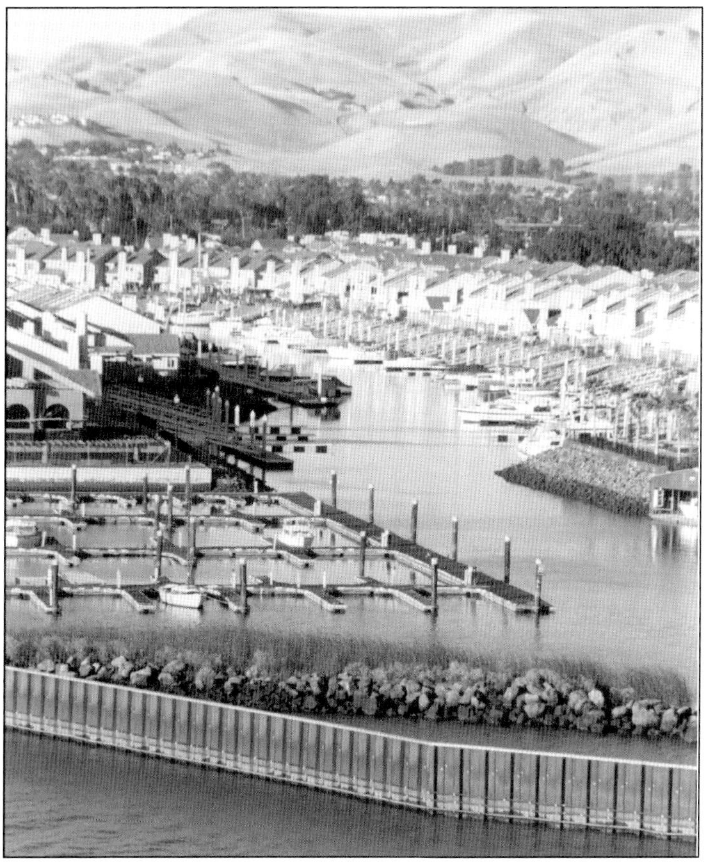

This photo shows the northside riverfront. The harbor houses large boats that can accommodate living space for owners.

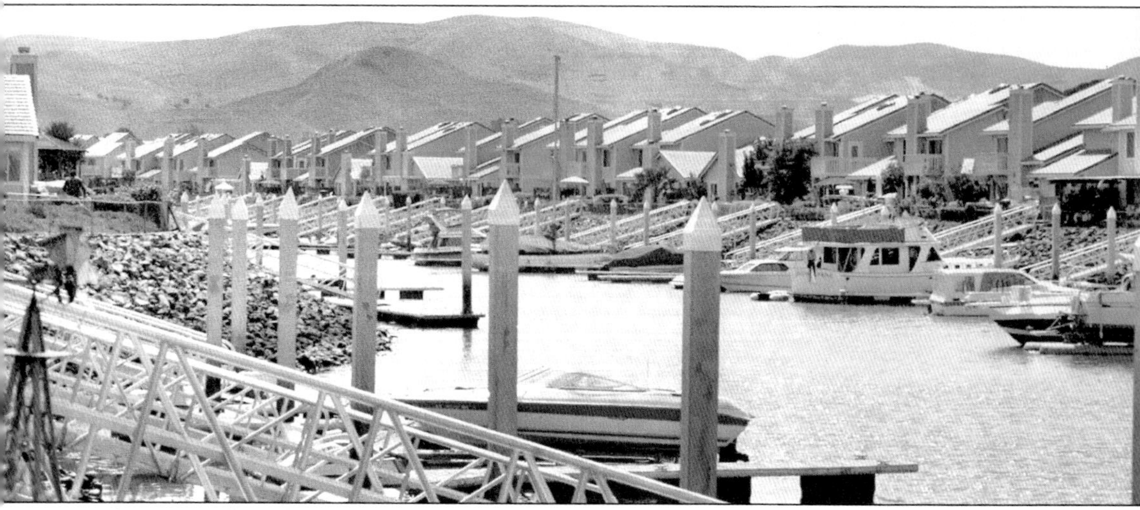

These waterfront homes have access to the river by way of small canals leading to the water. Small boats and watercraft can be moored at the back of the property with ramps leading up to the homes.

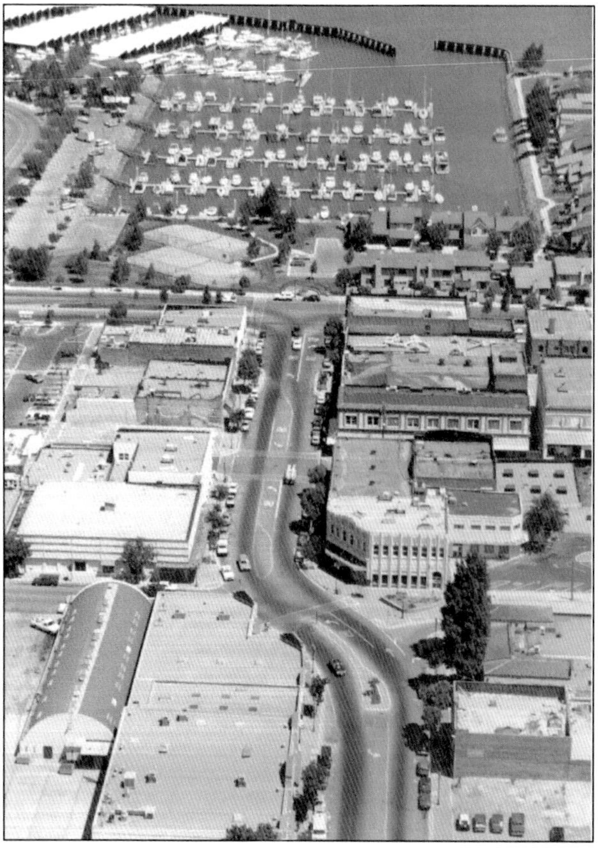

This view shows Railroad Avenue, the main street into the historic district of downtown Pittsburg, at Sixth Street, looking north toward the river. Visible on the right are the Pittsburg Historical Society Museum, the chamber of commerce, the Wells Fargo building, the McDonald Building, the California Theater, and a block of offices and businesses. On the north side are waterfront homes and riverboats in the harbor.